All *for*
Her

"Father Patrick Peyton exercised a ministry of 'new evangelization' before the term became a mainstay of contemporary Church practice. His thirst for holiness rooted itself in his Irish family's recitation of the Rosary. His confidence in the power of prayer sprang from his own sick bed chapel. He used the best methods of media communication known in his day. He had a message for the world and a passion to share it far and wide. *All for Her* describes his lifelong passion to bringing families to Jesus Christ through his Mother Mary. It was his path to holiness."

Father Robert L. Epping, C.S.C.
Superior General
Congregation of Holy Cross

"Father Patrick Peyton's boldness, creativity, enthusiasm, and passion for the Gospel shaped his life and ministry. They are clear signs of his holiness and his love of God and neighbor. As we remember him, may his devotion to Mary, his promotion of family prayer, his service to families, and his commitment to the mission of evangelization inspire us as we discern and seek to carry out the mission that the Lord has entrusted to each one of us."

From the foreword by **Father Wilfred J. Raymond, C.S.C.**
President of Holy Cross Family Ministries

"Lively and entertaining; it captures all the energy and scope of a very holy man embarked on a unique spiritual journey."

From the introduction by **Reverend James Chichetto, C.S.C.**
Associate Professor of Communications
Stonehill College

"No matter where Father Patrick Peyton was—growing up in County Mayo, working in Scranton, evangelizing Hollywood, speaking in stadiums across the world—he was the kind of person who loved God wholeheartedly with a love that overflowed into ardent, unlimited love of others. He learned this type of love from the Rosary, where from his youth he meditated on the love of God for him and derived from that contemplation the entire pattern and purpose of his existence."

Reverend Roger J. Landry
Priest of the diocese of Fall River, Massachusetts

"Few activities influence a family more deeply than their prayer together. Family prayer opens the heart of each member to the Sacred Heart of Jesus and helps the family to be more united in itself, yet more ready to serve the Church and society."

Saint John Paul II

"Father Peyton's incredible story was an experience—an experience for which I'll be forever grateful! I found him to be a man of enormous faith, a man actually in love with our Blessed Lady. For me his message is still an inspiration: 'The family that prays together stays together.'"

Loretta Young (1913–2000)
Actress

"Father Patrick Peyton was one of the most extraordinary priests I have ever known. He always seemed to accomplish what he set out to do, no matter how difficult or visionary it was. I can only applaud the good works of Father Peyton and recommend *All For Her* as entertaining, inspiring, and spiritually refreshing reading."

Reverend Theodore M. Hesburgh, C.S.C. (1917–2015)
President Emeritus
University of Notre Dame

"His was the captivating presence of a man in love with God, a priest who knew Mary as a loving mother to humanity."

Sister Margaret Kerry, F.S.P.
Author, speaker, and contributor to *CatholicMom.com*

"Father Peyton's wise counsel to me in that summer of 1991 was the fruit of the Holy Spirit. I also believe it was the Holy Spirit who encouraged Father Peyton to invite me in, to give me the sacrament [of Penance], to give me hope."

Jim Caviezel
Actor

"I pray that Father Patrick Peyton's promotion of family prayer and the Rosary, his service to families, and his commitment to the mission of evangelization, will inspire us all.

Reverend Bill Lies, C.S.C.
Provincial Superior
Congregation of Holy Cross, United States Province of Priests and Brothers

The Autobiography of
Father Patrick Peyton, C.S.C.

Ave Maria Press AVE Notre Dame, Indiana

© 2018 by The Family Rosary, Inc.

© 1967 and 1973 by Patrick J. Peyton

All rights reserved. No part of this book may be used or reproduced in any manner whatsoever, except in the case of reprints in the context of reviews, without written permission from Ave Maria Press®, Inc., P.O. Box 428, Notre Dame, IN 46556, 1-800-282-1865.

Founded in 1865, Ave Maria Press is a ministry of the United States Province of Holy Cross.

www.avemariapress.com

Paperback: ISBN-13 978-1-59471-885-4

E-book: ISBN-13 978-1-59471-886-1

Cover image from the Holy Cross Family Ministries archives.

Cover and text design by Christopher D. Tobin.

Printed and bound in the United States of America.

Library of Congress Cataloging-in-Publication Data is available.

Contents

Foreword to the New Edition

The Pastoral Genius of Venerable Patrick Peyton

The noted Hollywood actress Loretta Young once said on camera, "I never met a man who loved a woman more than Father Peyton loved Our Blessed Mother." Venerable Patrick Peyton understood profoundly that Mary knew the Lord Jesus best and loved him most on this earth. He also knew that the shortest route to Jesus is through Mary.

His home in County Mayo, Ireland, was "materially poor but spiritually rich." The Congregation of Holy Cross, his second family, stretched and broadened the rich faith he received at home. In the order he received a fine education, discovered new words to express his deep faith, and embraced the tenets of Holy Cross spirituality: trust in divine providence; unity based on shared faith and love for each other modeled on the Holy Family of Nazareth; zeal for the mission; hospitality; and the Cross as our only hope.

Also in this new family, Patrick came to know the special patroness of the congregation, Mary, the Lady of Sorrows.

Father Patrick Peyton, C.S.C., was saved from death from advanced tuberculosis through the intercession of Mary the Mother of God and the Rosaries prayed by his two families in Mayo and at the University of Notre Dame. Given a new lease on life, he promised Mary that every moment of the rest of his life would be devoted to spreading devotion to her and the family Rosary. Consequently, his autobiography is perfectly titled *All for Her.*

Father Peyton's story is known to many. It includes the near-miraculous ways in which a humble, young priest inspired millions through massive Rosary rallies and many more millions through radio, television, and film in Hollywood. What are much less known and appreciated are his unique theological, spiritual, and pastoral abilities—these elements, though not unique individually, when combined, constituted and defined Father Peyton's ministry and genius as an apostle of the Rosary and family prayer.

He now seems to be on his way to beatification and, God willing, to canonization as the saint for family prayer. The following fourteen elements make up the pastoral genius of Venerable Patrick Peyton:

1. A Passionate Son of Mary. Venerable Patrick Peyton saw the essential role of devotion to Mary in the Catholic experience of discipleship and in Catholic popular culture and piety. Speaking in Nazareth on May 24, 1971, he summed up his deep connection to and confidence in Mary:

> For this have I come amongst you. For this have
> I invited you to come from far and near. For this

I have come to greet you, meet you, and pray with you. And through the Family Rosary Crusade, blessing is an awareness, consciousness of Mary's reality; thanks be to God, Mary is real for me; she is alive; she is somebody's daughter; she knows what it is to be on this earth of ours; she knows what sorrow is, what fear is, what poverty is, what deprivation and destitution are.

Mary is for me a great strength; she is my spirituality; she is my peace; she is my prayer; she is my purity; she is my sureness; she is my defense, my protection. From her heart and from her arms and with her strengths I respond to the Most Blessed Trinity and to our Lord Jesus Christ, and to my fellow-man; her strengths are mine—my feeble strengths become strong in hers.

2. A Promoter of the Rosary as a Powerful Tool. He promoted the Rosary as a powerful tool for nurturing devotion to Mary and underscored its special place as a Catholic icon in the life of ordinary Catholics. Through the Rosary, elderly grandparents, infant children, and all ages in between could join in one prayer as a family.

3. A Man of Prayer. Throughout his formation for religious life and priesthood and during more than fifty years of priestly ministry, he placed great emphasis on the role of personal and communal prayer in his own life and in the lives of other Christians, especially in family life.

4. A Visionary for Family Prayer. Father Peyton, in his genius, envisioned family prayer as the tool for healing, renewing, and strengthening families when he said, "The Rosary has saved the world in the past, and it will save the world again by saving the family. The Family Rosary is a practical way to strengthen the unity of family life, so easily weakened by the modern way of living." He intuited that the health of this basic cell of society was necessary to the health of society as a whole when he wrote, "What was needed was not simply an end to the fighting but an atmosphere of true peace, peace in the heart, peace in the home, peace in the family. Yes, I told myself, here was the key: Family prayer, and in particular the prayer that had consistently brought God's favor through the centuries, that had saved Christendom at Lepanto, that had been preached and practiced and promoted incessantly by saints and popes, the Rosary."

5. An Apostle of Family Life. Father Peyton believed and often stated that nothing is more precious than the family, which is our greatest treasure. At the end of World War II, when millions of troops were returning home to families, many other families were mourning the loss of husbands, fathers, sons, and brothers. The fragility of the family surfaced as families, especially some couples, struggled with reunions made difficult by years of separation and post-traumatic stress, and other families dealt with their losses. For the healing of these spiritual and emotional wounds, Father Peyton reminded people: "The family is the greatest treasure the earth possesses. God is the greatest treasure of heaven. The Rosary is the link of steel that has the power to unite them both together for time and eternity."

6. An Auxiliary Priest to the Local Church. Father Peyton participated in the Holy Cross tradition of Blessed Basil Moreau by serving the local and universal Church in an auxiliary fashion with respect and subsidiarity to build up and strengthen what is already there. His first visit to a diocese was always to the bishop to greet him and receive his blessing and authorization.

7. A Witness in the Public Square. Father Peyton saw the value of the robust public witness of the Church in the midst of society. He said that faith must not be confined to the home and the church building, but must be shared and open to all. Hence the rallies in ballparks, stadiums, and other public gathering places in San Francisco, New York, São Paulo, Cebu, Manila, and Bombay. He saw the Church as a leaven in society that should be visibly, dynamically present in the world. At a moment when many forces seek to exclude religion from the public square and limit it to the private and individual realm, Peyton's intuition about public witness is particularly relevant.

8. An Initiator of Lay Collaboration. Even before Vatican II, Father Peyton's Family Rosary Crusade sought and trained lay collaborators to assist in the preparations for the rallies and, in the post-rally evangelization, through the films on the Mysteries of the Rosary—in keeping with the Holy Cross tradition of hospitality, inclusion, and collaboration with clergy, religious, and laity. His team carefully selected men to visit the homes of people of all faiths, inviting them to pledge to pray as a family and to attend the central Rosary rally. Thousands of lay catechists and lay leaders were equipped as "educators in the faith." These efforts were made in the Holy Cross tradition of assisting the local Church's ordinary work. Family Rosary usually left behind an office structure, a core of trained pastoral agents ready to spread the message in person and through the use of film and radio.

9. A Visionary for Families around the World. In keeping with the Holy Cross vision of global ministry, he responded to postwar threats to the family, the most basic unit of Church and society. He founded Family Rosary Crusade in Albany, New York (1942), and Family Theater Productions in Hollywood, California (1947). "To share with families of the world that peace, the prayer, the love and the togetherness I experienced in the Rosary home, would be my thanks. This would be my mission. This would be my priesthood's power and energy. And so was born the Family Rosary Crusade," he said.

10. An Evangelizer of the Masses. Father Peyton came to recognize the power and promise of large public events to inspire commitment to daily family prayer and the Rosary. He held his first such event in 1947 in London, Ontario. After that, his events became strategic, well-planned, massive Rosary rallies for family prayer in many major cities of the globe. More than twenty-eight million people participated in the rallies over the years, heard Father Peyton's personal witness to the faith, and experienced Mary's intercession through the power and promise of praying the family Rosary in the home.

11. A Pioneer in Media and Marketing. Father Peyton saw the immense possibilities and promise that mass media offered for evangelization and the effective advancement of his mission to offer family prayer, especially the Rosary, as the bedrock for unity and peace in the family and in society. Therefore, he kept abreast of cultural and technological advances by consulting such influential figures as Marshall McLuhan, a pioneer in the study of media theory, as well as the eminent Hollywood radio and film producer Tom

Lewis, and many others. It was a Hollywood copywriter, Al Scalpone, who delivered two powerful phrases to Father Peyton that summed up perfectly his mission: "The family that prays together stays together" and "A world at prayer is a world at peace."

12. An Influencer at Vatican II. At Vatican II, Father Peyton actively promoted the role of Mary, Mother of the Church, the family as the domestic church, and the importance of family prayer for the fulfillment of the family's God-given mission. The Council documents on the Church (*Lumen Gentium*), on the Church in the modern world (*Gaudium et Spes*), and on the apostolate of the laity (*Apostolicam Actuositatem*) were all influenced by Father Peyton and his friends in the hierarchy. Consequently, Vatican II clearly stated that the family has a social and ecclesial reality of primary importance. Father Peyton was delighted by the presentation of Mary's unique place in the Church:

> It seemed to me that Pope Paul's decision, announced in the same speech in which he promulgated this decree, to proclaim Our Lady as Mother of the Church was a logical outflow of the Council's own action. It clarified that Mary is the Mother of the family of God, the Mother of the members of Christ, the Mother of the Mystical Body. Her honored and indispensable role in the Family of God is thus the same as that of the mother in any family who pours herself out in selfless love for her children.

13. A Memorable Witness for Personal Holiness. Father Peyton's personal holiness left the most memorable impression with those encountering him, even if only once. Longtime supporters and collaborators and other faithful exposed to his witness retain a considerable ongoing devotion to him and his work. Millions of people were drawn to God, Jesus, the Gospel, and the Church through the fifty-one years of his priestly ministry. Often he referred to himself as Mary's burro, carrying her everywhere. His devotion to Mary, to the Rosary, and his daily holy hour before the Blessed Sacrament, as well as his faithful and devout celebration of the daily Eucharist and his constant prayer, all fit together to make him a man of heroic virtue worthy of emulation by all.

14. A Bold Intercessor for Families Today. The impact of Father Peyton's legacy continues today as he intercedes for families from heaven. He has been declared venerable and hopefully is on his way to beatification and to canonization. Venerable Patrick Peyton's boldness, creativity, enthusiasm, and passion for the Gospel shaped his life and ministry. They are clear signs of his holiness and his love of God and neighbor. As we remember him, may his devotion to Mary, his promotion of family prayer, his service to families, and his commitment to the mission of evangelization inspire us as we discern and seek to carry out the mission that the Lord has entrusted to each one of us.

Rev. Wilfred J. Raymond, C.S.C.
President of Holy Cross Family Ministries

Preface

When Father Patrick Peyton, C.S.C., died on June 3, 1992, he was no longer a well-known religious figure. However, few if any did as much as he did to promote the Rosary and family prayer throughout the world. His fifty years of fostering family unity by encouraging daily family prayer, especially the Rosary, have not been forgotten. Today, his legacy continues under the sponsorship of the Congregation of Holy Cross.

The hard work and dedication of Father Peyton have been recognized and honored by four popes, including Pope John Paul II. His many accomplishments include worldwide Rosary Crusades in forty countries drawing twenty-eight million people as well as more than six hundred dramatic and variety radio and TV programs that have had ten thousand broadcasts. Three-and-one-half years after his death, on October 7, 1995, the feast of the Holy Rosary, Pope John Paul II gave a talk on family prayer before leading the Rosary at St. Patrick's Cathedral in New York City, during which he said, "To use a phrase made famous by the late Father Patrick Peyton: 'The family that prays together stays together!'" In 1992 Pope John Paul II named Cardinal Roger Mahony, archbishop of Los Angeles, as his personal envoy to the fiftieth anniversary celebration of the Family Rosary in Manila, the Philippines. The outdoor Mass in December 1992, at which Cardinal Mahony presided, drew more than 1.5 million people.

Throughout his half-century of ministry, Father Peyton expressed his conviction that Catholics and non-Catholics alike needed to restore the Rosary and family prayer in their homes and in their very hearts. Such a restoration, he believed, would help people express their deepest yearnings for God, which would also strengthen families in overcoming the social pressures that were eroding family unity. He also believed that praying families throughout the world would achieve world peace as evidenced by another of his famous messages, "A world at prayer is a world at peace."

Father Peyton was an untiring evangelist for the Lord Jesus Christ and also an advocate of Mary chiefly because he believed that Mary was the most effective evangelist for Jesus in the modern world and that she was "omnipotent in the power of her intercession" with her Son. Consequently, Father Peyton's life's task, as he once stated, was to "devote every minute of it to restoring the family Rosary in America." His efforts didn't stop with America, however, as he went on to become an international leader of millions of people searching for God in their lives.

Although Father Peyton wrote *All for Her* some twenty-three years ago, the modern reader will find it lively and entertaining as it captures all the energy and scope of a very holy man embarked on a unique spiritual journey. The book reveals to us poignant stories about his father and mother and their devotion to the Rosary and family prayer, as well as stories of his saintly sister Nellie and of his anger and despair as a young man. We then follow Father Peyton to Scranton, Pennsylvania, where he served as sexton of St. Peter's Cathedral and began to pursue his priestly vocation; then on to the seminary at Notre Dame University, the Congregation of Holy Cross, his lifelong religious community; and in his life-threatening struggle with tuberculosis and his reliance on Mary to pray to her Son for a healing. Finally, Father Peyton takes us on some of his Rosary Crusades throughout the world, and he gives us a captivating account of his first national radio program that led to the creation of Family Theater Productions. Here he describes how he successfully recruited more than one hundred of the great stars of Hollywood to perform in his radio and TV productions designed to foster spirituality, prayer, and family unity.

All for Her is not only spiritual but entertaining reading. Father Patrick Peyton, who produced hundreds of dramatic programs, relates in his own words the real-life drama of his life and ministry and how all that he did, he did for her—believing that through the spiritual power of Mary's Rosary, families would be strengthened to withstand the secular obstacles to family unity and would be spiritually nourished to reflect the love and life of Christ in their daily lives.

Rev. James Wm. Chichetto, C.S.C.

Introduction

How does one possibly introduce a book on the life of Father Pat Peyton? Not easily done, but the best I can do is to recall my relationship with him over many years and simply tell the story as I recall it, so many years later.

When Pat Peyton was studying for the priesthood in the Congregation of Holy Cross, I was a fellow seminarian. We spent a year together at Moreau Seminary on the grounds of the University of Notre Dame. One day our horse ran away, and Pat and a fellow seminarian were sent out to look for him. Just to the east of us was a section of town that was then called the "dog patch." It was made up of people who were very poor during those Great Depression days. In the course of their search for the horse, Pat and his fellow seminarian talked to a good number of them. Pat, of course, was immediately concerned about their faith and used to ask them, after they made their inquiries about the horse, "What religion do you belong to?" Most of them said, "Catholic." Pat would then ask, "Do you come to Mass at Notre Dame?" Practically all of them said no because they didn't have decent clothing and they felt they would be embarrassed by coming to Sacred Heart Church at the university.

They finally found the horse, but Pat was troubled by the circumstances in which the people in the "dog patch" found themselves. If they couldn't come to Sacred Heart, they ought to have a chapel of their own. Pat and some others of us began by taking a census of the "dog patch," which had several hundred people living in it. The census proved quite clearly that, while practically all of them were Catholic, none of them were going to church on Sunday because of their embarrassment about their clothing. Pat immediately came to the conclusion that we should build a church for them where they could go without embarrassment, because all of them had poor clothing.

We spent most of that summer building the church. All of the seminarians chipped in with what little money they had, and we managed to buy some cheap lumber in North Carolina. It turned out that many of the seminarians were pretty good carpenters, and before the summer was finished, we had the church built. It was modest but quite beautiful to us in a humble kind of way.

I remember the day in August, the feast of the Assumption, when Pat and I and others greeted the then president of Notre Dame, Father John O'Hara, who later became Cardinal Archbishop of Philadelphia, after heading up all of the Catholic chapels during World War II as auxiliary bishop to Cardinal Spellman. It was a day of great triumph when he blessed the church, and the people attended in large numbers in a new parish called "Little Flower," after Saint Thérèse of the Child Jesus.

During all of that time, Pat was so zealous in visiting the families and completing the survey that he often wanted to do one more house before returning to the seminary. I would often say to him, "Pat, they are giving us a lot of leeway in letting us do this work. If we get back late, we will be in real trouble and miss prayers, and the superior may very well call off the whole project." Pat was stubborn in his way, and he would just say, "Only one more house." We did "one more house," and it took longer than we anticipated, and we arrived back at the seminary at a time that should have been halfway through the evening prayers. To my surprise, the seminarians were recreating, and when I asked why they weren't at prayers, they said, "We don't know, the superior just called them off for today." Pat just let that famous grin of his suffuse his face, and he would give me a wise look. I found then at an early stage that you just couldn't beat Pat when he really wanted to do something good, even though it was running in the face of other good things. Somehow it always worked out for him.

I left to study in Rome that fall and didn't see Pat again until after he had become a kind of legend in the seminary. He was told that he was dying of tuberculosis, and he prepared for that, but one of his old Irish priest friends told him, "You just don't have enough faith in the Blessed Mother. Put it in her hands, and everything will be all right." By a kind of miracle, it did become "all right." During one of his visits to the doctor who had predicted his death, it turned out that he was completely cured of tuberculosis, although he would be weak for some years to come.

When I returned to our theological seminary in Washington, DC, Holy Cross College, after the war had broken out in Europe and we were forced to leave, Pat came down to complete his theological studies before ordination. He had to spend most of his days in bed recuperating, but on the other hand, there was nothing the matter with his mind and spirit. I saw a great deal of him during those days because I was his tutor. After each morning of classes, I would go to his room and give him the gist of the theological lectures we had just completed in the morning. Pat had a memory like no one else I have ever known. It only took one pass through the morning's lectures, and he had it all, not just for then, but for life.

After the tutoring, I would sit and talk with him for a while. His mind was always on this or that project that he might do for the glory of Mary. Some of his ideas were a bit harebrained, but I had become wary enough by now not to discount them completely. After the discussion about a number of such projects, he one day said to me, "Now I have the right one. I have written a letter to Bishop O'Hara of Kansas City asking him if he would approve and promote my idea which I call 'the Family Rosary.' As my spelling is a bit Irish," he said, "I would appreciate it if you would edit my letter to Bishop O'Hara and post it."

I did so, and a few days later a response came back from Bishop O'Hara saying that he totally approved the project and would be happy to sponsor it. That was the beginning of a worldwide crusade, and at that point it was only in Pat's head. He had to get well and be up and about again, which he was shortly after my ordination in 1943. That summer I was helping out at St. Patrick's parish in Washington, DC, preparatory to beginning my doctoral studies in theology at Catholic University. It had been a difficult year, and I was looking forward to a couple of weeks at our summer camp in Maryland, following my duties at St. Patrick's.

The day before I was to leave, I had a call from our superior at the seminary, Father Christopher O'Toole, who subsequently became superior general of the order. He told me quite simply, "Father Pat has been chaplain up at the Catholic high school in Albany, New York. He has a chance to get some people to start promoting his Family Rosary Crusade, but he needs to convince some well-known people in Hollywood to help him. He hopes to go there this week, but he needs someone to take his place in Albany. You're it." There went the vacation, but what could one say?

When I arrived at Albany, Pat had already left. I asked what this was all about, and the pastor there told me that Pat had simply put in a phone call to Bing Crosby. One did not simply call Bing Crosby in those days and get him on the phone personally, but that is what happened. When Pat, in his lovely brogue, told Bing what he was about, Bing just said, "Come out and talk to me about it." So Pat was on his way, and so was the Family Rosary Crusade. The pastor also told me I had to begin a three-day retreat for the high-school students the next day. No one had bothered to mention that, but in Pat's mind things just worked out as long as the Family Rosary was moving ahead. I had my doubts about that retreat, but I did the best I could with zero preparation and never having given a retreat before, especially one requiring three one-hour talks each day plus all of the confessions. Somehow it worked out. Somehow everything Pat wanted to accomplish worked out, so I guess it overflowed on me, too, at that time.

As World War II went on, Pat would come to Washington to interview the Secretary of Defense, no less, so that
he could get the Family Rosary included in the materials
sent to the troops around the world. I told him that was a
wild and impossible idea, but somehow that worked out
like everything else that Pat touched. I guess my role as an
advisor was to tell him what ideas were wild and wouldn't
work, and then he would go out and make them work. As
time went on, I became less and less confident about giving
him advice. Somehow he had an inside track with the good
Lord and His Mother, and that was something that seemed
to assure success even though it seemed impossible from
a rational point of view. What all of this adds up to is that
Pat had an enormous faith in Our Lady, and she did not let
him down. I began to think that maybe she was inspiring
him in the "wild idea" department. That is a hard combination to beat.

As the years passed following the war, those initial and
tentative successes bloomed not only nationwide but worldwide. The top stars in Hollywood seemed to be standing in
line to help him and enjoyed doing it as well. He had them
all mesmerized and, I am sure, inspired them with a great
faith in Our Lady as he did so. Because of the attraction
of these stars, the Family Rosary Crusade blossomed on
radio and later with even greater success on television. His
marvelous films on the Mysteries of the Rosary appeared
on television around the world, and this accompanied
by massive rallies of millions of people in places as distant as Manila, Buenos Aires, Caracas, and Spain, as well
as throughout the United States and Canada. It took the

largest stadium in New York just to accommodate the group there, and Cardinal Spellman gave the opening talk.

It should be noted that Pat had some wonderful Holy Cross priests helping him in a very unselfish way, both here and abroad. I think they, too, had my earlier experience of having to tell him that he was crazy with this or that idea, but somehow he prevailed and somehow the idea became reality. Even Rome took notice, and the Family Rosary was given generous approval during the sessions of Vatican Council II. All of the popes from Pius XII to John Paul II welcomed him with great cordiality and favor because they knew of the great work he was doing to inspire devotion to Our Lady all over the world.

All of this, of course, required money, but somehow through his collaboration with J. Peter Grace, a great New York businessman and financier, there always seemed to be money there when needed. In fact, there is a good deal left even today. I can only say that Father Pat Peyton was an extraordinary man with an extraordinary devotion to Our Lady that led to a whole string of extraordinary happenings all over the world. There is certainly no Catholic priest who has addressed more Catholics and inspired them with his simple faith in Our Lady and his devotion to the Rosary. It was also important that he did this in a family context, promoting not just the Rosary but the "Family Rosary" said together each day in the heart of the family. He had learned this simple lesson at the knees of his parents in Ireland.

I must conclude by saying that Father Pat was one of the most extraordinary priests I have ever known. While I often disagreed with him, and even argued with him about the viability of his ideas, I must say that I lost more arguments than I won, and in general he always seemed to accomplish what he set out to do, no matter how difficult or visionary it was. As one who has spent practically his whole life at a university dedicated to Our Lady, I can only applaud the good works of this good man and hope and pray that his influence will continue across the years after his death as it certainly did during his life.

Rev. Theodore M. Hesburgh, C.S.C.
President Emeritus
University of Notre Dame
July 24, 1996

One

These Were My Parents

Carracastle in the first decades of this century was a straggly little village of thatched one-story cabins set in a fold of the foothills of the Ox Mountains, a few miles from the Atlantic Ocean in the bleak western part of County Mayo, Ireland. The higher land was stony and barren. The valleys were soggy from the almost continuous rain that swept in, warm and soft, from the Atlantic. It formed a misty medium, neither air nor water, in which land and stream and sky merged into a single ghostly vagueness. Harsher winds from the mountains in winter stirred the brown rushes bordering the many little lakes, home of the water hen, the mallard, and the goose. On a rare day in summer, the sun asserted his kingship, and then the pasture land shone with vivid greens that contrasted with the lustrous gold of the ripe oats and the bright yellows of the ubiquitous furze.

I was born in one of those cabins in 1909, and it was my home for the first nineteen years of my life. I always think that this was a great grace, not because it was a thatched

1

cabin, but because it was a home of prayer. Starting on their wedding day, my parents knelt each evening before the hearth to say together the family Rosary, that God and Mary might protect and bless their home and fill it with the laughter of children. God heard that daily prayer. He blessed my parents with a large family. They, for their part, expressed their gratitude in the way they knew best. In all the years of their married life they never once failed to gather the family every evening for the recitation of Mary's centuries-old prayer.

We were extremely close-knit as a family. It would have been hard for us to survive if we were not. There were eleven of us in all, four boys, five girls, and our parents, and we lived in this three-room thatched cottage in which my father's father and his father before him had raised similar families.

In the West of Ireland people are not demonstrative of their feelings, and the unity of this family was expressed less in high-sounding words or in gestures of friendship than in deeds. We all worked together, each carrying from earliest childhood his or her share of the unending round of labor involved in eking a livelihood for eleven persons out of fourteen acres of stony land worked without benefit of machines or sophisticated agricultural techniques. In that country, a child is raised once he learns to carry two sods of turf or peat from the rick at the gable end of the house to feed the open fire at the hearth. So runs a common saying. And from the time we were able to toddle, we all had our daily tasks and made our contribution to the common effort.

But our help to one another and our commitment to a common and mutually beneficial goal were something more than the organization of an anthill or a hive of bees. It was deep down a sense of love for each other based on a series of spiritual and moral ties, which made the well-being of the others more important to each individual than his own. When the swarm takes off, the new colony of bees forgets all about the hive from which it came. That was not the way in our family. Those who grew up and left home were still bound by unbreakable links. They continued to put the advantage of the others ahead of their own. They were ready to forego any personal benefit for the promotion of common purposes. And in fact, as I shall recount in more detail later, several members of my family literally sacrificed their lives to support me when I was in need and to help me toward a goal which represented not only my own heart's desire but the wish and ambition of all.

Such attitudes express the deepest tradition of that region and that culture. They are bound up with its religious sense and with its scale of values. But in our case, I believe they were intensified by the spirit and the spirituality of my father. This John Peyton, who married Mary Gillard of Rathreedane, Bonniconlon, in March 1899, when he was thirty-two years old and she twenty-seven, was an extraordinary man. He was himself the eldest son of sixteen children, and his father's premature death had catapulted him as a teen-ager into the responsibility of breadwinner for his mother, brothers, and sisters. Both before and after he was married, he went to work on various occasions in England, as was the practice of the young men of all the West of Ireland. After the heavy work of preparing the land and planting the crops, mostly by hand, they would earn additional money by hiring themselves out as harvest laborers in England, sometimes staying on as coal miners through the winter. Meanwhile the women and children would save the hay and oats of their own little farms, bring home the turf from the bog, and dig the potatoes.

My father also worked on building construction in England and learned the trade of stonemason. He practiced this trade in our own neighborhood, too, taking contracts to build dwelling houses, stables, and walls for local farmers and also to keep the local dirt roads in repair. But the grueling work begun while he was still a child quickly extorted its toll. About the time he was married, or not long afterward, he began to get acute attacks of bronchitis, and he became progressively less capable of physical exertion. So he was forced to restrict himself to supervision and direction, riding the horse out to the fields to watch while the rest of us worked.

The three eldest in the family were girls: Bridget, Mary, and Ellen. Bridget and Ellen are known in the family as Beatrice and Nellie respectively. These three girls and my mother had to carry the entire load for a long time. The earliest recollection I have of these three girls is seeing them as teen-agers doing the work of men on the farm, along with their mother. They were the ones who took the scythe to cut the oats, harnessed the horse and yoked him to the cart to bring out a load of stone to repair the holes in the road, and quarried the sand for the same purpose. I took it for granted that women cut the oats and plowed the fields. That was how we kept going until the three boys who followed,

Michael, Thomas, and myself, reached in turn an age at which we could make a significant contribution.

We all did our best, but the inability of the one who possessed the skills, my father, to take the active lead was inevitably reflected in our economic level. To fill eleven mouths and clothe eleven bodies from the produce of so meager a farm is not easy, and there was no revenue from other sources until the two eldest girls left for America in 1920 and began to send money home. After that, things looked up a little, in spite of the general disruption of the economy caused by the Black and Tan War and the Civil War that followed in the early 1920s. But in the meantime the going was rough, and we were lucky when we had our fill of potatoes, cabbage, turnips, soda bread, butter, eggs, and an occasional mouthful of fat bacon. The Peytons are big-framed, large-boned, energetic people, with rapid metabolisms. In my late fifties, I can still eat a second dinner without putting on weight. Am I, perhaps, subconsciously compensating for the hunger which was then my frequent companion?

My father grieved much that he could not do more for us. It hurt him particularly when the time came for one of us to leave home. He felt that it was his duty to hold the family group together until he was satisfied that each had acquired the maturity to stand honorably on his own feet. During his various stays in England, he had seen how some young Irish people had abandoned their moral principles and religious practice once they were away from the supports and safeguards of home. He himself had not made that mistake. On the contrary, he had deepened his religious experience. He was, for example, the very first to introduce in the neighborhood the practice of receiving Holy

Communion on the first Friday of each month in honor of the Sacred Heart. I remember from my early childhood that the two oldest children, Beatrice and Mary, used to go to the early Mass in the church at Ballina. That was long before the devotion had been established in our own parish of Atty-mass. But my father feared that if we left home too soon, we might not be strong enough to withstand the temptations to which we would be exposed. He wanted to keep us near him, and I believe he found it hard to reconcile himself to his poor health mainly because the resultant poverty forced some of his children to go away to work at an early age.

If he could not do everything for us that he wanted, he did what he could. He was a man of total integrity, so that we could always look up to him. Although we were the only family of our name in the village and had no close relatives in it, everyone there respected my father. He was tall and powerfully built, and a heavy mustache and deep, penetrating eyes gave him an air of distinction. He spoke two languages fluently and correctly—Gaelic and English— and he had natural qualities of leadership. The neighbors consulted him on their problems and welcomed his views on political and other issues. He was scrupulously honest in all his dealings.

He was strict with us as children, but he was honest and open in the circle of the family as well as outside. From about the time Beatrice was fourteen, he put her in charge of activities in the fields, while my mother worked mainly in and around the house, caring for the animals and poultry, as well as preparing food. We engaged in typical mixed farming. We kept a horse for the farm work, raised cattle, pigs, chickens, turkeys, ducks, and geese, grew potatoes, oats, turnips, cabbage, and onions.

Beatrice received the orders for each day's work, and the rest of us were instructed to obey her. Whatever the job, we were expected to do it thoroughly. Each evening, she made a full report of the day's accomplishments and received instructions for the next day. Beatrice was a perfectionist, and she insisted that we measure up to her own performance and standards. But she was no tyrant. My father knew how to maintain discipline without violence. He never raised his hand to us, nor would he have allowed Beatrice to treat us harshly had she wanted to. It was a different spirit entirely, a sense of a cooperative effort in which each gladly played his part. At the end of the year, when all the crops were harvested and the cattle and pigs sold, an inventory was taken. My father gave a full report to the entire family, even the youngest. We knew how much money we had and how it would be spent. We all sought for ways to stretch our meager fund, to increase the total, or to lighten the demands on it.

The dominant quality of my father, the one that gave a unity to all the rest, was his great spirit of faith. This, of course, is characteristic of the culture in which I was raised. The language is sprinkled with expressions of piety. Heaven and earth are intertwined in the mind and the imagination. We lived among holy wells, the memories of saints who had labored in the same fields, the hiding places of persecuted priests, and the rocks on which they had celebrated the Mass.

All of this was embodied in my father to a high degree. In his presence, one felt uplifted, almost like being in church.

I don't mean that he preached to us. What impressed me was the way he lived and the way he prayed, especially when each evening we all knelt together to say the Rosary. If there was one inflexible rule in our home, it was that every one of us had to participate in the family Rosary led by my father. It didn't matter how hard or how long the day's work—digging potatoes, cutting turf, or repairing a road. Often one or another would drop to sleep on his knees. But he was always brought back into the prayer, kindly but firmly. It was the entire family praising God, asking Him through His Mother to protect it, to guide it to the destiny He had intended for it. That nightly scene constitutes my earliest memory and the most abiding. From it I derive the entire pattern and purpose of my existence.

Other than the Rosary, we did not engage much in formal prayer. We went, of course, to Mass on Sundays and Holy Days, climbing on foot to the parish church at Attymass three miles away, in which I had been baptized on January 13, 1909, just four days after my birth. And, as I said, we went down to Ballina, a little farther in a different direction, to make the First Fridays before that devotion had become known in our parish. Later, our pastor introduced it, and we then began to attend in our own parish church of St. Joseph at Attymass. In addition, there was the major event twice a year, about Easter and in October, when the pastor came for "the stations." That was a custom going back to the days of persecution in Ireland, when there was neither church nor resident priest. A priest would then come in stealth at infrequent and irregular intervals to hear confessions, say Mass, and distribute the Eucharist in a secluded spot. The practice had survived in "the stations." Each time, the priest selected a different house in the village, and all assembled there to confess their sins, assist at Mass, and receive Holy Communion. Each family was proud when its turn came, and no effort was spared in whitewashing the walls inside and out and otherwise making the place spotlessly clean for the occasion.

In our dealings with our father, we could never forget that he was the one who made the decisions. Our mother, on the other hand, was a peaceful loving woman. I don't remember ever seeing her get mad except once, and that time she had plenty reason for it. She loved Michael, the eldest boy, more than any of us. Sometimes, when we were growing up, I would set out mischievously to provoke him, until one fine day Mother decided I had gone too far and told him to let me have it. He gave me a real walloping, and after that I was a little more respectful. But she herself never once laid a hand on me in all the years, no matter how great the provocation.

Because of my father's illness, she worked even harder than most of the other women in the village, and God knows they all had to do their share. I recall, for example, seeing her out in the field spraying the potatoes, a job that had to be done twice or perhaps three times in June and July, depending on the weather and the incidence of the blight. The metal knapsack sprayer with its hand-operated pump held nearly four gallons of spray. As a child I would help to mix the lime and copper sulphate in the barrel of water at the end of the potato field and ladle the mixture into the sprayer. She would then hoist it on her back and march up and down the rows of potatoes to cover the stalks with the blue liquid, a task which on each occasion required several grueling days of effort to complete.

In spite of this and similar tasks, she was as straight as a ramrod. Though not as tall as my father, she was taller than any of the neighboring women. She wore the same long wide skirts as they did, and like them wrapped her head and the upper part of her body in a heavy black shawl when she went out. But even that rough clothing could not hide her beautiful face and lovely figure. She had long silky hair, which she would often let me comb for her when I was a boy. When I was saying good-by to her for the first and last time in 1928, she was fifty-six years old, yet her hair was still black. Nor was her character soured in the least. On top of all the work, she had a hard time trying to anticipate the moods of my father, for it is not easy to be the wife of an invalid, even if he is a good man. Yet my last memory is of a woman still with the beautiful qualities of peace, joy, radiance, and balance. And she was full of fun, always ready for a prank or a joke. We were never afraid of her. We could confide our secrets to her and count on her to win some little privilege for us that we would hesitate to ask directly of our father.

It was a common practice in Ireland for one or another of the children to go for a time to live in the home of a relative. Usually, there was some practical reason. It might be to ease the burden on a mother who had several tiny children by taking one of them from under her feet for a while. Or it might be that the other home lacked a young boy or girl to run messages and help around the place. I was sent twice to stay with my mother's parents, Robert Gillard and his wife, Kitty, of Rathreedane, Bonniconlon. The first time was before I started school, so I guess the reason was to get me off my mother's hands. She nearly died of puerperal fever when I was born, and although she recovered completely, it was not long until Sarah came along, to be followed by John and Kitty.

I returned to my parents' home in time to be enrolled in the grade school at Bofield, less than half a mile away, in May 1914, when I was just over five years of age. The school was known as the national school, and it was in fact a public school. Teachers and children were all Catholics, however, and the local pastor was the school manager. Under the Irish system, a half hour is set aside daily for religious instructions, Catholic, Protestant, or Jewish, according to the religion of the pupils. In our neighborhood at that time there were no Protestant families. The Bofield school, accordingly, was to all intents and purposes the equivalent of a parochial school in the United States.

Apart from the church, which was in a category all its own and which we didn't think of as a building in the ordinary sense, the school was by far the most impressive construction in the neighborhood. It had big windows and high ceilings supported by cobwebbed beams. The slated roof further distinguished it from the thatched cottages around. It was, I suppose, the size of a four-car garage, but in my young imagination it figured as the biggest and most important building in the world. This was the home of learning for some fifty boys and sixty girls ranging in age from five to fourteen or fifteen years. We were divided into three classrooms, the oldest group under the charge of Tadhg O'Leary, the principal, the middle group under his wife, and the smallest ones under Maria Loftus. Tadhg was an outsider, a native of County Kerry, but his wife was Maria Kelly from Bonniconlon. In addition to the grade school, Tadhg conducted an advanced school in a separate room in the same building. Boys and girls from over a wide area came to be coached for entrance examinations to teacher-training colleges, the girls living in dormitories in the O'Leary home and the boys boarding out in neighboring homes.

Here it was that I took my first hesitant steps on the royal road to learning under the guidance of Maria Loftus, helped at times by a "monitor" from among the teacher candidates. We sat on long wooden benches, the timbers of which bore the names or initials of earlier generations of pupils. Maps on the walls identified by color countries and continents which meant nothing to us and also the two countries which we all knew vaguely would one day beckon most of us—England and the United States. Heating in the winter was provided by an open fire in a single grate, a fire for which each of us carried sods of turf from his home along with the couple of slices of soda bread that made his lunch.

Maria Loftus took me through the first three grades, teaching me the rudiments of reading, writing, and arithmetic. Yet it was not what she taught that affected me as much as the way she taught it. She treasured her innocent charges, made us feel important, left a warm mark on us. Among all my teachers, she stands out in my mind. Only Father Cornelius J. Hagerty, my professor of ethics at Notre Dame, left a greater mark on me, making a decisive contribution in what I regard as the supreme crisis and turning point in my life.

I went to live with my grandparents at Rathreedane for a second time in the summer of 1917, and now I was enrolled at the school in Bonniconlon, where by coincidence a brother of Maria Loftus was my teacher. This time the reason for sending me to my grandparents was to give a hand about the house. My grandfather was not only old but an invalid and practically blind. It was dangerous to leave him alone in the house, and it often fell to me to keep an eye on him while the others were out at work. In retrospect, the period I then spent with him was very important in my life. Dominick Melvin, the village blacksmith, was a frequent visitor. Nell Gallagher, a neighbor, would come in at night to sit by the hearth and smoke her short clay pipe when her work was finished, and her husband, Patrick, would sometimes come with her. Then my grandmother would light up my grandfather's clay pipe for him, and the conversation would range far and wide, always eloquent. As I sat spellbound in the warm recess of the fireplace, I learned things about the family and the community which otherwise I'd probably never have known.

The Gillards were people of some distinction in their village. In fact that part of it where they lived was often known as Gillardstown. According to a strong local tradition, the first Irish Gillard was a Napoleonic soldier. During his war with England, Napoleon had invaded Egypt in 1794, and he simultaneously sent a small diversionary force to Ireland, where conditions for revolt were ripe. A thousand Frenchmen, with arms for a much bigger force, landed in August at Killala, about thirteen miles from our village, were joined by a big but untrained force of local farmers, and quickly drove the English garrisons from Killala,

Ballina, and Castlebar. While the main force marched east toward Dublin to be defeated by a strong English army at Ballinamuch, County Longford, a smaller party moved northeast through Bonniconlon toward Sligo. Learning of the defeat and surrender of their comrades at Ballinamuch, they tossed their arms into a small lake in the Ox Mountains near Bonniconlon, still known as Lough na Gunnai or the Lake of the Guns, and dispersed. Most were repatriated, but some went home with their Irish comrades-in-arms and in due course married Irish wives. One of these was my grandfather's grandfather.

Life in the Gillard home was very like that in Carracastle. My grandfather was a man of the same deep spirituality as my father. The family Rosary was here equally the dominant moment of the day. While there was no artificial piety about his conversation, religious themes formed an integral part of it, even when he was recounting for me the local folklore.

A major feature of the village of Rathreedane, for example, is a prehistoric fort about forty yards in diameter and surmounted by a granite pillar some twelve feet high known as the Pillar Stone of Ruadhain's fort. The Ruadhain family, as my grandfather explained to me, were local chieftains at the time of St. Patrick in the fifth century. This, of course, was country evangelized by the saint in person. Only twenty miles away to the southwest, near Westport, is Croaghpatrick. On the top of this cone-shaped mountain, tradition says, Patrick fasted forty days and forty nights until he wrung from God a promise that Ireland would, until the end of time, cling to the faith he had brought it. One of the Ruadhains joined St. Patrick to work as his chief herdsman.

The society was semi-nomadic, so that it was normal for Patrick to travel with his flock of goats and maintain himself while he preached the Gospel. This Ruadhain established a church in our neighborhood when Patrick moved on, and he is still revered as a saint.

We had other saints among our neighbors, too: Muredach or Molaisse, Garbhan, Fechin, Cumian, Olcan, Attracta, Nathy, and Gerald, and many whose names I no longer remember but who were associated with ruins of churches and abbeys. They were my constant companions, as during the infinitely lingering twilight of those long summer evenings of 1917 I wandered along the winding little roads fragrant with new-mown hay or sat with my grandfather by the fireside and with my childish questions drew up from his long memory the traditions of fifteen hundred years. It was a home like my own. Living there confirmed the image I already possessed of what life was and should be in a normal Christian family. I could happily have remained there indefinitely. Instead, this second stay with my grandparents lasted only some months. I was fetched home again to Carracastle before the end of 1917.

Two

A Boy Becomes a Man

There was more than one reason for my abrupt return to my parents' home. The reports of my progress in the Bonnicon-lon school were less than satisfactory. Besides, I had reached an age at which I could make a significant contribution to the work of the house and farm. My father's health had deteriorated to a point where he could do little or nothing. I would go back to Bofield school, of course, as I was still only nine years old, but in the evenings, at weekends, and during vacations, I would be expected to pull my weight from now on.

The nature of the work changed with the seasons, but there was always something to occupy us. No doubt the most important crop was the potato. In spite of the famine of the 1840s, it had continued to be the staple food, and once the Bordeaux mixture, or the "spray," as we called it, had been discovered as a protection against blight, people were assured of a crop that would keep their stomachs full nearly all the year round. The land was plowed or turned

with a spade as soon after St. Patrick's Day as the soil had
dried out enough to be worked. Holes were opened at regular intervals on the prepared ridges by a man using a simple wooden instrument. A youngster then tossed a seed
into each hole, the seed consisting of a segment of potato
containing an "eye" or bud. These segments had been cut
in advance and dusted with lime to protect them against
insect attack. Another youngster followed with a spade to
cover the seed with earth. Later came two moldings with
layers of earth, the first spread before the stalks emerged,
the next carefully deposited around the young stalks to protect without damaging them. Preparation and application of
the spray followed, and the first potatoes were traditionally
dug on Garland Sunday, the last Sunday of July. In October
and early November the main crop had to be dug, picked,
and stored in pits to ensure the nourishment of humans,
pigs, and poultry until the following June.

Picking potatoes on a cold damp day was not a chore to
wish on your worst enemy. The squalls driving in off the sea
cut through to the bone. Boots became heavy with the wet
soil, which also stuck to the potatoes and chilled the fingers
as the picker tried to remove it. But when a late autumn sun
broke through, it quickly raised the spirits. One became
conscious of the geese that flocked to the fields at the sound
of the spade and fed on the small and rotted tubers. Seagulls
also zeroed in, searching for fat earthworms upturned by
the digger: bold, forward birds that did not hesitate to peck
at the blade of the spade. Crows were equally fond of the
earthworms, but they foraged down the line, always maintaining a cautious distance. The first wild geese crossed the
sky, forming changing patterns in response to mysterious

instructions from their leader. We would watch them as we ate the soda bread and jam and swallowed the strong hot tea carried by one of the children to the field to save time.

On Sundays and Holy Days, we performed only the essential tasks of milking the cows, feeding the animals and poultry, and cleaning about the house. But the rest of our lives was never idle, from early morning to dusk on Saturdays and during vacation, from after school on school days. Saving the turf on which we depended for fuel was a complicated process, often stretched out for months when the weather was rainy, as it was most of the time. The first step was to cut the sods with a winged spade, each sod about a foot long and five inches thick. Impregnated with water when cut so that each weighed six or seven pounds, the sods were spread on firm ground to dry the exposed side, then turned over, and later built up into footings consisting of four or five sods on end with another balanced on top, often juggled about yet again into larger units if rain slowed down the drying process. When it was finally cured, it was loaded into bags and carried on our backs across the soggy ground to the bog road where we dumped it into a cart for the journey home and final stacking.

Yet there was no day in all one's life to match that special day on the bog when nature regretted the long series of buffeting to which it normally subjected us in our Mayo backwater, and the sun smiled and the breeze laughed and humming bees danced in the fragrant heather and a skylark praised God infinitely high in the limpid air. On such a day the mid-afternoon meal became a banquet such as no Cordon Bleu chef has ever served. We would gather dry sods of turf to start the fire, draw water from a well or stream, prepare the tea in a tin can, and serve it in mugs. The bread had a flavor no master baker ever equaled, the tea a bouquet unknown to Burgundy or Tokay. When all were sated, the elders took a relaxed hour to gossip and doze, while we youngsters scampered across the open bog in search of the nests of the soaring larks or sloshed our barefoot way through the marshy places from which the turf had been cut, in pursuit of the big-eyed frogs.

Apart from such infrequent breaks, there was little time for games except on Sunday. Even on that day, however, I do not recall spending much of my time at the very simple games which alone were possible in the absence of equipment or facilities for organized sports. What I remember about Sunday is going to Mass. Literally everyone attended, winter and summer, rain or shine. Nobody had galoshes, and few had umbrellas or raincoats in those days. Many of the older people were stopped with rheumatism or the various back ailments which are the reward of shoulders that have carried too heavy burdens too far for too many years. But nothing short of total disablement would keep one of them away. If you pressed for a reason, you would most likely be told that their parents and grandparents had paid dearly for the privilege. And that was true enough. Within our parish boundaries were the remains of four old Catholic churches and monasteries, two of them founded by the Premonstratensians. The ruined church at Kildermott dates in part to the ninth century and is today preserved as a national monument. All of them had been vandalized by the Cromwellians in the seventeenth century.

There is an old story about the Kildermott church. Tradition says that it was originally situated at Killeen on the other side of a small lake called Ballymore Lake, that the monks decided to move it, stone by stone, across the lake to its present site, and that the final boatload of stones being rowed across at night by chanting monks sank, with the loss of all hands. The spirits of these monks were still believed to haunt the lake, putting out from Killeen on moonlit nights, their chant audible above the lapping of the water on their oars, and sinking without trace at the spot of the original catastrophe. Some of the old people used to say that in their youth they had witnessed the re-enactment, as perhaps, through poteen-bleary eyes, they had on their way home from an autumn fair in Ballina or a particularly gay wedding celebration. A curious detail in support of the tradition that the church was moved is that much of the stone is granite found only on the Killeen side of the lake.

The name Killeen is a corruption of the Gaelic *cillin*, meaning a little church. It comes from the same Latin root as the English word *cell*, and it originally referred to the home of a monk or hermit. As Irish place names indicate, many of these became burial grounds, and the Killeen in our parish is no exception. In fact, my parents are buried there. My father's family had traditionally been buried at Kilgarvan in Bonniconlon parish, but my father said he wanted Killeen because it was on the road from Carracastle to the church at Attymass. "When you are going up to Mass on Sunday, you won't be tempted to forget me," he would say. In pre-Christian Ireland, it was the tradition to cast a stone on the grave of famous people as one passed. Queen Maev at Knocknaree in County Sligo has a cairn the size of a mountain built up that way, stone by stone. Now it is a Hail Mary they recite for the repose of the soul, and surely a great spiritual cairn is rising week by week over the graves of my parents and other saints who sleep with them in Killeen, as their descendants pass that way each Sunday.

From the time the Cromwellians destroyed the four old religious foundations in the parish of Attymass, no church was available to the people until 1835. For long, the occasional Mass offered by some priest who passed stealthily that way was said in the open at Log na hAltora (The Altar Hollow) in my own home village of Carracastle, or at Cnoc na hAltora (The Altar Hill) near our present church in Attymass. Later, a priest was authorized in Bonniconlon, and he also served the Attymass parish. But he had no church building there, and when he came occasionally to say Mass in a barn, he had to get express authorization each time from a Protestant landlord whose writ ran over a wide area. One Sunday, as the story was handed down, the man could not be located, and after a long waiting period, the priest decided to proceed. Just before the Consecration, the landlord stormed in and halted the ceremony. Without a word the priest took the altar vessels and their contents and marched in procession with the entire congregation to the top of a mountain a mile away, where they were, or at least regarded themselves as being, outside the landlord's jurisdiction. There they completed the Mass without further interruption.

The bearers of such traditions held the Mass in reverence, and we children were not slow to follow their lead. To serve Mass was the highest possible honor, and I still recall how I was struck dumb when one of my companions, John Barrett, suggested to me one day that he could make the necessary arrangements. I was then about nine years old, and he was a year or two older. He was not a boy with whom I had been particularly close. On the contrary, I regarded him as something of a big shot, and I was amazed that he should make me such an offer. He brushed aside my protests that I could never learn, and before I knew, I was in fact initiated into the mysteries of lighting candles, swinging the incense censer, and answering the Latin responses.

Soon I was not content to serve one Mass on Sunday. I would go to the early Mass, then stay on in the church to pray, or drop behind the others on the road home and sometimes return to serve the second and final Mass. The unspoken conventions in our society were rigid, and high on the list was the prescription that nobody should do anything out of the ordinary. I knew the others made fun of me behind my back and sometimes even in my presence made me the butt of sly jokes about my excessive piety. But I could not help it. I had not only become enraptured by my job as Mass-server, but I had developed the secret ambition to become a priest. Soon it was occupying all my thoughts. I took less part in the conversations and games of the others. I was happy when I was sent to mind the cows, which meant that I was to confine them to grazing in one part of a field when the other part was planted to potatoes, oats, or hay. Then I could indulge my dream without fear of interruption, and I would think of God and His Blessed Mother and the beauty of heaven, and I would pray for the realization of my great ambition.

Nothing would have given my parents, and indeed all the members of the family, greater pleasure than to see one of us in the priesthood. But none of them wanted to raise my hopes. Some of the missionary-sending societies were able to accept a certain number of boys at the high-school level without charge. The competition for the free places was keen, however, and the standards were high. As for our own resources, they were non-existent. There was no question of going beyond the local school for additional education.

About a year before I became an altar boy, the idea of becoming a priest had already been suggested to me. Our parish had a mission once every three years, and I was about eight when two Redemptorists were invited by the pastor for this purpose. The mission was always a big event in the life of the parish. The people came out in hundreds each morning long before daybreak for the long walk to church for the confessions which began at seven o'clock, followed by Mass and sermon, then walked home to do their day's work, returning in the evening for another long and usually impassioned sermon. My mother had taken me one evening to the ceremonies, and afterward I had gone with her to the sacristy, where she wanted to speak to one of the missionaries. After their conversation, he turned to me. He was probably taking his heavy cloak off a hanger to put it on before going out into the cold of the night. In any case he threw it around my diminutive shoulders and said: "How would you like to wear a cloak like this when you grow up?" I was too shy to do more than smile and stutter some meaningless reply, but the seed had been sown.

Some years later there was another mission, this time preached by Capuchins. By then I was an altar boy in the thick of the activity, serving the Mass, assisting with cross or candle at the Way of the Cross, swinging the censer at the Benediction. The longing to be a priest, perhaps a missionary away in the depths of Africa, grew by the hour. I was particularly attracted to the younger of the two missionaries. One day I had climbed up on the altar in an effort to light some high candles. The older man began to scold me as lacking in reverence in the House of God, but the other defended me. After they had gone away, I decided that this was the order for me. So I wrote a letter to the young priest at his monastery in Dublin to tell him I wanted to become a member of his community. However, I never got an answer; either I had misaddressed the letter, or he had put it aside and forgotten it.

The unexpressed understanding in the family was that I would continue to attend Tadhg O'Leary's school in Bofield for as long as possible. At that time, the process of education was still quite informal in the West of Ireland. Attendance was not compulsory, and many families kept the children home to help on the farm once they reached the age of eleven or twelve. On the other hand, there was no cut-off age other than the economic need to make a living. It was not uncommon to see youths in their upper teens return to school for several months in winter after spending the summer and fall as farm laborers in England. In our village, the opportunity to continue to the secondary level was better than usual because of the advanced section conducted by Tadhg O'Leary for teacher candidates.

There were several reasons why my family wanted me to remain at school. I think the real one was that they all knew that I had my heart set on the priesthood, and they hoped that one day a situation would develop in which I could get into a seminary. But the stated reason, insofar as any reason was spelled out, was that I was not robust and that consequently I'd be more fitted to a teaching or similar profession than to manual labor. By this time, in addition, Michael and Tom had become available to carry the load of the farm work, so that the third boy could be spared.

Father Roger O'Donnell, our pastor, took a great interest in me and encouraged me to visit him. He would often give me a cup of tea after Sunday Mass or send me into his fruit orchard to help myself to gooseberries or apples in season. One day he gave me a big lift by asking if I'd like him to write to the mother house in Cork of the Society of African Missionaries to see if they would be willing to take me. "You know that your father could not afford the cost of Maynooth or any of the other big seminaries," he said, "but the people in Cork might take you on a scholarship basis, so that one way or another we could keep you there." I could not believe my good fortune. I felt sure they would not refuse Father Roger. But I was wrong. In due course the answer arrived, and it was unfavorable. "We are sorry," the verdict read, "but Patrick is not up to the required standards in mathematics."

I was devastated, and all my being rebelled. "What had mathematics to do with being a missionary in Africa?" I asked myself bitterly. Father O'Donnell tried to console me. "They have not turned you down," he said. "Stay at school a while longer and work harder at your mathematics. Then we can try again." But I would not listen to him. I did continue to go to school. But I told myself that I wasn't going to indulge my foolish dream of the priesthood any more. I would study to become a teacher or a bank clerk, get a professional job, get away from the mud and the bog, and become a wealthy man. So I continued at school. I wasn't learning very much, however, and that for a variety of reasons. I was restless and rebellious, suffering from the moods and vagaries which are the usual problems of the teen-ager. In addition, there was bitterness all around me. We had in Ireland reached the letdown of the Civil War after the glorious and heroic unity of the War of Independence. Neighbor was divided against neighbor, and often family against family. Even the school was affected. My father, though a sick man unable to take an active part in the struggle, was known as sympathetic to one side, and the opposing side was then dominant in our neighborhood and had the support of Tadhg O'Leary and his wife. The result was that we Peyton children felt isolated in the school.

Shortly before my fifteenth birthday, the situation came to a dramatic head in November 1923. Tadhg O'Leary hit me a whack over the head that hurt my pride more than my skull. "You're a lazy good-for-nothing," he said to explain the blow. Tadhg may very well have been justified in the punishment and the reason for it, but it came in a context which made it completely unacceptable to me. "You'll never do that to me again," I said under my breath, as I left the school. When I told the story to my father, he sided with me, and he told me to go and register at the school in Currower a couple of miles away. Bernie Durkin, the principal of the Currower school, however, was both a personal friend and political associate of Tadhg, and he refused to take me. Faced with such opposition, my father became furious, and he threatened to take legal action and to report Bernie to the education authorities in Dublin. Bernie finally capitulated and enrolled me in December 1923. But I never really got down to serious study in the

Currower school. In the circumstances, it would not have been easy, and in addition, I was in an unsettled frame of mind. The records at Currower show that I attended only fifty-two days and that I was struck off the roll on May 24, 1924, for having been absent on thirty consecutive school days without explanation.

What had happened was that, as soon as spring arrived, I just stopped attending and started to help my brothers full time in their activities on the farm and in repairing the local roads which they were paid by the county council to maintain. It was also about this time, perhaps the previous fall when I left Tadhg O'Leary's school, that I had my first absence from home as a worker and learned a lesson that was to remain with me the rest of my life.

A farmer who lived in an adjoining village needed a youngster to help pick potatoes for a week, and I was happy to oblige. It was a farm and a house like our own, and I got there in good time on Monday morning to start the work for which I would be paid two shillings a day, then the equivalent of fifty cents. The farmer used what was then still a new technique for digging the potatoes. He hitched his horse and plowed them out of the drills. His wife and I came along with buckets to gather the potatoes and dump them into pits where they were covered with straw and clay to protect them from the frost. They had three children of their own, two boys and a girl, but the oldest was only six or seven, and consequently they could not yet help.

The day was very much like a typical day back home. I was immediately a member of the family. I shared the same food, and I knew that when night came, I would sleep in the same bed as the bigger boy. But after supper, as we sat round

the turf fire in the kitchen, the horrible awareness gradually came to me that this home was not like my own. It was
a house in which the members of the family didn't kneel
down to say the Rosary together. I had sat on later than my
usual bedtime, heavy with sleep after the day's exertions,
yet confident that at any moment the man of the house
would say: "It's getting late, isn't it? Let's get on our knees
and say the Rosary to thank God and His Blessed Mother
for watching over us this day." But the words never came.
Instead, he finally yawned and got to his feet. "That's where
your bed is, down there at the end of the house with Bernie,"
he said to me. "You'll be in no shape for work tomorrow if
you stay up any longer."

I was thunderstruck, absolutely speechless at the realization that a Catholic home existed in my own neighborhood
in which the people did not kneel together for family prayer.
While I pretended to sleep, I prayed my own Rosary and felt
the pangs of homesickness, the bitterness of being among
people whose ways were different from my own, whose
sense of values failed to measure up to what all my training
and experience had told me was normal.

I must have been more withdrawn and self-centered
than usual that week. As I worked alongside the farmer
and his family in the fields, I could not bring myself to
join freely in their conversation. My mind was constantly
returning to the same indigestible fact. They talked together.
They laughed together. They lived together. But they did
not pray together.

Gradually an idea formed itself in my simple mind. I
had no right to condemn these people. It was no wickedness on their part, nothing more than a lack of knowledge.

Nobody had ever explained to them what a difference it made to kneel together in front of the hearth and tie the family together with God and Our Lady and the saints. I could see my duty clearly. It was not to be bitter or to be morose. It was to explain to this man what he was missing, what he was failing to give his children.

The urge to speak was strong, but so was the fear of the consequences. How could I ever do such a thing? Here was a grown man, a man on the level of my own father. I was a youngster just dropped from school as a failure, a "ladeen," to use the local expression. He wouldn't even listen to me. He would give me a clout over the ears, as was his right, and send me about my business. But I could not help it. I knew I had to talk or burst. And as I whispered my solitary Rosary in the darkness, my limbs numb from the dawn-to-dusk labor, I asked Our Lady to give me the courage to speak successfully.

And so I spent an interminable, unhappy week. Sometimes the opportunity would occur when we were in the fields, but always my courage would fail. Then Saturday evening came, and the farmer paid me the few shillings that were my wages. "I'll walk with you part of the way," he said. He was a kindly man. It was dark night already, and he knew that any child would be terrified of the ghosts who lurked in the shadow of every thorn bush, who congregated in the fairy raths, who rowed the phantom boat across Ballymore Lake. And so I got my chance. As we reached the point where he planned to leave me, I finally blurted out what had been all week on my mind. I don't know what I said, but it was my first sermon on family prayer, my first appeal to another Catholic to imitate the practice of my own family and reap the same rewards. I'm sure it was terrible, as I know my every appeal is terrible. But it came from love and conviction, and it carried love and conviction. I didn't get the clout I expected. The man heard me out. His comment was noncommittal, except that he indicated that he respected me for speaking my mind. And later I learned that they started to say the Rosary each night, and that they kept on saying it.

But the incident gave me no illusion that I might set myself up as a freelance preacher. It was just something that happened, and it altered in no way the reality of my situation. I had to find work. I was still too young to undertake the adventure of a spell in England, and besides I knew that my father was dead set against that. He had not allowed any of my older brothers or sisters to go there, and neither would he let me. Yet in our neighborhood there was practically nothing. The fact was obvious. The reasons for it, which I then understood only in the vaguest way, were that the national economy had been totally disrupted by the long struggle for independence, fought in large part by strikes and boycotts, by a passive resistance which had immobilized the machinery of government but had equally halted trade and commerce. The roads were cut, the railroads ripped up, the bridge destroyed, the courts paralyzed, the postal services disrupted. The Civil War had added the factor of internal dissension and bitterness, narrowing still further the number who might be willing to offer me a job.

No alternative, accordingly, was available to me other than to spend my days as an unskilled workman breaking stones to fill the ruts in the roads. At a much younger age than Job's at his arrival on his dung heap, I was deposited

on a heap of rocks on the margin of a mountain boreen, in
ragged pants, a hammer in my hands. What always stays
in my mind is the picture of John Naughton coming along
the road in the late afternoon, three or four books under his
arm, wearing a jacket and a collar and tie. John had been a
close buddy of mine at school, and we always stayed pals.
He would stop to chat with me on his way home. He was a
true friend and never said or did anything to rub salt in my
wounds. But when he had continued on his way, despair
would descend on me with its unbearable weight. "What a
fool I am," I would say to myself. "If only I had the self-con-
trol to keep my mouth shut, I could still be over there in
Tadhg O'Leary's school, and one of these days I'd be a bank
clerk or a teacher or something. But now I have found my
level, sitting on a pile of stones for the rest of my life, with
the harsh wind from Lough Talt coming through the Gap
at me to freeze the marrow in my bones."

In such moods I would become quite unbearable, and I
would turn to vent my spite on the ones I most loved. I even
turned on my father one day and hit him. I had been out
working with a horse and cart, repairing a road for which
we had a contract from the Board of Works. On my way
home I decided I'd take a load of sand and fill some ruts in
the little boreen running through our village. My father saw
from the house what I was doing, and he came out to stop
me. "This is a job for all the people who use the road to do
jointly," he said, "and I don't want you to do any more until
we get the others to agree to do their share." What he said
was reasonable enough, but I was in no mood for reason.
I just lost my temper. Raising my foot, I kicked him right
in the shin, left the horse and cart, and took off across the

fields. I had no idea where I was going, but I figured I'd spend the night in a neighbor's home and strike out for somewhere, Ballina or Dublin or England, the next day. I didn't go very far, however. Sarah had been watching from the door, knowing my mood, and she came after me up the hill until she finally persuaded me to stop my foolishness and come back home. I know my father must have been very upset, but he gave absolutely no indication, nor did he ever again refer to the matter.

In between the moments of depression, there would be spells when everything looked good. Then I would try to adjust my behavior and practices to those of my companions. I would join them in their simple diversions, the antics around the bonfire late into the night on St. John's Eve in midsummer, the Halloween games, the dances at the crossroads on Sunday evenings, the card games in each other's kitchens at night, the once-a-year horse racing at Gurteen, near Ballina.

Like everything else in our lives, association of the teenage boys and girls was highly formalized. There was none of the free-and-easy relationships which characterize the United States and which are today widely accepted in Ireland, too—that is to say, where in Ireland there are teen-agers. For much of the world that I knew as a boy no longer exists. In the little village that was loud with voices of children and young people, there is mostly today the brooding memories of old men and women leaning on their sticks and watching up the long dusty road for a sign of the wanderers they know will never come back. But in my time we did at least think of getting married, though we knew that it would be years before the boy could hope to set up for himself, or that the girl could leave the aged parents. We would meet at the dances, at the well when we went to draw water, in town on market day, exchanging perhaps only a glance and a few words.

For me there was only one girl ever. Her name was Katie Cummins, and she is dead long since, God rest her. We seldom met, and when we did I knew none of the ways of a lover, either to entice her or to express the deep longings of my heart. But for me she was the embodiment of all that was good and true and beautiful and holy in Irish womanhood. She would make me a good wife and fill our house with beauty and laughter and children. Wherever I went I would write her name for all to read. Our barn at home was scribbled all over with her initials. My mother didn't understand or perhaps kept her counsel, but Tom and Michael used to kid me all the time.

With this dream I fed myself as I sat on the pile of rocks and cracked them laboriously with my hammer into pebble-sized fragments to fill the holes in the dirt roads. But even my dream was often troubled. My mind would hark back to my earlier ambition to become a missionary. I couldn't get it fully out of my mind. "Dear God," I would say, "I did my best and it wasn't enough. It will be better to leave me free, and I promise that every child I have will be a priest or a nun." This would ease the pain for a while, but when I was about seventeen, another mission came along, and I remember a sermon one night on the transience of earthly happiness which upset once more all the calculations I had made. It was like a mission much earlier, when I was probably only eleven. On that occasion the preacher denounced the evils of liquor in such terms that then and

there I resolved no alcohol would ever pass my lips. Everyone was shaken by that sermon, and during the next few
days the moonshiners brought in their stills and smashed
them in the churchyard, though indeed some cynics said
that the only stills they could identify were ones so rusted
that it was past time to give them a Christian burial. But
I took the matter seriously, and that pledge I still observe.
This time the subject was the dangers of company-keep-
ing, and again the sermon so impressed me that I resolved
never again to go out with a girl. And I remember that on
the way home from the church, I was hailed by one of the
teen-agers. She was older than me, and I knew perfectly
well that she had no serious intentions. But I was in such a
state of shock that I wouldn't even give her the time of evening, walking past with my head down as though I wasn't
aware of her presence. After that I did go out once or twice
in moments of rebellion with a girl. But I never went with
anyone for long, and I never really felt free.

And so I went through those years, restless and defiant,
distressing my father because of my stubbornness, locked
in a prison of doubt and frustration, conscious only that the
walls were higher than I could ever hope to scale.

Shortly after the mission I have just mentioned, I made
a major decision. My father was as set as ever against any of
us going to England. I could see that there was no place for
me in the home. The land would go to Michael, the eldest
son, and it was little enough for him without any thought
to splitting it. The three eldest girls had gone off to America, Beatrice and Mary in 1920 and Nellie three years later.
But Tom was still at home as well as Michael to work the
land and handle the road contracts, and the three younger

than me were also growing up and able to do their share. So I cycled one evening into Bonniconlon and spent an hour convincing Martin Durkin that there wasn't a better or more loyal worker to be found in the seven townlands.

Sandy, as he was more commonly known than by his given name, was the big shot of the district—undertaker, butcher, storekeeper—involved in anything and everything that could turn a penny. He employed eight or ten young fellows to help in his many activities, and I finally persuaded him to take me on. The bargain was twelve shillings a week, all found. I would bunk with the other employees in his home under the watchful eye of his wife, and there also I would have my meals. The hours and the nature of the work were undefined. It might be cleaning out a barn, unloading groceries, bottling the stout for the fair day, bringing turf from the bog, whatever had to be done and whenever Sandy decided was the time to do it.

One thing, however, was different from my first experience away from home. About nine-thirty in the evening, Mrs. Durkin would close the store, where she had worked all day, and come into the kitchen where the staff was already gathered around the fire. "Get me a cup of tea, there's a good girl," she would say to the cook, as surely as she came in the door. When she had finished the tea, she would fish in an ample pocket for her beads, and down on our knees would go the entire company to say the Rosary. It was the touch of home which reconciled me to the distance from my own. In spite of the fact that Carracastle was only a few miles away, the nature of the work and the indefinite hours prevented me from visiting with any regularity.

Things might have gone on like that a long time, were it not for an incident that occurred on St. Patrick's Day. March 17 in Ireland is not only a national holiday but a Holy Day of Obligation on which everyone goes to Mass and is free from work, just like a Sunday. It was one of the big days of the year, and though it came in the middle of Lent, by custom immemorial it retained none of the penitential atmosphere which for us surrounded even Sundays during that season. The boys would go to Mass with bunches of shamrock and green harps on their jacket lapels, the men with the shamrock in their hatbands or cap peaks. Green ribbon adorned the hair of the young colleens, and many of the older women would have a green blouse or hat. In the afternoon we would flock to Ballina for the parade of fife-and-drum bands, cheering as they marched proudly down the main street to the strains of "Garryowen" or "Clare's Dragoons."

Now, however, I was working for Sandy Durkin, and it was no longer like the days of my freedom. "Pat," he said to me after Mass, "I want Pat Boyd and yourself to get a couple of sweeping brushes and go over to the dance hall. You know there's a big dance tonight, and it has to be in proper shape."

Pat Boyd didn't like the idea any more than I did, but there was nothing we could do. We took the brushes and marched glumly off. When we got inside, however, we started to let off some of our pent-up annoyance. Soon the two sweeping brushes were converted into lovely ladies in furbelows, and the pair of us were prancing up and down the dance floor in our best imitation of the swanks who would be enjoying themselves later. Unfortunately for me, or rather fortunately, Sandy chose that moment to take a guest on an inspection tour of his premises including the dance hall. He took a dim view of our performance. "What do you think you're doing?" he demanded angrily. "Haven't you eyes in your heads?" I snapped back with equal temper. "You're fired," he said. "I lived before I laid eyes on you," I said. "I'll live if I never lay eyes on you again." And so, on the feast of St. Patrick in the year of Our Lord 1927, I shook the dust of Sandy Durkin's empire off my shoes.

There was welcome for me when I arrived home, but worry too. Jobs didn't grow on trees, even if the national economy was slowly recovering, and it would be a brave man who would offer me another chance when he heard of the lip I gave to the great Sandy Durkin. As for me, I was now a man of the world, and I took the whole thing more lightly than any of the others. My stay in Bonniconlon had broadened my horizons. I had heard and absorbed the talk of the other young fellows who were using the training in Sandy's to catapult them to bigger things. I knew exactly what I wanted to do. Real estate in the United States was an even bigger business than in Bonniconlon. In next to no time one could parlay a persuasive voice and a quick wit into a million-dollar business. That was what I would do. I would go to America, and I could come home a millionaire.

The hardest part of the operation would be to get my father's consent. He was particularly reluctant to let me strike off on my own, because I had proved so self-willed and quick tempered. But Tom was willing to come with me, and I knew that would help to smooth the process. So I waited for an opportune moment, and it came one sunny afternoon in June when Tom and I were down in the field thinning the turnips. My father was by this time getting very severe bouts of asthma and bronchitis. Not too long before, we thought he was dying, and I dashed off to Atty-mass to bring Father O'Donnell over to give him the last sacraments. But in between he was quite healthy as long as he avoided undue exertion, especially when the weather was dry, and this afternoon he came strolling down the road in the sunshine to admire the soft green of the turnip plants and chat with us as we worked. He was still a striking man, walked straight without a stick, with a fine head of hair, a mere suggestion of a stoop about the broad shoulders.

It was my chance. We had more relatives in and around Scranton, Pennsylvania, than we had in County Mayo. Long before my three sisters had gone there, three of my father's brothers and three of his sisters had made the same journey, and several of them had settled down and raised families. My sister Beatrice had also married. Her husband, Michael Gallagher, was from the town of Crossmolina just across Lough Conn to the west of us, and they had a home of their own where Tom and I could live until we got on our feet. In addition, several of the Gillards, my mother's people, were in America.

I talked fast, and finally I overcame my father's reluctance. Little as he liked the idea, he was an intelligent man, and he realized that he had slight choice. So it was finally agreed that we would write to our sisters in Scranton to see if they could send us the passage money and make the arrangements to sponsor us for the visas. As to their willingness to receive us, that was not so much as contemplated. In our family a readiness to share was taken for granted.

Three

Welcome a New World

In 1927 it was no longer easy to get to America. At one time you could step on the boat and walk off in New York, if you had the few pounds to buy a steerage ticket. Restrictions imposed during and after the First World War, however, had been greatly expanded by a law of 1925, and I thought the word would never come. Although the fact that we had so many close relatives in the United States facilitated our application, it took long months to get the papers in order and obtain an appointment with the American Consulate in Dublin for the visas. In the meantime I helped on the farm and did such odd jobs for the Board of Works as digging drains, building fences, and repairing roads.

It was almost a year after I left Sandy Durkin's when in early March 1928 Tom and I set off for Dublin to get the visas. In my entire nineteen years I had never been farther from home than Ballina and Bonniconlon except twice, once when I went by bus to Bundoran, some fifty miles away, and again when I helped a neighbor bring cattle to the fair at Foxford seven or eight miles away in the foot-hills of the Ox Mountains. Not once had I ridden a train. The excitement of novelty was consequently the dominant emotion as I boarded the iron monster at Ballina, in fact a tiny three-coach local that took half a day to meander one hundred fifty miles across the fertile plains and alongside the lazy rivers and deep blue lakes of the Irish midlands.

Although we were coming home again before starting for America, I knew that one life was ended. But I did not grieve for long. I was young, and everything was new. I marveled at the richness of the land when we left the rocky hillsides and water-logged bogs of Connaught. The towns along the way, Claremorris, Athlone, Mullingar, each seemed a city full of excitement and promise, an anticipation of wonders ahead. And so they were. When we reached Dublin, snow was falling, and I was dazzled by the bright lights of the great city. I could not believe so many people, such fine houses, such endless rows of stores could exist in the world. The double-decker trolley cars and buses, the newsboys calling their wares, the endless lines of automobiles and cyclists on the broad paved streets, the countless pedestrians on the sidewalks. I asked myself where I had spent all these years. It was going to be a great life once I reached America. Surely in no time at all I'd be up there with the best of them in their fine clothes and their fine homes. Such were my reactions to Dublin, and such were my dominant thoughts as we returned to Carracastle with our passports and visas.

We were scheduled to leave home again on May 13 to join the liner at C'obh. The weeks after our return from Dublin passed quickly in a flurry of preparations and a

round of farewell visits and parties. Still, it was not all pleasure and plain sailing. As the decisive moment drew near,
I fell again into a deep depression, and I was capable of
lashing out without provocation at whomever was near me.
With typical perversity I hit hardest at those I loved most.
The very evening before we were due to leave, I behaved
unpardonably toward my dear mother. As I seldom went
out to dances or anything like that, I had been in the habit
of spending much of my time with her. And that last evening, as we worked in the garden, she asked me if I'd milk
the cows for her. I don't think she asked me simply because
she was tired, but more as a gesture of confidence in me, to
assure herself for the last time that she could always count
on her son to oblige her and be a help to her. That was the
way I understood it, and yet I refused her, just out of con-
trariness. I denied her that small reassurance.

Looking back over my whole life, I think that is one of
the things I most regret—having refused my poor mother
that small satisfaction at the moment she was suffering for
the loss of her two sons. And yet she was so generous, so
magnanimous, that she didn't even hold it against me. On
the contrary, the very next morning she gave me an evidence of love and sweetness such as to touch me and make
me recognize just how ungrateful a child I had been.

We had to leave home early to catch the train. Michael
and my mother went in on the horse and cart to carry the
few little pieces of luggage containing our meager personal
belongings. Tom and I followed on two bicycles, lingering
till the last possible moment with our father, who was not
well enough to accompany us to the station. He had been
visibly affected as the time of our departure neared, and

he was particularly worried about how I'd make out on my own. I remember the very last Sunday I ever spent with him in this world. I was alone in the house with only my mother and himself, when he called me into the bedroom. "Go down on your knees," he said in his most gentle voice, "and make a promise here before the picture of the Sacred Heart. From now on there will be nobody but yourself to advise you and to decide for you. But your first responsibility will always be to save your soul, and so I want you to promise to be faithful to Our Lord in America."

That is the memory I carried away with me of my father. As we parted he hid his sorrow behind an impassive face, but I knew that in his mind was the same thought he had expressed to me a short time before. "Be faithful," he had said, and I was determined to be faithful as I waved for the last time from the turn of the road to the brave man standing motionless alone in the half door of our cottage. I waved good-by to him, to the thatched cottages, to the little green fields, to the yellow primroses blooming in the sod ditch. I waved good-by, then pedaled madly away after Tom.

We caught up with my mother and Michael at the bridge over the Moy in Ballina. Tom and Michael went on ahead up the street to the railroad station, and my mother and I followed at a little distance. It was then she opened up her heart to me in that last minute and conveyed to me some of the heroism and great character with which she had borne with me through the years. Not till that conversation did I have any realization of what a worry I had been to my father and herself all through my teens. The outbursts of wickedness were bad enough, but they had been more concerned by the periods of scrupulousness and religiosity, when I used to spend so much time praying, even on my knees out in the field or in the barn. "Thanking God I am today," she said, "that it's off to America I'm sending you healthy and sane." The way she spoke indicated to me that she counted as nothing her sorrow at losing me in comparison with her joy that I was safely through the trials of youth, making me understand how much I had meant to her. It suddenly filled me with anguish to be leaving her, and my conscience reproached me for having hurt her so often. At the same time I was overflowing with happiness to know I had such a loving mother, a woman so valiant that she refused to be repulsed no matter what the provocation.

There must have been other families on the station platform saying good-by to sons and daughters starting off like us to catch the liner for America. But while we were leaving I was conscious of nobody but my mother waving her handkerchief, Michael supporting her, and we waving back as long as we could catch a glimpse. Similar scenes were enacted at Foxford and every station along the route, the overwhelming wailing and crying of mothers. It seemed to me that half the country was going with us, and each scene brought the lump back in my throat as I thought of my own poor mother huddled in the cart driving back to Carracastle, the shawl drawn tight around to hide her misery.

It was another long, tedious day's ride to Cobh, passing this time through Tuam, Limerick, and Cork. Most of our companions were innocent country boys and girls like ourselves, leaving home for the first time, unfamiliar with the world and its ways. We were to get a first and not too pleasant exposure to it when the train pulled into the station immediately before our destination. A swarm of brash, quick-talking youths came aboard and spent the last few miles wheedling and cajoling us into spending the night in the rooming houses of their respective employers. We were like so many cattle at a fair, dragged hither and thither by these competing schemers.

The next morning we were taken out by tender to board the ship. We were steerage passengers, of course, but for me it was all grandeur and luxury beyond my dreams. An occasional coastal steamer of a few hundred tons crossed the bar on the River Moy to tie up at Killala, shabby tramps with general cargo, or dirty coal boats. But who could have imagined anything like that transatlantic liner? Certainly not I. It added to the traumatic experience of the sight of Dublin and Cork and all the other visions of the marvelous world I was seeing for the first time. There was no limit to the possibilities ahead of me. As I walked the deck at night and heard the lapping of the waves and saw the majesty of the infinity of stars in the cloudless sky and felt the power of the tireless engines deep inside the ship, my imagination raced always ahead of me to the new shores. I felt daily more confident that I would never look back. All this I would conquer. In no time I'd be a millionaire. What a triumph when one day I'd return to Carracastle to let my father see for himself that he didn't have to worry about me, to let Tadhg O'Leary regret his failure to recognize the genius who once had graced his school, to end Sandy Durkin's tyranny and toss the ruins of his empire in the River Moy.

After a quick stop at Boston we sailed into New York Harbor in the early morning of May 23. I have none of the usual memories of the immigrant. We were berthed before I woke. It was not until much later that I first saw the

Statue of Liberty, and I have yet to visit Ellis Island. Neither did I see anything of New York. All the new arrivals were herded together by representatives of the travel companies and funneled to their various destinations. Tom and I were put on the ferry to Hoboken and from there, straight onto the train to Scranton. Nellie was working in the home of State Attorney General Harold A. Scragg, and he and his wife came with Nellie to the station in their automobile to welcome us and take us to the Gallaghers. It was our first experience of the generous friendly ways so typical of Americans, and it left an indelible memory. On our way through Scranton I was mesmerized by a great flashing sign: "Scranton, the Electric City," it said. I suppose it referred to the electric generating stations in which much of the area's coal production was used. For me, this advertising slogan, dancing in a variety of colors, seemed the triumph of a great magician. Afterward, at night, I would often go along and stand there entranced, never tiring of its magnificence. I did not then know it, but that sign was providing one of the strands that would ultimately be woven into the tapestry of my life. For the moment, however, all that this and the other wonders of the journey did was to make me want to know more about the fairyland into which I had wandered. If only I could get a job as driver on a long-distance bus running from New York to Los Angeles, I thought. Who could ambition anything more satisfying?

As I soon learned, my three sisters had very different plans for me. They had remained convinced that my calling in life was to the priesthood and that I would be restless and discontented in any other career. And just while Tom and I were on the sea, a chance encounter opened for them a way to promote their intention. They had gone to the evening service in the cathedral, as they often did. A young priest, hearing their Irish accents as they left, stopped to chat. His name was Paul Kelly, and he had just been made monsignor and put in charge of the cathedral parish. They told him that two of their brothers were on the way over from Ireland, that one of them had felt a call to the priesthood when a boy, but that circumstances had prevented his following it. "Bring him in to see me when he arrives," said Monsignor Kelly. "I'll look him over. Maybe we can still save that vocation."

I had scarcely reached Scranton when my sisters told me that Monsignor Kelly wanted to see me. I'm not sure if they stated explicitly that he wanted to discuss the possibility of my making another effort to become a priest, but in any case I knew exactly what the message meant. They thought they were doing me a great favor, but for me it was the first bad news since I left home. Everything had been sailing beautifully. I had put the past behind me, including the old dream of the priesthood. Twice it had deceived me. The last thing I wanted was a similar disillusionment in my new country.

They had arranged for us to stop into the rectory on Sunday night. There was a Holy Hour every Sunday evening, and Mary and Nellie brought Tom and myself with them. Beatrice had to stay home with her young children. When the girls announced that we were to visit Monsignor Kelly afterward, I had said nothing. I was reluctant to offend them when they were doing so much for Tom and me. But I now summoned up my courage. "I don't want to see this Monsignor Kelly," I said to Mary on the way to church.

"I'm not going." At the end of the service Nellie led the way from the cathedral and turned left outside toward the rectory, expecting me to follow. Instead I turned my back on her. "What's wrong with you?" she called after me in puzzlement. Mary took my part. "He doesn't want to go," she said gently, "and there's no use trying to force him." I remember so well what a cloud of darkness and disappointment covered Nellie's face for one fraction of a second. Then she shook it off and acted as though it was a matter of no importance. But I had seen that look, and it continued to haunt me. "For the third time," it seemed to say, "God is inviting you, and you are throwing His invitation back in His face." I knew perfectly well that I was in the wrong, but I was not yet ready to admit it.

So we left Monsignor Kelly with no explanation, although we knew he had seen the two girls and the two strange young men who had to be their brothers. Off we set for what was known as the Casey block or the Irish block. It was one location in Scranton where all the exiles assembled on a Sunday evening. We would stand and sit and walk around that block, all of the Irish in Scranton, looking for neighbors from the old country, exchanging gossip, and meeting acquaintances. For us, that was the highlight of the week. When I got down there among my friends, I thought it was as good as being in heaven, and it didn't bother me a bit that I had let my sisters down and disappointed them.

The next day I set out to find work. I was determined to go it on my own. I wouldn't be dependent on my sisters or on anyone. But I soon discovered that jobs didn't grow on trees. Day after day I went from place to place, to factories, to stores, to offices. The Great Depression was still ahead of us, but Scranton apparently was not sharing the prosperity that was still riding high in the country. Or maybe it was just the raw country lad with the Mayo brogue that failed to make an impression. In any case, there were no takers. All morning I would walk, and at noon I'd come back and sit in the courthouse square, discouraged. In the afternoon I'd continue my rounds. I had a brief lift when I found a small outfit willing to let me sell American flags on commission from door to door. But I couldn't even make a go of that. When I had only one sale to report after several days (it was to my uncle and aunt!), they told me to stop wasting their time. I was sorely tempted by an army recruiting sergeant one noon as I sat in the square. But one thing we knew in Ireland was that you never got rich in the army, so I determined to stick it out a bit longer.

I felt a grievance against Michael Gallagher, my brother-in-law. He was in the coal mines, and he had reluctantly got a job for Tom there. "It's not only dirty work with little future," he said. "It's bad for the health and dangerous as well." Tom was both older than me and hardier. "You're too big for your age," Michael would say to me. "You think you're a man, but you have no strength in you. It would kill you in no time." He was right, of course, but I couldn't admit that. I was becoming desperate. It was an awful shame for me to go on week after week living on my sisters, eating their bread, and giving no return.

All the time Nellie was reading my mind, but she kept her peace. She was kind to me beyond description, did everything she could to minimize the trouble and the burden I was on them all. That was Nellie down to the ground. She was a very striking girl, with beautiful features and a cheerful, open face. But she was utterly unspoiled. As a child she had been more of a tomboy than the other girls of the family, played football with the boys, climbed fences, was far more in the thick of things than I ever had been. Now she was more mature and demure, but her basic character was unchanged. Everyone who came in contact with her felt that she was more concerned to benefit them than to benefit from them.

So she watched me and bided her time. And her time came five or six weeks after my arrival in Scranton. Monsignor Kelly had not forgotten the appointment that was never kept. "Can you trace a girl called Nellie Peyton?" he asked his secretary one day. The secretary tracked her down at the Scragg home and put her on the phone to Monsignor Kelly. "Didn't your brother who was thinking of being a priest get here?" he asked. "He did," she said, "but somehow or other, with all the excitement, I have been very busy." She wouldn't tell him a lie, and still she wanted to take the blame. "Bring him in now," said Monsignor Kelly. "I may have a job for him."

It was the prospect of the job that brought me. By now I was deep in shame, fallen from the heights of the great elation of my first arrival. No matter where I turned, no door opened. It seemed to me that I was in as deep a trench as when I was down in the bog-hole back home throwing up the water-heavy sods to dry on the bank above. So I swallowed my pride this time and went along meekly to meet Monsignor Kelly.

Luckily he said nothing to me about being a priest. All he did was to offer me work as sexton in the cathedral. I didn't know what the word sexton meant, but it was all the same to me. Even when I found out that it was a fancy name for a janitor, I was still happy. I was on my own two feet again. I felt the noose loosening around my throat. So Monsignor Kelly gave me the key, and he told me when to open the doors in the morning and close them at night, and he instructed me on everything from sweeping the floors, to stoking the furnace, to decorating the altar. He was a grand man. I took to him instantly.

The interview with Monsignor Kelly was in mid-June and the starting date as sexton was July 1. In the meantime one of our friends named Tom Manley, a steam-shovel operator, got me a job on his crew on a construction site. I might easily have stayed with that, but Manley warned me that the prospects were very uncertain, that men were being laid off from one day to another. And in fact I was less than a week there when the boss notified two of the men that their time was up. I had got to know the two of them, and the news made me feel bad. One had the responsibility of a family. The other was a sort of drifter but a good-natured fellow, and it looked as if he was making a serious effort to go straight. I went in to the boss. "Lay me off," I said. "I'm the last in, and besides I have a job lined up to start very shortly." "You're a fool," the boss said. "You're a strong, reliable worker. Stay here until the other job comes through." Manley wanted me to stay, too, but I wouldn't have it on my conscience to put the father of a family on the side of the street. It was a salutary experience, and it helped me to realize that there was a cloud behind the silver lining of making a fortune in the United States. I learned later that the boss did a little thinking for himself, too, when he realized I was actually concerned about the other fellows. He juggled things around and kept them both on.

Working in the cathedral, once I started on July 1, had an extraordinary effect on me. I never felt alone for a minute, even when the church was empty. All the joy and peace and sense of being at home which I used to feel in the little chapel at Attymass flooded back into my soul. As I swept or dusted or polished, I would turn toward the tabernacle on the altar and greet our dear Lord hidden sacramentally behind the veils. When I passed the statue of Our Blessed Mother, I would stop to talk to her and thank her for the delicacy with which she had treated me by bringing me so gently against my will to this place of happiness.

I couldn't say that my intentions were all purified right away. At the beginning what was uppermost was the relief of being economically independent again. Tom and I were still living with the others, but at least I could contribute my share to the upkeep of the family. Not only that, but I quickly realized that the job carried status, even if the pay was small. There were certain hours when my Uncle Pat was likely to be passing the cathedral, and I remember I would make it my business to be on the front steps all dressed up in a shirt and tie, reminding him that his recently arrived nephew was already in a white-collar job while he after a lifetime was still a laborer in overalls.

But living and working constantly in the presence of God soon made me think of more important things than pulling rank on my good uncle. Most of the priests at the cathedral were young, and I quickly got to know and like several of them. As I observed their dedication and the good work they did, as I admired the devotion with which they said Mass, the thought again took form that maybe it was not too late or too hopeless even at my age to try once more. It took form and grew and expanded until finally the moment came when it filled my entire mind. I was behind the high altar at that precise moment, a can of paint in one hand and a brush in the other, busy painting the back wall. I threw everything down on an impulse, ran to Monsignor Kelly's room, and blurted out the words that had long been on my tongue. "I want to be a priest," I told him.

He didn't seem a bit surprised. "What's a noun?" he asked with extreme practicality. "What's a verb, what's an adjective?" He had evidently made up his mind about the reality of my vocation, and his concern was to establish if I had any scholastic background at all to justify a new effort. Though taken totally by surprise by his questions, I managed to dredge up from the depths of my memory answers that he found adequate. "Go over to the Christian Brothers," he said, "and enroll for the first year of high school at St. Thomas's. I'll take care of the tuition." By another extraordinary coincidence, it was the registration day for the new academic year. While I was doing that, Monsignor Kelly was thinking. "Tell your brother," he said when I returned, "to leave that job in the coal mines and take over the keys of the cathedral from you. There are too many of them getting killed and maimed in the mines."

So Tom took the keys without a murmur and took over my job as sexton. He and I have always enjoyed a very unusual relationship. He was a much more outgoing boy than I was, good humored, pleasant faced, but with a definite streak of leadership. He was much closer to his older brother, Michael, than he was to me. The two of them were

inseparable. Although they were not alike in appearance
or in temperament, they thought as one. Yet, though Tom
was ordinarily a leader and ordinarily not too close to me,
and though he was a year and a half older than me, it was I
who told him what to do in the decisive moments of his life.
It was I who had taken the initiative in getting the two of
us to America that day when we were in the field thinning
turnips and our father came along and sat on the fence in
the sun. And now, once more, I had decided for him that
he should come out of the coal mines and take a job that
would lead him along a road to which he had scarcely given
a thought.

I started off with enthusiasm in my career as a freshman.
I wouldn't say I particularly enjoyed the books, though I
didn't dislike them either. Nor was it easy for a big giant
of a man like myself to sit at a desk with young whipper-
snappers of thirteen or fourteen and have them snigger at
me when I missed an answer or misspelled a word, or have
them make fun of my outlandish brogue. But it really all
went over my head. My mind was so firmly made up that,
even if they had all ganged up on me, I'd have still ignored
them. And this they never did. On the contrary, by a kind
of fluke, I became class president. Somebody put up my
name, probably as a joke. There were six contenders and a
secret ballot. I took the nomination seriously and voted for
myself. I won by one vote. But I had won, and this gave me
a status that didn't hurt.

Nearly every afternoon, when school ended, I'd drop
round to the cathedral to say my prayers, to chat with Tom,
to give him a hand if he was behind. He had been on the
job about a month when, as we walked home together one

evening, he made a remark which immediately set me to thinking. "A priest's life is wonderful, isn't it?" was what he said. It came out quite naturally in the conversation, and I don't believe he was even remotely applying the comment to himself. But it stuck in my mind. "Why shouldn't Tom be a priest too?" I asked myself. "If it suits me, it should suit him, and it would help me a lot if I had him as a companion."

I went in the next day, which happened to be a Friday, to Monsignor Kelly. "My brother wants to be a priest," I said. He had never actually used those words, but I had decided that this was how he had meant to express himself.

"Is that so?" he said. "Well, if he does, he'll have to go to school, too, and he'll have trouble making up the four weeks he has missed. So you tell him he has until Monday morning to make up his mind, and if he still wants to be a priest, I'll pay the tuition."

The Scragg family thought very highly of my sister Nellie, and one of her prerogatives was to invite her family from time to time to have supper and spend the evening with her in the kitchen of the Scragg home. That was where we were due to meet this particular Friday evening, and I burst in like a young bull to find Nellie, Mary, and Tom already assembled. "You have till Monday morning to make up your mind to be a priest," I said to Tom in the presence of the others, without even waiting to say hello to them, "and if you do, Father Kelly will take care of you."

The thing hit poor Tom like a bombshell, and I could see that the girls were taken aback by my impetuosity. "I'll think about it," he said. "We don't have to decide tonight." So he thought it over Saturday, and by noon on Sunday he had made his decision. "I'll try it," he said. Once again I had made his plunge for him.

On Monday he started high school. He had left grade school at a much earlier age than I had, and he had been longer away, so that it was a great heroism for him to face the little kids. But he stuck at it, and before long he caught up with us, and from that time the two of us managed to keep always side by side in the upper third of the class. We both graduated, magna cum laude from Notre Dame, and we were twenty-ninth and thirtieth in a class of 469.

Not only did Monsignor Kelly pay the two tuitions, but he suggested that we should between us continue to look after the cathedral so as not to be a burden on our sisters. We went at it manfully, but I think that year was the greatest challenge the two of us ever faced and overcame. Back in Carracastle we seldom had to get up before eight o'clock, because that was the rhythm that the work of the farm demanded. There was no light before that hour in the winter, and even in the summer one had to wait for the sun to dry the dew off the fields before starting to work them. Now one of us had to get up every second morning in turn at five o'clock and walk two miles to open the cathedral doors, then down to the basement to start the fires and shovel coal into the furnaces. Two tons of coal they swallowed every day throughout the winter. Then preparing the altar for the Masses and being busy around the place until it was time to take off for school. Frequently there was a wedding or a funeral, and that meant extra work. Often there was a novena and sometimes a mission. They were really hectic.

One of us would have to rush over again at noon to ring the Angelus, then devote the lunch hour to cleaning. When school was out, the two of us would return to the unending job of sweeping and tidying the church and grounds. But soon we found that the one who was up early couldn't take it. So we set up a cot in the basement, and he took a couple of hours sleep while the other carried the entire load. It was usually seven when we went home for dinner, then studied till midnight. Today's early bird slept till eight tomorrow, but the other was out at five. Ever since then I understand the longing of the alcoholic for the drink. That was my longing for sleep. Poor Mary would have to start calling me at four on my early morning. It took a whole hour to waken me. Each time she shook me awake, I'd collapse right back again. The same in school. I'd fall down in a stupor on top of the desk, and the teacher could hardly rouse me.

Yet through it all I was supremely happy. Later on it would appear that I had stretched myself beyond human endurance, starting the process which led to serious illness when I was a seminarian studying theology. But at the time I was ready to do whatever had to be done. And Tom never showed any desire to desert me. At that point, I think we were both thinking mainly of Tom as coming along with me, though indeed it gradually emerged that he had a firm vocation of his own, so that he persevered and has a great and growing priestly record to his credit. New circumstances intervened, however, to ease the strain of our studies, a strain harsh enough by itself after our long absence from the halls of learning.

In the spring of 1929, six or eight months after we had begun our ordeal, a group of Holy Cross priests from Notre Dame, Indiana, came to preach a mission in the cathedral. There were four or five of them, and I took a great fancy to them. The more I thought about it, the clearer my next step became to me. I went up to one of them, a big, tall giant of a man called Father Pat Dolan. "Father Pat," I said, "I want to join Holy Cross. I want to be a missionary."

Father Dolan was interested right away, but there were difficulties to be overcome. How could we win the approval of Monsignor Kelly? He was the one who had taken Tom and myself in off the street, the one who had been paying our tuition. How would he like it if some missionaries edged in to net the fish when he had them on his hook? On the other hand, though I didn't realize it at the time, my sisters knew that there could be a lot of opposition to our going to the diocesan seminary. Earlier they had been glad enough to get young men from Ireland when there was a shortage of priests for the growing Church in the United States. More recently, however, as the Catholics in America improved their position and achieved higher education, plenty of local young people were available to enter the priesthood. In consequence, some were saying that it wasn't right to give preference to immigrants. Finally, there was the practical problem that the combination of studies and work was exacting beyond all reason. Could we continue it for four years without killing ourselves?

Father Dolan undertook to talk to Monsignor Kelly, and he answered with the same unselfish generosity which had characterized him from the outset. He called me into his office. "I'd be the last in the world to stop you, Pat," he said. "If later you became unhappy, you'd only feel that things would have been different if you had been allowed to follow your wish." Then he read for me the recommendation he was sending on to the Holy Cross superiors. "I envy the community or the bishop that finally gets him," he said. It was a great encouragement to me to think that such a fine and holy priest thought of me in those terms. It doubled my determination to reach my goal and demonstrate for him that his confidence was not misplaced. Unfortunately he did not live to know that Tom and I both persevered, for he was called to his reward in 1934.

We finished out our first year of high school in Scranton, then set off on August 20, 1929, to start the second at the Holy Cross minor seminary under the shadow of Notre Dame University in Indiana. Once again I made Tom's decision for him. He would come with me. He came humbly, and I knew he never regretted it. He was like every other member of our family. He never refused me any sacrifice I asked of him, just as I never refused the request of any of them, if it was in my power to grant it. I would and could have gone alone. But I was convinced that Holy Cross was calling the two of us, that it wanted us, that we could help it in its work. So we both went there, and there we both still are.

Four

Lifted Up to Be Cast Down

The Notre Dame which welcomed Tom and me in September 1929 was far different from the Indiana mission deep in the forests where Father Edward Sorin, first Holy Cross superior in the United States, had decided to build a high school nearly a century earlier. It had become the site of one of America's great universities, and nearby was the thriving city of South Bend. But one thing had been preserved, the natural beauty that had enraptured Father Sorin, especially the beauty of the two lakes around which had been spaced the majestic buildings in a setting of trees now dazzlingly resplendent in their fall hues.

After the city life of Scranton, this was indeed a marriage of heaven and earth. I could once more feel the sense of the spacious countryside in which I had grown up, but a countryside vastly richer, proclaiming even more loudly the wonders of its Creator. At Notre Dame my heart filled with happiness. Here I was at home from the first instant. My eyes feasted on the lakes, on the golden dome dominating the campus, on the tiny chapel where the native people used to worship in the last century, on the grotto of Our Lady toward which I soon learned to turn my steps with each problem or disappointment. I thanked God and His Mother fervently for welcoming me to this earthly paradise.

The remaining three years of high school passed quickly and without incident for Tom and me. We returned once to Scranton to spend a vacation with our sisters, working in the cathedral and in the cemetery to provide pocket money and help to clothe ourselves and feed ourselves while on vacation. What was lacking, our sisters generously provided. There was nothing they would not have done to prosper our undertaking.

On graduation in June 1932, we immediately entered the Holy Cross novitiate, which was then located at Notre Dame. A year later we took temporary vows and began the four-year academic course for a B.A. It was a hard course, and I won't say that I really enjoyed the studies, certainly not to the point of throwing myself into them for the sake of knowledge in itself. What I saw was the goal of the priesthood, to reach which I had to climb this mountain. And climb it I did, and would have gladly climbed it had it been ten times higher and thrice more rugged. I fought my way through everything—Latin, Greek, literature, physics, biology, philosophy. I was more successful with philosophy than with any of the other subjects, thanks largely to the encouragement of the professor of ethics, Father Cornelius Hagerty, a man who would later give me providential guidance in the crisis that I then little thought was just ahead of me. He was the teacher who left the deepest impression on me in all my schooling from start to finish.

I had a tremendous memory, which I suppose I inherited from my ancestors. The old people back in Ireland could recall folk tales handed down by word of mouth from generation to generation. They could repeat them word for word and go on every night for a month without once coming back to the same story. It was much the same in the grade school, where we learned a tremendous amount of poetry by heart, especially Shakespeare. I now began to reap the benefit of that training. Father Hagerty would from time to time get me up in class and ask me to deliver the day's lesson from the philosophy manual, and I would start at the beginning and reel it off page after page to the end. "Why can't the rest of you do that?" he would ask the other students. "Because you don't know how to study, or because you are too lazy." Well maybe he was hard on them, but he admired my ability to get the stuff into my head and to keep it there. It was always his idea that I'd make a fine professor of philosophy, but even though I liked the subject better than any other I studied, maybe even better than the theology which followed, I never had any ambition in that direction.

During those years, too, largely without realizing it, I was absorbing the spirit of the Congregation of Holy Cross. Like every other order and congregation in the Catholic Church, it commits its members to a life of perfection and demands from them the traditional vows of poverty, chastity, and obedience. But it has its own well-defined characteristics, so that to be a member of the Holy Cross family is not the same as to be a Jesuit or a Capuchin or a Trappist. Let me note three points which I regard as particularly significant: its understanding of the vow of obedience, its concept of help to the diocesan clergy as one of its primary purposes, and its family atmosphere.

In one sense obedience is very precise in Holy Cross. No member undertakes any activity without written instructions from his superior—his obedience, to use our technical term. The superior can cancel this obedience at any time and substitute a new one. Yet from the outset it has been well established that ours is not a "blind obedience." We must use initiative and judgment, and take the consequence of our actions. The balance between obedience and conscience in Holy Cross is a delicate one. Father Basil Moreau, our founder, had many bitter tussles with Father Edward Sorin, the trusted friend he sent from France to make our first foundation in the United States in 1841. Father Moreau himself had equally deep conflicts with his close associates in France, and the atmosphere finally became so embittered that he was forced to leave the community. It was not until long after his death that the rights and wrongs were fully sorted out and the memory of our saintly founder vindicated. It is not easy to live the tension of Holy Cross obedience. Yet, as we who live in the Church of the Second Vatican Council realize today, Holy Cross was always in this respect ahead of the times. It started with the idea of reasoned obedience which the Council has now told us is the only kind fully consonant with the spirit of Christianity.

Another of our characteristics is our tradition of availability to the Church for whatever tasks it judges most urgent at a given moment. In this sense, our objective is a very special one. When the Congregation began in France in the 1830s, the Church in that country was still feeling the effects of the French Revolution. Priests were few in number and inadequately trained. Father Moreau's first project was organizing a group of what he called "auxiliary priests," men who would be available to help pastors whose needs exceeded their resources. The group gradually institutionalized as a religious congregation, but the original concept survived. The result is that the Holy Cross vocation provides for extraordinary flexibility of action. Holy Cross priests are engaged in a great range of activities, the limits imposed only by the needs of the Church at different times and in different places.

In this respect, Holy Cross is like the Jesuits who pride themselves on being always available for whatever work the Pope may determine. They differ, however, not only in their notion of obedience, to which I have just referred, but also in the personality of the two bodies. St. Ignatius thought of social groupings in terms of the army, a strong esprit de corps supported by strict discipline. Father Moreau took the family as his model, and the strengths and weaknesses of his organization were those of a family bound more by common aspirations, common experience, mutual affection, and sharing of sufferings than by the cold words of a contract. I had always lived in that kind of a family, both back in Ireland and in Scranton. It was one of the things that immediately endeared Holy Cross to me.

Not very long after my first profession, I began to feel a strong urge to become a foreign missionary. I realized that my superiors would decide, when the time came, whether or not I was suited for that work, but I was confident that they would put no obstacle in my way. Of all our foreign missions, the one we regarded as most specifically the vocation of Holy Cross was Bengal. It had been assigned to us in 1852, and it had been a place of trials and sacrifices from the outset. One of the first group of three priests died on the voyage, a second survived only two years, and in the same month in which he died, a newly arrived priest and a Sister were drowned in an accident to a river boat carrying them to their destination. The level of attrition was such that we were forced for a time to withdraw in the 1870s. After an interval of sixteen years, however, we had recouped our strength and were ready to renew the struggle. The diocese of Dacca, which is today in East Pakistan, was assigned specifically to the Notre Dame province. A practice was established that those members of the Congregation who felt a special call to the foreign missions would take an additional vow committing them to go to Bengal or any other foreign mission to which the superior general might assign them. This vow was optional, and those who did not take it remained free to refuse any obedience outside the United States. For me there was no problem. With my perpetual vows, three years after first vows at the end of the novitiate, I included the fourth vow for the foreign missions. Tom decided that he would remain in the United States.

One effect of this decision was that we were separated a year later, after our graduation from Notre Dame. We have two houses for theologians in Washington, DC, one for those who are preparing for work in the United States, the other for prospective missionaries. Tom went to the former, known as Holy Cross College, and I to the latter, to which we usually refer as the Bengalese.

Those were happy days at the Bengalese. I had reached the home stretch. The frequently denied goal of the priesthood was finally in sight. I threw myself into my studies with a greater abandon than before. In addition to theology and canon law, we were starting to acquire the specific knowledge that would be needed in our chosen work, to get the feel of the strange languages and customs of a far-off people. I was full of energy, and I was determined to extract the maximum value from these last four years, so that I might emerge as fully qualified as lay in my power. That determination kept me studying constantly. When I went on walks in the afternoon along the country roads about the Catholic University campus, in my mind I was studying. When I played handball with my companions, I was still with my books. When I swept my room, cleaned the chapel, or dug up a flower bed in the garden, my thoughts were always on the one important issue. I had just this short time to complete my education. The measure of my dedication would be the measure of my success as a missionary.

In this way a year went by with the speed of a single day. I was well into the second when indications of possibly serious trouble began to develop in October 1938. From the early part of that year, I had been finding it harder to drive myself. The grueling pace was taking its toll, but I had refused to read the signs. I just forged ahead, a glutton for work, both physical and mental, with no rest or no willingness to rest.

So it continued until one day in October I noticed a speck of blood on my handkerchief. At first I thought nothing of it. As a boy I had frequent nosebleeds, and I told myself it was simply a recurrence. Several times, however, the symptom was repeated when I coughed. I had to face the fact that I was spitting up blood. To anyone from Ireland that could mean only one thing in those days, the disease whose name was seldom mentioned but which everyone knew. Tuberculosis was endemic, and its progress through lingering years of idleness and discomfort to early death was taken for granted, once it was diagnosed. That my illness was indeed tuberculosis was confirmed for me beyond the possibility of doubt one day in November, a day that opened like any other, with morning prayers, attendance at Mass, breakfast, classes, and lunch. At one o'clock in the afternoon I felt very tired. The next class started at one-twenty. I decided to stretch out on the bed for five minutes before class. No sooner had I done so than I felt the warm blood in my mouth pumping up out of my lungs in a hemorrhage. I jumped up immediately, my whole being alerted to fight the verdict which my reason told me was clear. It could not be. I would not allow it. The goal was now too close. I wasn't going to be cheated again.

I went to class as if nothing had happened. And for several days I went around with my oppressive secret. Finally, however, I realized that it was an obligation of conscience to inform my superior, and he immediately sent me to the community physician, Dr. John F. Harrington. On the way I formulated several alternative theories to explain the bleeding. Perhaps they impressed the doctor, because—although he examined me carefully—he came up with the answer I wanted to hear. "You don't have to worry," he said. "Your lungs are strong and sound."

Between November and January I had several other hemorrhages which I did not report. By the beginning of February they were becoming so frequent that I knew I couldn't go on much longer. Things came to a head in my room late on the night of Monday, February 6, when everyone was in bed. The hemorrhage was so violent that I had to find a receptacle to hold the blood. Stars gathered before my eyes, and my knees trembled under my weight. I believe that if I had fainted and fallen on the affected side, I'd have bled to death then and there. While I waited for the doctor, the blood seemed still trying to burst through the tissue, the sensation one has that the least movement will renew a severe nosebleed when it is on the point of stopping.

This time the doctor was a specialist, Dr. Malcolm F. Lent, and when he arrived he shared my apprehension. Later he told me that he did not expect me to survive the night. Several times he almost decided to puncture the lung so that its complete collapse would ease the pressure and possibly save me. First, however, he propped me with pillows in a reclining position, and gradually the danger of further hemorrhaging ceased. Eventually, I fell into a troubled sleep.

The next day it was possible to carry me down three flights of stairs to an ambulance which brought me to Providence Hospital nearby. They had summoned my brother from Holy Cross College. "I'm afraid I'm finished," I gasped when I saw him. "There's life in you still," he reassured me. "The Peytons take a lot of killing." His remark must still have been in my mind when they wheeled me into the elevator at the hospital. There were several nuns in the elevator and one lay woman. The nuns were standing with demurely downcast eyes, but the lay woman looked me straight in the face and said: "I'm proud of that smile. Keep it up and you'll pull through." They were the words of encouragement

I had been needing. They made me feel brave enough to fight again.

For three months I lay on the flat of my back in Providence Hospital. There was no question about the diagnosis. I had tuberculosis, all right. The report of the radiologist on the x-rays taken on February 7 was that I had "an advanced tuberculosis of the right upper lobe, with consolidation and a small cavity," together with a generalized pneumonia-type inflammation of both lungs. But as recently as 1939, the doctors were still groping for a cure. The wonder drugs, which have since just about wiped out the disease in most countries, had still to be found. Rest, good food, and fresh air were the principal recommendations, and the process of self-restoration was greatly facilitated by a procedure called pneumothorax. This involves the repeated injection of air into the lining of the thoracic cavity, causing the infected lung to collapse gradually and rest. It doesn't always work, but when it does the prognosis becomes more favorable.

Pneumotherapy was started almost immediately, but progress was slow and doubtful. X-rays taken about two weeks later confirmed the advanced tuberculosis of the right lung, with cavitation in the upper lobe, and "a marked increase in pathology since the previous examination." Subsequent x-rays showed that the lung was not collapsing as it should under the pneumotherapy. Adhesions to the lateral chest wall kept it about 50 percent expanded, and consequently it was not getting the rest required for a cure. In May it was decided to transfer me to the infirmary at Notre Dame, then located in the building which earlier had been my novitiate house. I had recovered sufficiently to permit continuation of the treatment at Healthwin Sanitarium, about three miles away. This sanitarium specialized in treating tuberculosis victims, and my superior hoped that the specialists and the change of air would hasten my recovery.

The infirmary at Notre Dame was so crowded that I had to share a room with a fellow seminarian, William Ford. He also was a tuberculosis patient, but his condition was less acute than mine, so that after some months he was able to return to the seminary. He and I were ordained together in 1941. Willie, however, worked so hard after ordination that he shortly suffered a relapse and died. In the infirmary he was always in good spirits, and his company was a joy and consolation to me during what was otherwise a very uncomfortable summer. The trouble was not merely the oppressive heat, though it was extremely trying. The progress of my illness was getting me down. The doctors at Healthwin were continuing the treatment started in Washington, intended to collapse the affected lung. I went out there once a week for an injection of air into the pulmonary sac. Things would go well for a while, and then I'd have a setback; another period of encouragement, and another letdown. Even prayer no longer brought me any happiness. In fact it was an effort to pray at all. I would turn on the radio, but I soon got bored. I would read the funnies, but that also tired me. More serious reading was not only forbidden but out of the question. I could not concentrate on anything. So I lay on the bed all through those burning summer months and stared at the ceiling day after day, week after week, month after month, knowing all the time that I was getting worse instead of better. Late in July I got a letter from my sister Nellie to tell me that she was coming soon to visit me. The news gave me great pleasure. Although we did not have the opportunity to see each other often, I had kept in close touch with my family in Scranton, and especially with Nellie. I felt that I owed the fulfillment of my vocation to her more than any of the others, and I also knew that she regarded her life as committed in a special way to the furthering of Tom's progress and mine toward the priesthood. Just how total this commitment was I would not learn until later. Shortly after Tom and I had gone to Notre Dame, Nellie had moved from the Scraggs to work for the bishop and the ten priests who lived with him. She was infinitely happy in those surroundings, close to the cathedral, where she could attend Mass and receive Holy Communion every morning, and where she could frequently visit when she had a break in her duties during the day.

By the time Nellie arrived I had a private room, and I recall that it was like the sunshine entering when she walked in. I had found a beautiful picture of Our Lady thrown in the corner of the room when I first moved there. It was dirty, covered with paint spots, but I took an instant fancy to it. I got a companion to clean it up for me and hang it at the end of my bed. Looking at that picture helped me to pray, and so did Nellie when she came. She gave me several novena books and got me to promise to join her in novenas to Our Blessed Mother. Her extraordinary faith and serene trust raised my spirits. While she was around, my illness seemed more endurable, and confidence that I would recover began to revive.

We talked a lot about my mother, who had been a widow for five years, my father having died in 1934 at the age of sixty-six. We had felt it necessary to tell her that I had to take a rest as a result of excessive application to study, not mentioning the nature or seriousness of the illness. But she apparently had read between the lines and suspected more than she knew. As I learned later from my Aunt Annie, my mother's sister, the two of them had several conversations which revealed what was on my mother's mind. The first was in late July or early August, shortly after my mother had a slight stroke. "Your mother's constant prayer at that time," Aunt Annie said, "was that your sufferings would come upon her, that you would get well and go back to your work." The context in which Aunt Annie placed these remarks for me was that it was not simply the expression of the natural love of a mother for her son, but over and above, a supernatural motivation which inspired her to sacrifice her own life willingly if it would save the life of another who could do more than she could to help others and to save souls for Christ. It was not easy for her, Aunt Annie said, but she was able to rise above her human weakness. "I was never a good soldier," she quoted her as saying on one occasion, "but now I have to be one." Within a short time she received what she and those around her regarded as an answer to her prayer. While Nellie was still with me in August, we received word that she had a second and far more serious cerebral hemorrhage. From that time it was obvious that her days were numbered. She lingered on for just a few more months.

A short time after Nellie's return to Scranton in September, I had another setback that scared me. When I reported it at my next weekly visit to Healthwin, Dr. John A. Mart said it was time to make a full evaluation of the treatment. He ordered x-rays and blood tests. A week later I returned full of anxiety for the verdict. It was just about as gloomy as it could be. "My colleagues and I have studied the x-rays and samples. We have reviewed the entire history of the case. I am sorry to report that the treatment is a failure."

"And is there nothing else you can try?" I asked dejectedly. "There is a possibility, but it is a possibility of desperation," he answered. "My colleagues and myself would be prepared to undertake an operation. The pneumotherapy is not working, and we are now convinced it will not work for you. The only alternative is to remove several ribs and break several others. It will involve three major operations, and the effect will be to make your shoulder blade fall in, giving your lung the rest that is essential for recovery."

"It's a desperate mutilation of a man's body," I said. "It would leave him handicapped for life, even if it worked."

"I know," he said, "and that is why my colleagues and I want you to think the thing over and make your own decision. You are a man dedicated to God. Your choice now is to put yourself in our hands and trust to our efforts, or to write us off and put your trust in God and in prayer."

It was a shocking confrontation for a young man recently initiated into the spiritual life. God would want me to try everything possible, I thought. Yet I resisted the idea of my whole side being permanently maimed. Then a thought struck me. "Would you mind getting the opinion of Dr. Lent in Washington?" I asked him. "On the contrary," he said, "we'd welcome it. I'll have the entire record sent to him." It was agreed that the pneumotherapy would meanwhile continue.

Dr. Mart reported to Dr. Lent that the fluid which had been present in the right cavity when they had first examined me was still present and that the adhesions then also present were continuing to interfere with the collapse of the lung. In addition, I was still spitting up blood from time to time. "We reviewed the situation at our staff conference and came to the conclusion that the pneumothorax would never adequately control the tuberculous processes and consequently have recommended thoracoplasty."

I was grateful for the postponement of a decision, and the delay was actually longer than I had dared hope, because Dr. Lent was moving his office and did not get round to a reply until the middle of December. By then the entire situation had altered radically and providentially, as I shall now describe. When I left Dr. Mart's office I remember it was a dreary October evening. I went back to my room at Notre Dame in a state of utter dejection and emotional confusion.

I closed the door of my room, and the tears coursed down my face. "This is finally the summit of Calvary," I told myself. My heart was torn. At best, even if the operation were successful, I was going to lose another whole year. I might easily be forced to abandon altogether my dream of the priesthood. Still I didn't want to yield to despair. I tried to think of myself as being really on Calvary, really willing to share in Christ's sufferings, and to accept my own fate as coming from the hands of God.

The next day I reported the situation to my superior at the infirmary, Father Thomas Irving, and he was all in favor of the operation. More than that, he wanted to get the business over before the ice and snow of winter set in. I was ready to obey, but my spirit still revolted. One point I could not get out of my mind was that three medical doctors, one Jewish and the others Protestants, had challenged my belief that my fate was in the hands of God. I knew that they were good doctors and honorable men. In their own minds they must have little hope of success, if they were leaving it to me to choose. But what an agonizing choice they offered me!

Five

I Call and Mary Hears

The news spread quickly across the campus, and it brought Father Cornelius Hagerty running to me. As he stood in the doorway of my room that night in late October, a distant memory flooded back, filled me with joy, and put me in a state of receptivity for what he was going to say to me. I recalled the first time I had ever set eyes on him. It was, I believe, my first year in the community, and I was out for a walk at Notre Dame one afternoon with several of my companions. "That's Father Hagerty," one of them said, pointing to a priest in the distance. Although we did not exchange a word, the mere sight of him left a mark on me: his serenity, his dignity, his peaceful face. All our subsequent relations had confirmed that first impression. Here was a man who would never wear a false face. He would say what he believed regardless of the consequences. I welcomed him to my room with open arms.

Father Cornelius and I have more than once tried to reconstruct what exactly passed between us that night. The precise words have vanished forever, and it may well be that I read more into them than he intended by them. If I did, I believe that we both are now agreed that this was providential. For he forced me to face squarely the issue that the doctors had presented to me: Was my faith a sham or a reality? He handed me the correct answer, and all I can do is to thank God and Mary for the rest of my life that I had the grace to accept it.

About certain parts of the conversation I am quite clear. He may not even have known about the choice the doctors had offered me, though he obviously did know that they had given me bad news. But what he said fitted perfectly into my situation and gave me the key to my decision. "You have the faith, Pat," he said, "but you're not using it. You brought it with you from Ireland. Your mother gave it to you, just as her mother had given it to her." He dwelt on that point, recalling a passage in which St. Paul describes how the faith is transmitted from mother to son.

Then he explained to me how meaningful prayer to Our Blessed Mother would be, if only I used the faith I possessed. "Our Lady will be as good as you think she is," he said. "If you think she is a fifty per-center, that is what she will be; if you think she is a hundred per-center, she will be for you a hundred per-center. No one of us ever does as much as he is capable of doing. We always fall short, stopping on the near side of our total effort."

It was startling to be addressed in such words, but not nearly as startling as what he said next. "Even Our Lord and Our Lady do not do as much as they could do," he added, "but the reason is that we think they are not able. We limit them by the extent of our faith." Then he made me another wonderful statement. "I will begin a novena of Masses for you tomorrow, and that's the greatest thing on earth. It is not just some holy man or some holy woman praying for you for nine days. It is Jesus Christ praying to His Father for you. And that is power infinitely greater than any power on earth."

He went on talking for a long time in this vein, restoring my confidence in the goodness and mercy of God, insisting that the way to reach God was through the intercession of Mary. As I listened, I felt that he was building a bridge for me over the chasm that spelt the difference between theory and reality, that he was leading me across that bridge so that I could see Mary, could walk with her, talk to her, realize that she was a real person who would listen, love, respond. I will not say that I really saw Mary for the first time while he talked, but I know I saw her with a new clarity and intensity, so that I could say in my heart: "Mother, I believe that you are alive, that you are real, that you are a woman, that you have eyes, a face, a smile, a memory, an intelligence, a heart. You have a mother and father of your own. You have a son, who is truly God, who loves you, who will deny you nothing you ask."

Many beautiful things Father Hagerty said. But what really captivated me was the way he summed up his entire thinking in three brief statements. "Mary is omnipotent in the power of her prayer," he said. "Mary is omnipotent in the power of her intercession with her Son. Mary can do anything God can do." Then he went on to explain the meaning of these three statements. "The difference is not in what God can do and what Mary can do. The difference is in the way they do it. God wills something and it happens.

Mary prays to Him for something and He does it. He will never say no to her."

The total impact of what Father Hagerty said was to add a new dimension to the love I already had for the Mother of God. To a greater extent than ever before, he helped me to realize how human she is, how approachable, how sensitive to our needs, so that she could never be haughty or turn her back when we call her. I saw how strong my own position was in dealing with her. All those years, from the time I was able to lisp the prayers, I had joined with my family in praising her and paying tribute to her. It was like a man who had paid an insurance over the years on his house. Now the house was burning down and he could come and claim on his insurance.

I knew what I had to do. There would be no operations. I would put my trust in God, and I would approach Him through His Mother and mine. She would cure me.

There was still the problem of my superior, but I was confident that he would not insist, when I explained the entire situation to him.

Father Hagerty's visit was about October 25, and during the following days my peace of mind and confidence grew. I prayed constantly to Mary to cure me, and it was on Halloween, the Eve of All Saints, that I knew that she had decided to do just that. I was eating my supper in bed, and the radio was playing some Irish tunes, transmitted from London. Just then the oppression and the depression and the darkness were swept from my soul, to be replaced by a lightness and freedom, and a hope. I had been up and down many times, but this was different. The fog had finally lifted.

I was due to go to Healthwin the following Monday, November 6, for my weekly treatment. I decided to say nothing to anyone until the doctors found out for themselves. But interiorly I was at peace. I remember in particular two visits I had on the Sunday afternoon. One was from two ladies, Mrs. Ladewski, the mother of a seminarian from South Bend, and Mrs. Rossi, the mother of a Notre Dame student from California. They were very cheerful, and when they left they promised that they would go directly to the grotto of the Blessed Virgin on the campus to light candles for my recovery. The other was from an old priest living out his last days in the infirmary, a Father Hugh Gallagher. He had noticed the beginning of the optimism that now filled me, and he feared that I was in for a letdown the following day when I went again to Healthwin. He tried to moderate my enthusiasm, and I was grateful for his concern. Secretly, nevertheless, I knew I had nothing to fear.

The first procedure, each time I went to the sanitarium, was to put me under the fluoroscope to determine how much gas should be pumped into the pulmonary sac. Two of the doctors were present, and the moment they took the first look, one of them beckoned the other to withdraw to a corner where they could talk without being overheard. They didn't have to tell me. I knew that something wonderful had happened. Here were the men who a few weeks earlier had told me it was hopeless, and now they were back out of the corner, turning me this way and that, checking, examining, making notes.

"How is the fluid?" I asked. The presence of fluid in the sac was a complication which prevented the collapsing of the lung. "It's not all gone," one of them said, "but it's going."

With joy I reported the news to Father Irving and to Brother Michael the nurse, when I returned to the infirmary. They were delighted. Father Irving told me to go straight to bed, but the chapel was my first stop, and there I made a long thanksgiving to God and Mary. I decided not only to redouble my own prayers but to enlist the prayers of others in a concentrated storming of heaven. I knew that Nellie, Mary, and Beatrice were already on their knees night and day. Now the seminarians of Notre Dame and the nuns of a Carmelite convent joined them. With such backers, I knew Mary could not fail me.

A week later, on November 13, I was back again at Healthwin. "How is the fluid now?" I asked with mounting confidence. "It's all gone," they said. "There's not a trace of it left." "In that case," I said, "why don't you discharge me as cured? You must realize what happened. You challenged me to put my trust in God, and that is what I did. It was Mary, the Mother of God, who heard my prayers. She does not do things by half. She wants me to go back to my studies, and you mustn't stand in my way."

They were very polite. They agreed that they had no way to account for the sudden improvement. But they were also quite firm. "Now we must continue the treatment," they said. "You must wait until the end of the six-month period from your last full examination. Until that study of your condition is completed, you must follow the regimen we have laid down."

That same evening I had a visit from a young student priest, Father Richard Sullivan, who many years later was to be my provincial. "I am going to offer a novena of Masses for you," he told me, "to end on the feast of the Presentation

of Our Lady, November 21." Lying in my bed each morning during those nine days, I joined in spirit with Father
Sullivan, and I looked forward with anticipation to Mary's
feast. I was not disappointed. The evening of November
20, I knelt for a long time before the picture of Our Blessed
Mother in my room, and I then took Lourdes water from a
bottle and rubbed it on my chest. In the morning the sputum cup which is the constant companion of the victim of
tuberculosis was clean. I had not coughed up a single taste
of poison from my lungs all night, nor did I ever again use
that sputum cup. On Our Lady's day, I was allowed up for
a while. I was weak and pale, but I wanted to be a member
of the community again, and it was a great happiness to go
to the recreation room and chat with the priests.

I was more determined than ever to force the issue with
the doctors at Healthwin, but they were equally adamant
that I would have to wait out the full six months before
repeating the major examination which I was confident
would give me a clean bill of health. My dilemma was
quickly resolved by Father Christopher J. O'Toole, who
subsequently served a term as superior general of Holy
Cross. He had been ordained a few years earlier and had
gone for further studies to Louvain University, Belgium.
With the outbreak of war in Europe in September 1939, he
had been brought back home and made assistant to Father
Irving at the infirmary while awaiting a new assignment.
Day by day he had followed my rapid improvement, and
he now made arrangements to have Dr. James McMeel of
South Bend examine me independently. The x-rays and
other tests were made at St. Joseph's Hospital, South Bend,
on December 5. Two days later Dr. McMeel called Brother

Michael. "Tell Pat Peyton," he said, "that he can get up for Mass tomorrow."

Tomorrow was the feast of the Immaculate Conception of Mary. It was a Mass I had always attended with love, but never before did the Scripture readings affect me as they did that day. The tone was set by the opening words of the Introit: "I will heartily rejoice in the Lord, in my God is the joy of my soul, for he has clothed me with a robe of salvation" (Is 61:10). And when the priest came to the final words of the Epistle, I thought it was more than my heart could contain. "He who finds me, finds life, and wins favor from the Lord" (Prov 8:35). It was indeed true. Finding Mary, I had found life and had been clothed with a robe of salvation.

Armed with this assurance, I pestered the Healthwin doctors until they finally agreed to move up the examination. They were still understandably skeptical, and they went about their task methodically and thoroughly. They completed their examinations and tests on January 15, 1940, and a few days later they mailed me the verdict. I shall never forget the moment it reached me. For a long time I held the letter in my hand, not daring to open it. I felt like the man in the dock as the jury files back into the court to announce its findings. I knew that I was cured, just as the man in the dock may know that he is innocent, but that doesn't mean that the verdict will go in his favor. My terror was that they would be overcautious, that they would insist on keeping me in bed, force me to lose another year. Finally, however, I prayed and summoned my faith. I tore the envelope open with shaking hands. Mary had not deceived me. "After discussing your situation at our staff conference," the letter read, "we came to the conclusion that you could safely take eleven hours a week. It is important that you get as much rest as possible, and if at any time new symptoms develop, you should contact us immediately. Pneumothorax will be continued with refills every two weeks." The letter was signed by Dr. John A. Mart. I was lifted to heaven in delight by the news, yet it also frightened me. This was Mary's own doing, and she would bear the responsibility. "Mary, I hope I will never disgrace you," I cried aloud, my heart full of gratitude that I was free to continue toward my goal.

I packed my suitcase and went back to Washington. Because of my health record, it was decided I should give up any idea of going on to the Bengal missions, so my destination was this time the Holy Cross College, where I would once more be close to Tom. I traveled through the night, and he was at the station to greet me in the early morning. It was Monday, February 5, exactly a year from the Monday I had been carried from the Bengalese to Providence Hospital.

Tom stuck close to me from that moment. He had been assigned to ensure that I limited my activity to the absolute minimum to keep up with my class work, and he watched over me like a hawk. But there was nothing hawk-like about his sentiments. He had suffered with me, and he was conscious of all the family had suffered with me and for me. We already had the news that our mother had died early in December, at the very time that Dr. McMeel was making the tests which had finally convinced everyone that my health was restored. It was not long until we got further evidence of the enormous price that my family was paying, and paying gladly, for my recovery. My sister Nellie died.

Oh, my dear Nellie, what an emptiness that news left in my soul. For years she had been praying fervently that God would make priests of both her brothers. When, through her assistance, we were finally on our way at Notre Dame, she was still aware of the many difficulties involved in the routine of study and obedience for two full-grown men accustomed to their own way, especially one so stubborn as her brother Patrick had turned out to be. She, accordingly, made a vow that she would never marry, provided that her two brothers would succeed in their vocation. That was her supreme concern. I was given a slip of paper found in a drawer in her room after her death. "I, Nellie Peyton," it read, "offer Thee, dear Lord, all my thoughts, words, and actions of this day, and every day, and even life itself, for my two brothers, Thomas Francis Peyton and Patrick Joseph Peyton, that if it be Thy Holy Will that they become priests, that never in their priestly lives will they commit a mortal sin." It was her morning offering.

Even life itself, she had written. And God had accepted her offering. She underwent major surgery on April 28, and everything worked out fine. Four days later the doctors put her on the recovered list, but the very same day she had a totally unanticipated heart attack. It was Saturday afternoon, and by Sunday morning the condition was so serious that word was sent to our superior, Father William J. Doheny, now a member of the Roman Rota, the curial tribunal which deals with marriage cases. "I am sorry to have to tell you your sister Nellie is dying," he said. "Go and pack immediately." Tom and I ran to our rooms, but before we had put our few things together, Father Doheny came with another sad message. She had died at 11:02 a.m. We reached Scranton that same afternoon and received additional details. When it became apparent that there was little or no hope of recovery, Monsignor William Farrell, then chancellor of the diocese and a good friend of Nellie's, who was also a patient in the hospital, had requested permission to prepare her for death. The regular chaplain agreed, and the monsignor went to her room at nine o'clock on the Sunday morning. "Nellie, you are going to die," he told her. "Yes, I know," she replied with the greatest calm. He administered the sacrament of the Anointing of the Sick and gave her the Holy Eucharist. "Have you a message for your brothers?" he asked her afterward. "I do, Monsignor," she replied. "Tell them that if it be God's Holy Will that they become priests, I pray that they will be true priests like Jesus Christ."

For us it was a sad homecoming, yet we were deeply consoled to find how all who had known her esteemed our Nellie. The bishop of the diocese, Bishop William J. Hafey, not only presided at the funeral Mass but spoke at the end. His theme was the message Nellie had left for Tom and me. "We all learned from this humble maid," he said. There were thirty-two priests in the sanctuary. Monsignor John H. Vaughan, the celebrant of the Mass, sobbed aloud several times, unashamedly.

After the funeral on May 8, one of the priests for whom she had worked in the bishop's house called on us at Beatrice's. "Every one of the priests loved her," he told us. "She was a most unusual woman. We could tell her our innermost secrets, not just me, but others too. She advised and consoled us, and she did not hesitate to tell us to improve on our own nature."

Among the anecdotes he told us was one which perfectly illustrated her approach. He was waiting at the front door
one morning, somewhat impatiently, for another priest
with whom he had arranged to make a long trip. Nellie was
sweeping off the steps. "Father is making a long thanksgiving after his Mass today," he commented a little sarcastically.
"Yes, isn't he?" Nellie answered with her most charming
smile. "One time, you did the same."

Listening to this priest, I realized more clearly than ever
before how important a contribution Nellie had made and
would continue to make to my own life. I was permanently
obligated to her because of the vow she had voluntarily
made and gladly fulfilled to give herself, even her life, for
my spiritual and temporal welfare. The least I could do in
return would be to lead a life which, in its intensity of love
for God and His Blessed Mother and in the totality of its
concentration on the work of God, would not only justify
my own existence but would leave a surplus to equal all the
good Nellie would have radiated around her, had she lived
the normal human span. "I'll not forget that little story,
Nellie," I said in my heart. "You will never have to reproach
me during my priestly life in the way you had to reproach
that priest for growing cool in his dedication."

Back in Washington after the funeral, and constantly
thinking of the stronger ties my sister had forged for me
by her death, I became possessed by a new restlessness.
I realized that I ought to be more than satisfied with the
extraordinary favor Mary had done me in restoring my
health so that I could continue my studies in defiance of
all available medical opinion. But in my heart there grew
an uncontrollable desire, and I began to pray incessantly

to the Blessed Mother to humor my whim. I wanted to be ordained with Tom, even though I was now a year behind him in my studies. We had come together from Ireland. We had worked together as laborers. We had set out together for the priesthood. It was the kind of human, family situation that I knew the Mother of God would understand, and I was not deceived.

I took no action other than prayer to achieve this result. No doubt my colleagues and my superiors knew what was in my mind, but I made no formal request. Imagine, then, my delight when in May 1941, about a month before Tom and his classmates were to set off for Notre Dame, where the ordinations were scheduled for June 15, a cablegram arrived from Rome. "Special dispensations are granted," it read, "for the immediate ordination to the priesthood of seminarian Patrick Peyton." My prayers had once more been heard. I packed my bags and went off with the others. When in due course our names were called, Tom and I stepped forward side by side in the gray Gothic church of the Sacred Heart at Notre Dame. The bishop extended his hands over each of us in turn and called down the Holy Spirit on us to guide us always in our priestly lives. To minimize the strain, in the light of my health record, I was instructed to sit during most of the long ceremony.

I did not hesitate when I heard my name; yet when the bishop's hands touched my head, I felt almost crushed by the weight of the burden they were placing on me. Henceforth I would always have to carry that burden, not only in time but through all eternity, or as the Book put it, "even in heaven, even in hell." The bishop told me that Christ's yoke was sweet and his burden light, but how could such a one as I carry it worthily? All my past life welled up in a single vision before my eyes. Here was I, a farm boy from Mayo village, a road worker, a general handyman, a helper on a steam shovel, an obstinate and often ungrateful son. Now I was being transformed into another Christ. I was being given power to make Christ present in the Christian community under the appearances of bread and wine. I was being authorized to forgive sin in His name. I was being commissioned to preach His word, so that those who heard me heard Him. I could enroll new recruits in the ranks of the people of God by pouring on their heads the saving waters of Baptism. I could strengthen the dying for their final journey by anointing them with the holy oils of the Sacrament of the Sick.

It was a terrifying experience but a supremely salutary one. For when the vision passed, what remained was that I was now by ordination another Christ and that consequently Christ's Mother was, more than ever before, my mother. If in the past she had behaved with such delicacy toward me, what could I not now expect from her, now that I was another Christ, the very fruit of her womb? The thought filled me with consolation and exaltation beyond all describing. If I had the heavens in my hand at the moment, I'd have given them right to her. At Notre Dame that day, I gave my heart and soul in love to Mary. I promised her all the merit of my priesthood until death. The merit and the glory of every action I would ever perform would be hers and hers alone.

Six

Decision for a Lifetime

As yet I had no clear idea of how I would spend my life in repaying to Mary the gifts she had showered on me. But that such was my duty and my need was clear beyond questioning. It was in this mood I journeyed with Tom to Scranton, where we were to celebrate our first solemn Masses in the company of our family and friends, and in the same mood I offered that Mass to her as the expression of my gratitude and the pledge of my commitment.

Father Tom was sent by his superiors into parish work in New Orleans, in South Bend, Indiana, then once more in New Orleans. Since then, we have never lived and worked together, although it is my pleasure to see him at irregular intervals. Our careers have been very different, his in a fixed spot, mine like the gypsies, wherever my compass guides me. Of him I can certainly say that he has lived up to the hopes and expectations of Nellie, for he is a true priest. I have never regretted the part I played in steering him toward the altar.

The dispensation to advance my ordination did not release me from the obligation to complete the regular course of studies. Consequently, I went back to Washington for another year of theology. All the other seminarians were away for the summer, and I used to spend a lot of time sitting alone on the lawn of Holy Cross College, alone but never for a moment lonely. I was in the highest heaven, because my dream had finally come true. I was a priest. I was not even worried about the enormous debt I owed Our Blessed Mother for having given me this gift. I knew she would in her own time and way tell me how to make a small return. Still the debt was never far from my thoughts, for I had definitely committed myself in my own mind to do nothing else in my entire life but work at paying it off.

Pearl Harbor had not yet come, but the news from Europe was terrifying, and the influx to Washington grew daily as the country girded itself for the test of endurance that now seemed inescapable. From where I sat, I could see the endless ebb and flow of traffic on Harewood Road at the bottom of our lawn. At the rush hour in the evening, it piled up endlessly. I used to wonder how many of those people, sitting there fuming while their motors overheated, used the time to think of the Mother of God and pray to her, how many of them perhaps never gave her a thought in their whole lives. One day I had an idea. It would be terrific, I thought, if a statue of Our Lady could be erected on the lawn in full view of the road, at a point where the lights of the cars would illuminate it at night. I had no understanding of finance, no administrative experience, no idea of how to take the first step. But I figured, as I always have, that if Mary wanted the statue, and if she wanted me to be the means by which it was realized, the rest would work itself out. So I canvassed my fellow seminarians, who by this time were back from their vacations, to see who could help in raising funds. Soon it became clear that I couldn't even start until the superior gave his approval. He didn't give it. So that was the end of my first bright idea.

The months passed, and the war spread from Europe and Africa to the Pacific. The thought of the carnage and the slaughter was constantly on my mind. So was my debt to Mary. How it grieves her, I thought, to see so many of her children killing each other, filling their minds with hatred of fellow children of God, destroying the earth instead of building it up. Surely there was something I could do, something I should be doing that I was neglecting. I had read of Lepanto, the great battle in the Mediterranean in 1571, when a Christian fleet had stopped Muslims as they advanced toward the very heart of Christendom. The Christian soldiers and sailors had knelt and prayed the Rosary before committing themselves to battle. In gratitude for the victory, Pope Pius V had proclaimed October 7 as the feast of the Most Holy Rosary for the entire Church. The thought kept coming back to my mind that somehow the Rosary was called to play a part again in the victory of justice and restoration of peace to the world.

I can fix exactly the day in which what had been a vague thought coalesced into a concrete idea. It was the last Sunday of January 1942, the day we spent as a monthly day of recollection in the seminary. I was alone in my room, and it was the middle of the morning. Suddenly the thought struck me that here in this house we had ten priests and sixty young men who would be ordained priests over the next few years and that if all of us prayed fervently enough, we could put an end to the war. "But how should we pray and what should we pray for?" I asked myself. What was needed was not simply an end to the fighting but an atmosphere of true peace, peace in the heart, peace in the home, peace in the family. "Yes," I told myself, "here was the key: family prayer, and in particular the prayer that had consistently brought God's favor through the centuries, that had saved Christendom at Lepanto, that had been preached and practiced and promoted incessantly by saints and popes, the Rosary." My mind ran forward with the idea. I would enlist in a great Crusade for the family Rosary not only these seventy men with whom I lived, but all the millions of servicemen, like the soldiers and sailors before the battle of Lepanto—and not only the servicemen, but their mothers and fathers and brothers and sisters, every family in the United States, every family in the world, all giving just ten minutes a day to recite the same prayer as the men at Lepanto, a prayer drawn from the Scriptures, breathing the inspired Word of God.

I have it, I thought jubilantly. It can't fail, this is God's will for me. Then and there I knew I had found my lifework. Here was something worthy to occupy my entire efforts, something that would repay Mary's many favors to me, that would transform the world by binding the family close to itself every single day on its knees in the presence of God.

A second thought followed the first. Why stop simply with the family Rosary? Why not also develop a campaign in favor of daily attendance at Mass? The Rosary is good, but the Mass is better. Why not go the whole way?

I spent considerable time mulling over that idea, looking for a way to tie the two projects together in a unified package. Finally, however—and this decision was made the very same day—finally I decided that I was trying to bite off too much too fast. "One small step at a time," I told myself. If I asked too big a favor, I'd get nothing at all. Better start with the small thing, the ten minutes a day right in the home, no need to dress up, no need to go out in snow or rain or blazing heat, just ten short minutes in one's own living room or bedroom or kitchen. If I got that, I'd be on the way, and if God and Mary wanted more, they would show the way to it in their own time.

That was the decision I made, to devote my entire life, my every effort, to the promotion of family prayer, and particularly of family prayer expressed in the form of the Rosary said every day or every night by the family gathered together in its own home. I had no idea how I was going to do it. Here I was, still a student, with a health record that prevented me from doing even a normal day's work, without resources, without wealthy friends, without any broad experience of the country in which I proposed to work, a sophisticated country with the reputation of being materialistic, a complicated country where every activity required its own specialist. I knew I was going to be laughed at as a visionary or a fool. But I didn't care. I couldn't help it. This was what I was going to do, and I knew that I was going to succeed because Our Blessed Mother would see to it. It was not my reputation that was at stake, but hers.

The very moment my mind was made up, I ran out of my room to share my thought with one of our seminarians and ask his help to make it a reality. This was Charles

Sheedy, a brilliant young man who was ordained shortly afterward and who is today a shining light of Holy Cross as a professor at Notre Dame. I confided in Charley. I felt I could trust his judgment.

Charley's reaction was restrained but favorable. It was a fine idea. But how could we make it work? How even get the approval of the superiors to test it? I had already gone with one idea, and it had been shot down right away. We mulled things over, and I decided not to face Father Christopher O'Toole, who was now my superior, until I had something more concrete to offer him. I went through all that spring and early summer planning and plotting and figuring. And all we had to show for our efforts by the time that June came with the end of the school year and the end of my studies was one small article published in *Our Sunday Visitor*. Charley had written it, and the message was a call to the readers to retain or restore the family Rosary in their own homes. That was all, to encourage the idea. There was nothing to indicate that this was the first blow in a mighty effort that would spread out to the whole of America and ultimately circle the globe, so that no family could plead that it never was told what it could gain here and hereafter by saying the Rosary as a family every day. We could not say anything about such a program, such a crusade, because we had absolutely no way to undertake it. We didn't even have our superior's approval.

That came only late in June. I was sitting on the porch one evening with Father O'Toole. The others had left on vacation, and I had remained behind waiting for my first assignment, the obedience from my provincial which would decide the work I should undertake in Holy Cross. Father

O'Toole was in a particularly pleasant mood, and I decided the moment had come to spring my idea on him. "The one thing I want to do with my life," I told him, "is to devote every minute of it to restoring the family Rosary in America." At that time I had not projected the idea beyond the shores of America. That was where I saw my mission.

Father O'Toole was noncommittally sympathetic. It was a fine thought, of course. There probably wasn't a priest from Maine to California who wouldn't regard such an assignment as a worthwhile lifework. But how realistic was it? What concretely could one priest, with a bad health record, accomplish if he set out with a bag of rosary beads on his back to peddle the Joyful, Sorrowful, and Glorious Mysteries from door to door? "I don't think I could give you that kind of authorization, Pat," he said. "It would have to come from Father Steiner." Father Thomas A. Steiner was our provincial superior. An engineer by profession and longtime dean of the college of engineering at Notre Dame, he was a good and sincere priest, but not primarily renowned for his imagination or love of experimentation. He would be a tough nut to crack.

As he spoke, Father O'Toole continued to study my idea. "Suppose you did get approval," he said. "How would you go about starting?" That was my chance. "You remember," I said, "that a few months ago you invited Bishop Edwin O'Hara of Kansas City to talk to us. He spoke about the Confraternity of Christian Doctrine, which he had helped to establish in this country, as well as about the Catholic Rural Life movement in which he was also a pioneer. One thing he said impressed me greatly, because it fitted in so completely with my own experience in my home and my little community back in Ireland. He described the rural family as the great carrier of tradition in a nation. I think this is a man we could approach, and if we did, he would back us to the hilt."

Father O'Toole was obviously impressed. "What do you mean?" he asked me. "What would you want Bishop O'Hara to do?"

"What I'd like to ask him," I replied, "would be that he should present the program for me to the next meeting of the American bishops in Washington in November and ask the bishops to support it and recommend it. If the bishops went on record in a resolution, then the door would be wide open everywhere. The sky would be the limit."

"Write the bishop, by all means," said Father O'Toole. "But don't propose to him that he act as your spokesman. Just describe your idea and ask for his reaction. I can authorize that without consulting Father Provincial. It's not committing anyone to anything."

So I got to work. I drafted a letter, and I got Ted Hesburgh, a seminarian and a friend, to revise it and type it up. This seminarian is now Father Theodore M. Hesburgh, president of the University of Notre Dame. Even before that time, I had adopted what is my continuing practice of picking a feast of Our Lady for an important action. This letter was dated and mailed on July 2, the feast of the Visitation.

Bishop O'Hara's response was enthusiastic beyond all anticipation. "I agree completely that the family Rosary will be the strongest safeguard of tomorrow's families. Thanks to your suggestion, I have underlined it in my program for the Confraternity of Christian Doctrine for the coming year. I was also impressed with your observation that Our Lady of Lourdes said the Rosary with Bernadette, or at least as much of it as she could properly say. It is a sign of heaven's approval of the family Rosary."

Joyfully, I showed the letter to Father O'Toole. "Go right ahead with your planning," he said. "So long as you are under my authority, you have full permission."

On August 15 Bishop John F. O'Hara, the former president of Notre Dame, visited us at Holy Cross College. I asked to speak to him, and I explained my project. "You have a wonderful idea," he said. "I will order all the chaplains in our armed forces to preach the family Rosary on four consecutive Sundays, and I will ask them to urge the servicemen to write home and urge their own families to say the Rosary for their safety for as long as they are in service."

Such success gave me courage. I began to go around Washington to the headquarters of the big national Catholic organizations, the National Council of Catholic Men and the National Council of Catholic Women. Everywhere I went I was well received. Everywhere they promised me that in their publications and in speeches to their members they would stress the value of the family Rosary. I also made personal contacts which would later be valuable. But before I had got very far along with this task, word came from Father Provincial that he had decided what to do with me. As I was still convalescent and under doctor's orders to take things easy, I was to go to Albany as chaplain of the Holy Cross Brothers at the Vincentian Institute. The Institute is a high school for boys, and it shares a building with a high school for girls conducted by the Sisters of Mercy.

I thought I was hopelessly sidetracked from the work to which alone I wanted to devote myself. I couldn't have been more wrong. Our Lady was sending me to the spot where helpers were waiting to project my Crusade to heights I had never imagined. First among these in time, and still among the giants who have done most to carry the message of the family Rosary to the ends of the earth, were Sister Magdalena, then head of the secretarial department of the girls' division at Vincentian and now mother general of the Mercy Sisters, and Father Francis F. Woods. I first met him at a Mass at the cathedral in Albany. He was a tall man, very refined, with a pleasant manner and distinguished appearance. He was big and strong and good-looking, just a year or two older than me. In addition to being secretary of the matrimonial court, he was chaplain at the College of St. Rose and lived only a few doors away from me on Madison Avenue. A front room on the second floor of the brick house in which the Brothers lived at 923 Madison Avenue was now my home. It had a desk and a chair in the bay window, a telephone on the desk, one other chair, a chest of drawers, and a bed. That was all, except for one treasure, a reproduction of a Murillo Madonna over the bed, a picture that millions would later admire when I reproduced it on the cover of a little pamphlet entitled "The Story of the Family Rosary."

Once I left Washington, the authorization from Father O'Toole lost its validity. Armed with the blessing of two bishops, however, I summoned courage to ask Father Provincial to renew it. He said he had no objection, subject to work as chaplain for the seventeen Brothers, and provided also that Bishop Edmund Gibbons of Albany concurred. I called on Bishop Gibbons, and he immediately gave me his blessing, a blessing which has been renewed by his successors Bishop Scully and Bishop Maginn.

It was through one of the Brothers at the Vincentian Institute that I met Sister Magdalena and two of her colleagues, Sister Bernice, head of the Catholic Youth Organization at the school, and Sister Borromeo, then the school principal and later mother general. Sister Magdalena's qualities impressed me from the first time I met her. We knocked on the door of her classroom, and out came this youthful, cheerful nun, goodness radiating from her entire personality. She had been a secretary before joining the Congregation. Her family name was Buckley. Later I enjoyed the friendship of her mother, a widow, now dead.

It was about the same time that I met Sister Bernice. She introduced me to Mother Adrian, who was then the mother general, and she in turn invited me to talk to a group of Sisters from the many schools they conducted in the diocese. The Sisters went back to their schools full of enthusiasm for the family Rosary, and they began to urge their students to preach it in their own homes. Within a short time, when Mother Adrian asked for a report, she was informed that about nineteen hundred families had been won to the practice.

My initial success with Bishop Edwin O'Hara and Bishop John O'Hara had convinced me that the way to expand the Crusade to the whole of America was through the bishops. So I enlisted Sister Magdalena's help. I had no office, no typewriter, no supplies, no secretarial help, not even money for stamps. But Sister Magdalena recruited her commercial students. I dictated letters to them. They typed and stenciled and addressed envelopes, and between one way and another we begged money for stamps. Again I chose a feast of Our Lady, I believe it was November 21, the Presentation. Our Lady did not disappoint me. The first reply was from William Cardinal O'Connell of Boston promising his full support. Gradually letters came from many bishops, several of them containing not only words of approval but such concrete evidence of action as pastoral letters and diocesan newspapers carrying appropriate editorials.

One such newspaper was the *Brooklyn Tablet*, and its message was so overwhelming that I wrote Bishop Thomas Molloy that I would be in New York on a certain date and that I would be honored if I could thank him in person. I still remember how frightened I was as I waited in his reception room. I wasn't used to talking to bishops. The impression his appearance made did nothing to help me. He was a heavy-built man with an austere face. But I was put at ease quickly enough when we began to talk. If what he had written was overwhelming, it was nothing to what he said. "When I was a boy," he began, "I lived in a New England village that was Irish at one end and French at the other, with anti-Catholic elements in between. The hostile elements kept the Catholics conscious of their religion, and all Catholic families said the Rosary every day. Today the hostility is gone, and so is the family Rosary. My own brother doesn't say it. Yet the Rosary is as valuable as it ever was, though for different reasons."

He paused and rubbed his chin, studying me with an enigmatic smile. "You need money, of course, to get this thing off the ground," he said finally. "How much will it take for a start?"

How much? I had absolutely no idea. We had never made up a budget, never done a projection. I might have said five dollars or five million. I pulled a figure at random out of the air. "Five thousand dollars," I said, as though I knew what I was talking about.

"I'll give it to you," the bishop replied without batting an eyelid. "I'll be glad to. It will come back to me."

That commitment sent me home to Albany walking on air. It was not just the money but the assurance of Bishop Molloy. If a man like that believed in what I was doing, I need not fear to face anybody. But the money also meant responsibility. We had to think in bigger terms. So Father Frank Woods and I sat down with Sister Magdalena, and we made some hard decisions. We still had no office, no typewriter, nothing. But Sister Magdalena's girls had been roused to a level of enthusiasm where they were willing to do whatever had to be done. One of them in particular, Eileen Soraghan, couldn't do enough for us. When she finished her course, she got an excellent job as secretary with a business firm. But we all felt she was the one we needed. Sister Magdalena finally called her. That was in October 1944. "Eileen," she said, "Father Pat needs you. Will you leave that security and fly blindly? He has no source of income, nothing but work that needs doing." Eileen came from her security to insecurity, and she stayed with me four years until she married a fine young fellow named Eddie Gerwin, a graduate of the Christian Brothers Academy.

The Dominican Sisters nearby gave us the free use of a room intended for a chaplain in their mother house, to serve as an office. When we grew out of that, the Sisters of St. Joseph came to our rescue with a bigger room in the

College of St. Rose, on Western Avenue. I thought that surely it would more than serve our needs forever. We were able
to partition it off so that the many workers could operate
without falling over each other.

Even there, nevertheless, we were soon feeling a squeeze.
I remember that we were close to the storeroom for the
groceries, and we were forever begging the sister in charge
of the cafeteria to move some of her supplies so that we
could steal space from her for the overflow of our stocks of
booklets and paper. That was how much the mailing operation had grown. On December 8, 1942, shortly after my
interview with Bishop Molloy, we sent letters to the national
presidents of the Catholic lay organizations of America,
some of whom I had earlier contacted in Washington. The
concrete results were not as great as I had hoped, but we did
get very firm commitments of support from the Catholic
Daughters of America, the Legion of Mary, the Ancient
Order of Hibernians, the Knights of Columbus, and the St.
Vincent de Paul Society. Several of these were followed up
in significant ways. The Knights passed a resolution nam-
ing the promotion of the family Rosary on a nationwide
scale one of their objectives. The St. Vincent de Paul Society
distributed half a million pieces of our promotional literature, thanks in large part to the personal efforts of William
Drennan, its executive secretary.

Our next mailing was to all the pastors of the country.
We began early in January to address 12,600 envelopes.
With Sister Magdalena and Eileen Soraghan in command,
the pages were ripped from the Catholic Directory and
passed out to the girls of the Vincentian and the novices
of the Sisters of Mercy. A circular letter was drafted and

duplicated. The mailing date was set for February 11, the anniversary of Mary's recital of part of the Rosary with Bernadette at Lourdes. Bishop Molloy's promised contribution had not yet arrived, and we didn't have a single dollar, but we decided to send the letters first-class, with three-cent stamps, and with no return address on the envelopes. That way, we figured, the pastors would be at least curious enough to open them and find out what they contained.

By February 1 the letters were piled mountain high, but not a stamp for even one. On February 2, feast of the Purification of Our Lady, I began a novena of Masses to end on February 10, eve of the feast of Our Lady of Lourdes and of our mailing date. I did not start the novena of Masses with the intention of getting the money. I never want money associated with the Mass. I never accept a Mass stipend, because I feel it would commit me to offer my Mass for the special intention of the donor of the stipend and not for the special intention of Mary, which is what I then sought and what I always seek when I say the Mass. I feel that Our Lady needs our help, just as we need hers, and that the greatest way I can respond to her need is by giving her the total allocation of the precious fruits that come from my Mass. And it is only subject to this unconditional offering of those fruits to her that I carry in my mind to the altar my two other constant concerns, that the Family Rosary Crusade will succeed, and that the needs of its friends will be taken care of. So all I asked Mary during the novena was that she would make those letters her own and decide in her own way how they should be disposed of.

All I got on the first day were a few bills. The amount was small, but as far as I was concerned, it could have been in the millions, because I had absolutely not a dime. But the second day money began to flow in from all sides. It was under my plate when I came to table. It was in the corner of my room under the chair. It was wrapped in packets found lying on desks in the school. Sometimes I'd put my hand in my pocket and out would come a fistful of dollar bills. I was so thrilled that I didn't stop to ask where it was all coming from, and it was not till much later that I pieced together the entire story. The two friends primarily responsible were Mother Adrian of the Sisters of Mercy and Brother Thomas, superior of the Holy Cross Brothers. They passed the word of my plight in all directions. Mother Adrian got in touch with the various convents under her jurisdiction, and the Sisters got the children to contribute nickels and dimes and to beg quarters and dollar bills from their parents. Brother Thomas got his colleagues to inspire their students to do their share. And so it came in day by day. We needed $380 worth of stamps, and $380 worth we had by February 10, and a three-cent stamp on every last envelope. The sacks were carried triumphantly to the school chapel and deposited for the night near the statue of Our Lady. A post-office truck hauled them away in the morning.

While that letter was on its way, penetrating the minds of the pastors of the country and preparing them to participate later in the expansion of the Crusade, as so many of them did, Bishop Molloy delivered the first installment on his promise. It was a check for $2,500, and it was mailed on the last day of April to reach us just as Mary's month of May began. We decided that we would spend the money on the production and distribution of additional promotional material.

I started that operation at Deer Park, in northern Maryland, where I was assigned as confessor during the summer
vacation of our seminarians from Washington. The Albany
Brothers went to Notre Dame for the summer, so I wasn't
needed there until schooltime in the fall. I took the replies I
had received to my various mailings over the previous nine
months to Deer Park, and a group of seminarians set to
work to analyze them and prepare a report on the reactions
of the Catholic leaders of America to the Family Rosary
Crusade. We got it down to twelve typed pages, and we
sent it out on August 15 and September 8 to the bishops,
the major superiors of religious orders and congregations,
the presidents of Catholic lay organizations, and editors of
Catholic newspapers.

When I got back to Albany in September, I found that
Father Woods had reached a point where he was willing
to devote himself to the Crusade as fully as I had always
been. He had from the start been sympathetic but not too
deeply involved. Even then, however, he had given me a
tremendous new opening when he invited me to talk to
the students of the College of St. Rose about the family
Rosary. That provided a whole series of contacts not less
decisive than those already made among the Mercy Sisters
at Vincentian Institute. Later, he was deeply affected by the
consolation of a dying girl which was a result of her devotion to the family Rosary and by the wonderful way that
brave child offered her suffering and death to further the
devotion. Mary Grace Reutemann was this girl's name, and
one of the things that had impressed Father Woods about
her was that she was a natural leader in her age group and
radiated an extraordinary influence around her. She had

been elected class leader for her junior year. "If the family Rosary devotion can mean so much to a bright young girl like Mary," he said to himself, "then maybe there is more to it than I have realized." That was one of the things that decided him. Another was his own experience as secretary of the diocesan marriage court. He was constantly having to discuss the problems of couples whose marriages were in jeopardy, and he soon discovered that when he could get a husband and wife to say the Rosary together each evening with their children, a new atmosphere was quickly developed and the prospects for saving the marriage rose immediately.

So he made his decision to come with me 100 percent. It was no easy decision for him to make. As chaplain at the College of St. Rose and as secretary of the matrimonial court, he had a brilliant scholastic record and a high reputation among his fellow priests in the Albany diocese. All he had to do was to continue in the career on which he had embarked, and in due course he could count on becoming a bishop. But once he saw that he was being called instead to poverty and uncertainty, to struggle and wandering, to the vicissitudes of the gypsy for the sake of Our Lady and the sanctity of the home, he did not hesitate for a moment. He came with me, and he stayed with me until shortly before God called him to his reward.

During the fall of 1943, Father Woods was involved in two projects. The first was the preparation of three folders, each of which developed a series of reasons why every family should say the Rosary in common. They were supplemented by a pledge card, by signing which the members of a family would commit themselves to practice the devotion.

We sent samples to all pastors in America, and the orders that came back to us during this and the following year totaled 1,200,000. The packet was reprinted in Australia and distributed widely there. We also got many orders from Africa.

The other Woods project of that fall was the first small step on a path which still stretches infinitely before us, our introduction to the world of radio which would before long become the world of radio and television. Every Wednesday evening at nine, an Albany radio station, WABY, transmitted a program known as *The Voice of the College of St. Rose*. The participants were students of the college. For some time previously, they had been dramatizing sections of the Baltimore Catechism. Father Woods and I talked to them, and the upshot was that in October 1943, they began to devote this radio time on a regular basis to the recitation of the Rosary. There had been some doubters, but the public reaction from the word *go* was excellent.

The following summer Father Woods came with me to Deer Park, where I returned as vacation confessor for our Holy Cross seminarians. We had decided to work on a more ambitious pamphlet, "The Story of the Family Rosary." We enlisted a group of outstanding seminarians headed by Paul C. Bailey, now a Holy Cross priest teaching psychology at Notre Dame High School, Niles, Illinois. Prominent in his team were Robert Moher and William Evans, both now also Holy Cross priests, the one attached to St. Patrick's Cathedral, New York, and the other a missionary in East Pakistan. Father Bernard Ransing, the local superior, not only gave complete freedom for the work but made an active contribution, even taking his turn at a typewriter. Father Ransing is now an official of the Congregation of Religious in Rome.

The group at Deer Park did a tremendous job, but first Paul Bailey forced us to face an issue which was basic to our position. Paul thought the Rosary an excellent devotion, but he preferred its private recitation. He wasn't sold on the whole family getting together at a fixed time. I guess Father Woods and I didn't know as much as the Second Vatican Council's Decree on the Liturgy has since made common knowledge about the social aspects of prayer, or as the Constitution on the Church explains about the community of the People of God. But we gave him common-sense arguments which finally convinced him that family ties are important in the modern world and that family ties are strengthened by family prayer. We had to keep repeating the same kind of answer to all kinds of people until the Council. Since then, however, our answer is ready-made. We simply quote from the Constitution on the Church in the Modern World. "With their parents leading the way by example and family prayer," it says, "children and indeed everyone gathered around the family hearth will find a readier path to human maturity, salvation, and holiness." And for good measure we throw in a few words from the Decree on the Lay Apostolate, where it says that the family will fulfill its mission to be the first and vital cell of society, "if it shows itself to be the domestic sanctuary of the Church through the mutual affection of the members and the common prayer they offer to God."

Well, in any case, we persuaded Paul Bailey, and he put his whole heart and head into the pamphlet. A first edition

of 100,000 was printed in October and samples sent out
to the pastors in November. Meanwhile, we had also had
other seminarians working all through the summer in Deer
Park and flooding the mails, and they did this for us each
summer, so that within two or three years we shipped so
many bags of mail that from being a little country post
office, Deer Park moved up into one of the top circulation
categories. The response from the pastors was such that a
second printing of 250,000 was soon needed, and that was
followed by a third of 500,000, and after that I had to write
to the War Labor Board in Washington begging them for
a special allocation of forty-four tons of paper to supply
the demand. It was also distributed in French and Slovak
translations.

Early in 1945, while all this was mounting to a crescen-
do, I met Monsignor Fulton Sheen for the first time. He was
not yet a bishop, but he was already a famous radio orator. Much earlier he had been converted by our promotion
material to the cause we were promoting, and both in 1943
and 1944 he had spoken out in favor of the family Rosary. Finally I met him, and we entered into an agreement.
He said he would return to the issue on the third Sunday
of Lent and would announce on a network program that
he would send without cost or obligation a copy of "The
Story of the Family Rosary" and rosary beads to any listener who wrote in. I was to supply the pamphlets and the
rosary beads, and he warned me to be ready for a response
of ten thousand. The Wednesday after the talk, he called
me and said I'd better get busy and send an additional ten
thousand pamphlets and sets of beads. "In just four days,"
he said, "we have six thousand requests, and they're only

starting." We struggled to fill that order, and two weeks later he almost gave me a heart attack when he notified me that the number had reached fifty thousand. They had come from every nook and corner of the country, not only from Catholic listeners but many from Protestants and even some from Jews.

Long before this extraordinary demonstration of what the radio can do when you have a national figure to drive home to the listener what prayer should mean to him, I had been convinced that the response to our fifteen-minute program in Albany warranted a national hookup for the Rosary. We were now nearly two years on WABY, no longer in the time allocated for *The Voice of the College of St. Rose*, but at a separate time of our own. The two people who directed the program were a brilliant college student named Warren Brockley, who had first become interested while at high school at the Vincentian Institute, and Mary Kilfoil, a teacher in a public school. They continued to use the format we had developed at the outset. They would come each week to the station with the members of a family, and they would all say the Rosary, just as they would in their own homes. We never had a priest to lead it. We wanted to convey the atmosphere of a typical Catholic home.

My original authorization from Father Steiner, my provincial, was to work only in Albany, but in the summer of 1943 an incident occurred which caused him to broaden that permission significantly. While I was staying at Deer Park as vacation chaplain for the Holy Cross seminarians, I was invited by Sister Mary Carmel, an Ursuline nun, to speak at St. Theresa's Convent, Morgantown, West Virginia. That talk in turn brought an invitation to speak at the mother house in Louisville, Kentucky. When I arrived, however, I was informed that Archbishop John A. Floersh of Louisville had forbidden me to speak even to the Sisters unless I had written authorization from my own superior. So I got on the phone to Father Steiner, fearing he was going to bawl me out for getting myself into such a spot without having consulted him. Instead, he was most gracious. He wrote a letter telling me I could speak at any time in any diocese, so long as the bishop agreed. "I want every possible effort made," he said, "to move Our Lady to bring this terrible war to an end."

Other talks about this time were to the national convention of the St. Vincent de Paul Society in Buffalo, and to the pupils of the Notre Dame Academy in Cleveland. It was when I went to Cleveland that I approached Wilbert J. O'Neill, president of the National Council of Catholic Men, to see if he would give me time on *The Catholic Hour* to say the Rosary on a coast-to-coast network. He was a grand old man, and he received me well, but the final answer was no. It was too repetitive, too monotonous. It would be bad radio, and they would only lose the audience they had built up at great cost and great effort.

Back in Albany, however, the word that I was trying to get a network to carry the Rosary reached James Connors, local reporter for *Variety*, the bible of the entertainment industry. James was impressed by the favorable reaction to our program on WABY. He called me shortly after my return from Cleveland and told me he had heard I had bigger ambitions. "I have," I said, "but I'm not getting very far. I tried for 'The Catholic Hour,' and they turned me down flat." "I'm not surprised," he said. "I know you are getting response here, but a network is different. It's not only that they think the Rosary is bad radio. It is identified in the public mind with the Catholic Church and Catholic practice, and there are parts of the country where you'd have a storm of protest. They won't take that kind of risk."

I had the feeling that James himself was interested, in spite of his negative evaluation of the prospects. "I'm not giving up yet," I said to him, "and I'd appreciate your advice. You know more about this than I do."

"There's only one bit of advice I can give you," he said. "There's a fellow up in Schenectady, George Nelson, part owner of WSNY and of an advertising agency. He's a Protestant, but if anyone can figure this out for you, George is the one."

That is how I was brought into the presence of one of the finest and most loving people, one of the most gentle Christians I have known. He was in his early thirties and looked younger: a thin, athletic, self-possessed man, full of fire and energy, and yet a courteous gentleman. Enthusiasm was his dominant characteristic, and once he heard me out and agreed to help, he refused even to consider the possibility of failure. "I'll give you an introduction to Edgar Kobak, president of the Mutual Broadcasting Company in New York. Ed is a friend of mine."

In due course I had a reply from Mr. Kobak telling me that the director of religious programs, Miss Elsie Dick, would see me. I took the train to New York. Although I had traveled around quite a bit in the previous two years, it was always in the atmosphere of rectories and religious houses and schools. My first plunge into the vast, unknown world of New York business terrified me, and I trembled as

I stood outside 1440 Broadway and looked up at the massive outlines of that center of entertainment and information. "Blessed Mother, guide me," I prayed, and I repeated the words of my favorite appeal to Mary, the Memorare: "Remember, O most gracious Virgin Mary, that never was it known in any age that anyone who fled to thy protection, implored thy aid, or sought thy intercession was left unaided. Inspired with this confidence . . ."

Inspired with that confidence, I was ushered into the presence of Miss Dick. She was businesslike and to the point. I suppose she had a dozen similar problems a day. But in my ignorance of business procedure, I thought it awfully abrupt. "You're coming for free time?" she asked. "I am," I said. "You can't get it," she said, and before I could protest, she launched into a litany of difficulties. Not only Protestant ministers and Jewish rabbis would complain, she said, but so would Catholic priests. I had no organization behind me. If they gave time to individuals, they might as well go out of business.

I quickly realized that I was wasting my time, that there wasn't a chance of concocting answers that would meet her objections and convince her. So I said what was in my heart, not giving a hang how deeply I might offend her. "It's extraordinary," I said, "how preoccupied we are with other people's problems, so long as it doesn't cost us anything. It is a pleasure to hear you speak theoretically about the problem of the family, about the decay and disintegration of family life, so long as nobody asks you to raise your hand to help save it. And that's what you are now refusing, because I'm not coming in here to glorify your network by having some great orator talk, but I'm suggesting some husband

and wife, some father and mother, to pray and ask other families to join in prayer, and you won't have it."

I guess nobody had ever before talked like that to this honorable Jewish lady. "I will have it," she shot back to me. "I have no choice. When you put it like that, I can't say no." Then she lifted the telephone. "I'm not the only one involved," she explained. "You have to get clearance from Monsignor McClafferty." Monsignor John J. McClafferty was director of the division of Social Research of the New York archdiocese and Archbishop Spellman's contact with the radio industry. He was also executive secretary of the National Legion of Decency. Elsie was lucky enough to find him in his office and arranged an appointment for me to see him. "My mother is Irish," he said, when I explained my plan, "and it would be the end of me if I ever said no to the Rosary or to you."

When I told him that the date allotted to me was Sunday, May 20, he said: "Wouldn't it be wonderful if you could get the previous Sunday instead? It's Mother's Day, the perfect day for your program." He called Elsie Dick. "That day belongs to a Protestant group," she said, "but I'll ask them if they will switch." In a short time she called back. They had no objection.

Everything had happened so quickly and so contrary to all reasonable anticipation that I think it was only on the train back to Albany I had time to sort out the details and realize just how fantastic was my success. And when I thought of the undiplomatic way I had dealt with Elsie Dick, I shuddered. Nine people out of ten would have been outraged and shown me the door. But here was a person with the goodness of heart and greatness of soul to ignore the affront and see through to the reality. I thanked Our Lady for having inspired me to get her message across in a way so unconventional.

Now I had what so many had assured me was impossible, free time on a national network. I had it for what the professionals had assured me was "bad radio," because it was a monotonous and repetitive prayer, the Rosary. As I thought over these aspects, I was again filled with apprehension. I had myself and Elsie Dick and Monsignor McClafferty out on a limb. I had what I had asked for, but now I had no idea how to use it. I didn't know how to start putting a show together.

In my panic I turned again to George Nelson. "We got it," I told him, as soon as I reached Albany, "and now I have no idea what to do with it." George had still only a vague idea what the Rosary was. When I first met him, his own thought was to make the opening for me. "Tell me about the Rosary," he said. I told him, and he called in his staff and put them to work. They all rallied round, but particularly Cecil Woodland and Jim Healy, his publicity man. Something that happened at this time made a tremendous impression on George. His daughter Georgia, then age twelve, became seriously ill with cellulitis and scarlet fever and had to be isolated in a hospital ward. When Father Woods heard about it, he went right over and insisted on going in to kneel by her bed and pray for her and console her. After that courageous and faith-inspired gesture, George couldn't do enough for us.

We had to decide who would lead the Rosary on the program, and we asked the advice of Bishop John O'Hara, the future cardinal. He made some suggestions, but without

coming up with a name that we felt would make an immediate dramatic impact on the national consciousness. So we
kept discussing alternatives until one day the Sullivans were
mentioned. I don't know which of us mentioned them first,
but immediately we both knew we had a winner. These were
the Mr. and Mrs. Thomas F. Sullivan who had a short time
previously lost five sons in one naval battle in the Pacific.
I got on the telephone. "I'd like to speak to the Sullivans,"
I said, "the ones who lost their five boys. They live somewhere in Iowa." I don't know how the operator did it, but
in no time at all, I was talking to Genevieve Sullivan. Her
parents were out, she said, but if I left my number, they
would call back. It was Genevieve herself who called, within
a few minutes. She had contacted her parents at a neighbor's
house. "They'll be there, Father," she said, "and so will I, if
you'll have me."

George and his team had not only been working out
the format of the program but also conducting a massive
campaign of advance publicity. Now that he had a big name
like the Sullivans, he redoubled his efforts. News stories
went out every few days to the news agencies and the major
newspapers and magazines. A telegram was sent to each
Mutual station and affiliate, urging it to clear time to carry
the program to be transmitted by the parent station in
New York. Then news came of the Nazi surrender and the
end of the war in Europe in the first days of May, and the
proclamation by President Truman declaring May 8 as V-E
Day and a day of national thanksgiving. The promotion
campaign hit a new high. All over the country people were
hearing and reading that the Sullivan parents would recite
the Rosary on a national hookup as part of the celebration.

Down in New York, meanwhile, Elsie Dick and her associates were getting worried. They had got into this as a Sunday morning religious program, a public service at an hour that was unlikely to have many listeners or draw much attention. Now they had a tiger by the tail. They called me to New York for a conference. "Our reputation is at stake," they said. "This could be an awful flop. And who is the Nelson character anyway, who is pumping out all the publicity? We must get the whole thing under our unified control."

I gave them a quick rundown on George Nelson, and I showed them what he had brought together. We had one of the finest choirs in New York, the choir of the Blessed Sacrament Church conducted by Warren Foley, to sing the hymns. Archbishop Spellman would participate and give a short talk. It was curious how he became involved. Father Woods and I had discussed asking him, then decided we'd better leave well enough alone. A few hours later, we had a call from the Chancery to say Archbishop Spellman would be not only willing but honored to participate. Apparently, one of the people we had earlier consulted had passed word on to him. In addition, I announced proudly, we had the Sullivan parents and their daughter.

At this point, a member of the Mutual staff, Adolph Opfinger, made a flip comment which—as so often happens in my life—was to have immeasurable consequences. "So you have the Sullivans," he said half jokingly. "It's a wonder you don't get Bing."

I heard the remark but I let it pass over my head, and we completed our business. Mutual approved in general what we had done, and it was agreed that they would now take a bigger part in pulling it together and that they would let us have their Broadway theater for the broadcast, so that we could invite a live audience of distinguished guests. But after I went out, the thought kept whizzing around in my head: Why not get Bing, why not indeed? It was Good Friday, April 20. I got on the telephone. "I'd like to speak to Mr. Bing Crosby in Hollywood, California," I said. The answer came back that he was away for the weekend. On Monday I called again. "He's on the lot right now, filming *The Bells of St. Mary's*," I was told. "Leave a number and he'll call you." I left the number. Inside half an hour I heard Bing's voice on the phone. I told him who I was and what I wanted, that I was trying to put the family Rosary back in the home, that I had got this wonderful chance of a lifetime on a network, that his participation would increase the audience impact immeasurably. "You have me," he said, just like that. "Write me a letter to confirm our conversation and to tell me what to do."

On Tuesday I walked into Mutual again. "We have Bing," I said, "and I'm proud of him, because he is ready to put his name, his fame, and his reputation on the line for Our Lady, for the Rosary, and for the family."

"Now," said George Nelson, "let's get the president." I got on the phone to the White House and I called and I called and I called. On one occasion, the operator left the key open, and I heard her say: "It's that Peyton again." Of course, poor President Truman had his hands full in those days, and I don't suppose my request ever got near him. Still, we had him on the program, for he recorded a special message for the day of national thanksgiving, and I believe that George Nelson excerpted it and fitted in a couple of sentences in the right place.

The whole thing had been done with practically no money. George Nelson never charged a penny for all his own time and effort and that of his staff. My principal costs were my travel between Albany and New York and the telephone calls. In New York Father Woods and I could always count on a bed and a bite to eat at the French Hospital, then run by the Marianite Sisters of Holy Cross. We got down to New York on Saturday morning, May 12, and the first thing I did was to arrange with the manager of the Commodore Hotel to accommodate the Sullivans. A mutual friend, Frank Walker, former postmaster general, had given me an introduction, and the manager gave them rooms for little or nothing. Then Father Woods and I went to see the theater, where a rehearsal was to be held at four that afternoon. "It looks awfully bare," he said. We were thinking of the nine hundred invited guests, clergy and leaders of Catholic organizations. If we made a good impression, they would be sold on the family Rosary. "It does," I said, "look awfully bare." So the two of us went down to Barclay Street, and in the window of Benziger's religious-goods store, we saw just what we were looking for—a beautiful statue of Our Lady of Providence to make a centerpiece for the stage.

We walked into the store and introduced ourselves to Mr. Bernard A. Benziger. "We'd like to borrow that statue," I said, "to dress up the stage at Mutual while we say the Rosary for a live audience and a national hookup. We'll give you a mention." He not only agreed but got a truck to transport it and gave us twenty-five dollars for flowers. As we walked out we spotted two candelabra, and he lent us those too.

The decorations had not arrived by rehearsal time at four o'clock. The stage was drab, and so was everything

about the rehearsal itself. It was a delicately timed and highly intricate program, with more than fifty participants, all
amateurs except Bing Crosby. Bing was not there. His part
would be piped in from the studios of KHJ, Mutual's Los
Angeles affiliate, the following morning. After several hours
of coaching, there was a complete run-through which was
recorded and played back. It sounded terrible. The production was ragged, the timing poor, the pace uneven,
the participants self-conscious and mike-shy. "We need
hours more of rehearsal," Elsie Dick wailed. "This is the
end for all of us." Father Woods and I could only agree, but
it was already eleven o'clock and everyone had gone home
except the three of us. With dejected hearts we decided we
too should get some sleep, and with dejected steps Father
Woods and I tramped our way through the streets to the
French Hospital on West Thirtieth Street. Our own humil-
iation we could bear. What crushed us was that the cause
of the family Rosary, instead of being advanced, would be
set back ten years. If any possibility existed, we would have
canceled the whole thing then and there. But even that exit
was blocked. We had to go through with it.

Only prayer could save us now. We crept into the chapel
and said the Rosary. "There were two men in Our Lady's
life," Father Woods whispered to me. "Let us ask them not
to let her down tomorrow." So we prayed to Mary's spouse,
St. Joseph, and to her Son. We also invoked the Blessed
Trinity with all the fervor of our souls. In the morning we
offered our Masses and said fifteen decades of the Rosary
with the same concentration. Then with heavy steps we
went to the broadcast.

We were first. We fixed the shrine, putting one table on top of another and placing the statue of Our Lady of Providence on top. We set out the flowers and interspersed them with two hundred vigil lights. Warren Foley arrived with his choristers in cassocks and surplices, followed by Archbishop Spellman and his secretary, Monsignor Francis X. Shea, and of course the Sullivans. We had another quick rehearsal, and just before we were to go on the air at 10:30 a.m., I asked participants and guests to join in one Hail Mary.

Then the orchestra was playing, the music swelled. From the moment the red light flashed I was at ease. I knew it was a success. The choir was singing the Magnificat. The archbishop was speaking. The parents who had just lost their five boys were leading all America in the family Rosary. The treble of sweet voices rose again in the familiar beauty of "Hail, Queen of Heaven." From thousands of miles away came the voice of America's favorite singer. He was not singing now, but his words were a song that spoke the true glory, the true greatness, and the true significance of the family Rosary. They were written for him by a great Christian friend of Our Lady, George Nelson.

The gloom was gone from the faces of the Mutual executives too. "We have a winner," Elsie Dick said to me exultingly. "I'm going to get the top religious award of the year for this program." When she spoke like that, dear Elsie wasn't complimenting herself. She even wrote me a letter the following day giving my associates and myself all the credit and apologizing for what she called her earlier abruptness. And when I tried to share the compliments in my reply, she wrote a second time: "I feel conscience-stricken over your gratitude when I really haven't done anything. You have really helped me to do my job better."

That was the kind of generous lady she was, but her judgment of the success of the program was absolutely correct. Thanks to the Nelson promotion, it had secured a phenomenal audience. Monsignor McClafferty had told me that we'd be doing very well if sixty stations carried it. Actually, it was transmitted by at least three hundred. The newspapers the following day gave it a great review. The Rosary recited by the Sullivans of Iowa was the most touching of all the V-E Day programs, they said. To the day of her death Elsie Dick used to insist that it was the best religious program ever.

Father Woods and I were jubilant. We had proved that a radio network could be got to co-operate in our Crusade for family prayer. We had proved that the Rosary was what they called "good radio," that it could get and hold an audience. Many obstacles remained to be surmounted, but the insuperable one had been overcome. We now knew we were on our way.

Seven

I Shoot for the Stars

The success of the Mother's Day program did not, however, ensure an automatic or immediate break-through into the world of national radio. It gave us an immense leverage, both with important churchmen like Archbishop Spellman and Bishop John O'Hara, and with professional radio people. But as every radio man knew, and as we were to learn, there is a big difference between a one-shot success and a continuing series. The formula had still to be found.

My more immediate concern on May 14 was to dig up the cash needed to take care of expenses incurred in the previous day's broadcast, as well as money for the continuing campaign of letter writing and production of pamphlets in Albany. Neither then nor at any time have I had any permanent source of income. The Congregation of Holy Cross has been very good to me. It has allowed me to devote myself for the past twenty-five years to the promotion of the family Rosary. But I have never received a regular subsidy from it. Even the various men they have assigned to me through the years as helpers have been assessed the standard annual contribution fixed as the cost of maintaining the Congregation's administration and training programs. I have never appealed for money on radio or television programs, nor have I ever authorized any collection of money in connection with the Crusades, either in the United States or overseas. Once or twice collections were raised for the local church without my knowledge. But I have never been the beneficiary, and I always took steps to stop the practice when I learned of it. I have seen too many good works destroyed or misunderstood because the taint of money became associated with them. My agreement with the local bishop now explicitly excludes any money-raising activities in connection with a Crusade. In principle, the bishop commits himself to pay the costs from general diocesan funds. If the diocese is too poor, I find the money elsewhere, in the same ways as I do for my other activities. I am determined that no suggestion of money-making will ever be associated with my preaching of Mary's Rosary.

Still, I require money in ever-growing quantities for the constantly expanding activities in which I am involved, and while my needs constantly outstrip my assets, I somehow manage to keep my head above water. It grieves me that I have to spend so much of my time persuading the wealthy to exchange a part of their material blessings for the greater blessing that comes from serving Mary. But I reconcile myself as best I can. I have found no better way to achieve what I am determined to achieve.

In those early days, however, I had not yet reached the hearts or the pockets of any significant number of such benefactors. Such showers from heaven as Bishop Molloy's generous gift were rare. So I was devoting much of my time to preaching triduums. The primary purpose of these triduums was to promote devotion to Our Lady and encourage the practice of the family Rosary. It was the first step at the parish level in what would grow into the diocesan and ultimately the regional, the national, and the international Family Rosary Crusade. At the invitation of the pastor, I would arrive in a parish on a Saturday night, preach all the Masses on Sunday, announcing that I'd be preaching again on Sunday night and Monday night, and winding up the triduum with a Holy Hour on Tuesday night. At this final service a collection would be taken up for the benefit of the Family Rosary Crusade. In that way I raised some money while promoting my primary objective.

It so happened that the day after the Mother's Day broadcast an event occurred which directly gave a great impetus to the program of triduums and which indirectly produced for me the formula I needed to get the radio network on which my eyes were now set. I went to Pittsburgh that day at the invitation of Bishop Hugh Charles Boyle. The bishop had been impressed by the letters he had been getting from Albany, and he invited me to talk to all his priests when they assembled for their monthly meeting. The day he fixed was May 14. This was the first time I ever spoke to all the priests of a diocese assembled in one place. The reaction was favorable, and many of the pastors invited me to give triduums in their parishes, thereby ensuring me a period of concentrated activity. Among them all, the one who opened himself completely to me was a great Kerryman, Monsignor Edward Moriarty, pastor of St. Agnes, Pittsburgh. He had been extremely impressed by the Mother's Day program, and he was delighted to know of my more ambitious plans. I had earlier met Fritz Wilson, a Notre Dame graduate, and Fritz began a money-raising operation in Pittsburgh which helped me significantly for many years. Fritz got a group of his friends and business associates to attend an annual luncheon, and each time he ended up with a substantial check for the Family Rosary Crusade. I told Ray Healy and Hal Coleman, Rochester businessmen, what Fritz was doing, and they started a similar club in Rochester. Ted Lemm, who was then manager of a department store in Rochester and is now similarly employed in Memphis, Tennessee, was active in this group, and he in turn talked about it to John Timothy Smith, a Syracuse lawyer. John Timothy became so enthusiastic that he not only organized a group in Syracuse, but made frequent trips for years to other cities of northern New York to promote similar groups in all of them. I got outstanding support in this way from cities in New York, Illinois, Pennsylvania, Florida, Ohio, Kansas, and California.

Meanwhile, I was getting invitations to preach triduums over a steadily expanding area of the eastern seaboard and from as far as Cleveland, Detroit, and Milwaukee in the Midwest. The work frequently took me to Pittsburgh, and each time, Monsignor Moriarty and Fritz Wilson would have figured out some new angle to launch the network radio program. From our continuing discussions and our exchange of ideas with others, it was becoming clear that we would not get anywhere unless we had big names to dangle before the radio executives. We thought that we should try to get a different archbishop or bishop as guest speaker each week. He would introduce a nationally known figure both to lead in the recital of the Rosary and to dramatize the Mysteries in such a way as to give the incidents of long ago in the life of Christ and His Mother a new meaning for the people of today. We were confident that this would make the Rosary intelligible for all listeners without offending the beliefs of any, that we could put it in a frame that would hold an audience of Protestants and Jews as well as Catholics.

As I went round like this from place to place, I began to ask each bishop I met if he would participate in a radio program of the kind I envisaged. All the bishops with whom I spoke from the New England states to Ohio were unanimous in approval. I didn't get a single refusal. Meanwhile, my almost constant travel meant that I was no longer able to serve as chaplain to the Holy Cross Brothers in Albany or even to keep an eye on the massive work being done by Eileen Soraghan and a host of volunteers. So one day I asked Father Steiner if he could spare another Holy Cross priest to help me. "How about Father Lawyer?" he suggested. Father Steiner was of solid German stock and nobody ever accused him of frivolity in his life, but for a moment I thought my Father Provincial was making a joke. Father Jerome Lawyer had been a close friend of mine in the Bengalese, although a couple of years ahead of me in his studies. Upon ordination, he was assigned to Dacca, but because of the war in Europe and Africa, he was sent by way of the Pacific and had reached the Philippines just in time to be captured and interned by the Japanese. Finally released from the prisoner-of-war camp in February 1945, suffering from malnutrition and badly shaken up, he had returned to Notre Dame to rest. Father Steiner called Father Jerry in. "Will you go up to Albany to give Father Pat a hand?" he asked him. "You can rest there just as well as at Notre Dame." Father Jerry has a subtle English sense of humor, and he thought the idea of getting a rest in my company was capital. "Well, if you don't like it, take the next train and come back," Father Steiner said in his matter-of-fact way. Father Jerry came to Albany. He got no rest. But he didn't take the train back. Instead, he stayed with me sixteen years and became one of the main architects of the Crusade.

My radio project was now like a jigsaw puzzle with each of the pieces slowly being put into place. I had what I believed would prove to be a winning formula. I had the word of the bishops. On a trip to Pittsburgh, another piece fell into place. My two friends were waiting with a gleam in their eyes. "Fritz and I have been discussing your plan to get nationally known figures to lead the Rosary," Monsignor Moriarty said, "and we have decided there is only one way it can work. You remember how Bing Crosby completed the package on Mother's Day. What you have to do is go out yourself to Hollywood and get a string of the stars. It's that simple."

It was simple to propose, and it made good sense. But as I rode back in the train to Albany, I felt in my soul that they were asking me an impossible thing, a fantastic, unrealistic thing. I knew nobody in Hollywood, knew nothing of its ways, had never been west of the Mississippi. Besides, I couldn't even get to Los Angeles if I tried. Since the end of the war in Europe, there was an unending movement of troops and supplies across the Atlantic and across the United States for the final great push that had started in the Pacific. The highest priorities were needed to get a seat on a train, and airplanes were entirely out of the question.

Once back in Albany, I put the whole idea to one side and concentrated on the work that had accumulated in my absence. The office was now located in the basement of the College of St. Rose. About the second or third day after my return, a nun came into the office with a big smile on her face. "We have the tickets for you, Father," she said. "What tickets?" I asked. "The tickets to Los Angeles," she said. "Two of them."

I was dumbfounded. "I never asked for tickets," I finally managed to say. "You didn't?" she said. "That's funny. Our Assistant Reverend Mother General was in from St. Louis visiting our community in Troy. She was in the community room when the phone rang and a man asked to speak to her. 'I'm Father Peyton,' the man said, 'and I must get to Los Angeles. With your influence in Chicago and St. Louis, I feel sure you can get me two reservations.' She came back to the community room. 'Who's Father Peyton?' she asked, and she repeated the conversation. 'If Father Peyton wants reservations,' one of the Sisters said, 'you'd better get them for him!' Knowing that I had just obtained two reservations through great difficulties to visit my father in California, Mother Anna Gonzaga, the Assistant Reverend Mother, asked me to come right down to the college and give my tickets to you. So here are the tickets, Father." And with that she laid the reservations on my desk, and to this day Sister Gerarda Joseph has not regretted the great sacrifice she made that day.

Father Woods and I discussed the matter for about a week. We tried to find out who had made the telephone call, but whoever did had not called back, and nobody could enlighten us. Much later I did learn that the caller was a Father John Tracy, and he had given up the effort when he got no reply from the Troy convent. One of the many things that caused us to hesitate was a fear that Archbishop John J. Cantwell of Los Angeles would think I was crazy and stop the whole thing before it got off the ground. Finally, we decided to give it a try.

I believe it was a Friday evening that Father Woods put me on the train in Albany. I can still see him, his hand raised in blessing, as the train pulled out of the station. I reached Chicago in the morning and had time to say Mass before boarding the train for the West. When I found my seat, the first thing that attracted my attention was a very snooty-looking person facing me. Her manners matched her haughty appearance. She was outraged at having to travel coach. She had been assigned the upper berth, and I the lower. As a gesture of friendship, I offered to change places. She accepted with alacrity but for the rest of the trip lost no opportunity of stressing that I was the gainer by the transaction.

There was an hour stop at Cheyenne, Wyoming. I had brought a list of cities in which bishops lived, and Cheyenne was on the list. I dashed out and was directed to the nearest church. It was only a few blocks away, and it was the cathedral. Bishop Patrick Alphonsus McGovern, however, lived six or seven blocks further up. The priest at the rectory had no car, but he found someone who dropped me at the bishop's house. The bishop was sleeping, and I had more trouble and delay in persuading the housekeeper to waken him. But it was worth the effort. He received me most cordially and assured me that it would be a privilege to participate in the type of radio program I described. By now it was only fifteen minutes to train time. "You'll never make it," he said, dashing out into the street with me to flag down a car for a ride. He himself had none. A taxi came along, but the motor stalled. Then a man and woman pulled up, but when they saw the bishop's pectoral cross they drove away quickly. At last a bus came, and it just made it. When I got back on the train, a marine was waiting for me with two sandwiches. I had told him my plan, and he knew I wouldn't have time to eat.

We had a similar halt at Salt Lake City, and there I was able to say Mass in the cathedral. The endless journeying through the Rockies gave me a sense of the vastness of America and of the splendor of God's creation surpassing anything I had experienced in my whole life. Yet, as we neared Los Angeles, my apprehension grew hourly. The whole business seemed more and more absurd. People talked about the silly star-struck youngsters who flocked to Hollywood hoping to be discovered, and they said that for every success, a thousand were destroyed. Those youngsters had something Hollywood wanted. What had I? All I had was faith, and it was surely being put to the test. I prayed and forced myself blindly ahead.

When I stepped off the train I knew what I would do. I got into a taxi. "Drive me to the nearest Catholic church, please," I told the driver. As we drove I said a little prayer, and in a short time he deposited me at the cathedral. Later I learned that the taxi driver had passed the old Spanish mission on the way. He had presumably decided from my accent that I'd make out better at the cathedral, and never in his life was he more right. Looking back, I can only thank Providence for giving this man, whose very name is unknown to me, a special guidance at a critical moment.

At the rectory I was told that the vicar general was out, so I went into the cathedral and said my Mass. As I knelt in the sanctuary for my thanksgiving, a priest walked through. He was tall, with a commanding appearance. From his robes and the biretta he was wearing I knew it was Monsignor John J. Cawley, the vicar general. He obviously heard my step as I followed him down the aisle, for at the cathedral door he turned to wait for me. "I'm Father Peyton," I said, "and I have just arrived from Albany." "What's the trouble?" he asked. "No trouble at all," I replied, "except that I'm looking for a friend to help me with a job I came here to do." "Where in Ireland did you come from?" was his next question. "A parish called Attymass," I said, "not far from Bonniconlon." "I said Mass in Bonniconlon not many years ago," he said. "That's where my mother and father married," I said. The monsignor himself, as I learned, had been born and raised in the town of Gurteen in the same diocese.

"This is your home whenever you are here," he said, and he meant it. From that time until his death, he was my father and guide in the western part of the United States. "I don't want you to make a single move until I make everything right for you with the archbishop." In a short time he arranged a meeting with Archbishop Cantwell, and after a short talk the archbishop pledged the fullest co-operation. "The family Rosary has been promoted throughout the entire archdiocese as long ago as 1939," he reminded me. "And in response to a letter you sent me several years ago, I wrote a pastoral letter to be read in all churches insisting once more that the place of the Rosary is in the home. You can count on me all the way." An official letter was sent to Monsignor John J. Devlin, the Chancery contact with the movie industry. The man who wrote it for the archbishop to sign is now Auxiliary Bishop Timothy Manning of Los Angeles, a native of County Cork, Ireland.

The first big Hollywood figure I met, however, was not reached through any of these sources. I had carried one letter of recommendation with me, an introduction from John Sheehan of New York to his friend Colonel Thomas Lewis, founder and first head of the Armed Forces Radio Service. Tom is Loretta Young's husband. He had been a top man in radio advertising before the war and would climb to greater heights later in advertising and other activities related to the management and operation of the ramified activities which go to make up Hollywood.

It was not until long afterward that I learned the whole story of that fateful interview with Tom Lewis. Tom had been working under almost intolerable pressures for several years in the armed forces, building up the worldwide network of information and inspiration for the troops. His job was now done, as the war in the Pacific was nearing its inevitable end. He was physically and emotionally exhausted. All he wanted was to get out of uniform, take a long rest with his family, and get back into his peacetime work as an advertising executive. John Sheehan was not only a good friend but the kind of man who would not make an unreasonable request. When Tom read the letter of introduction which John had sent, he assumed that here was another priest with a routine application to beam a message to the troops. That was something that could be handled by his adjutant. The formula was well defined. Every religious denomination was allotted its share of time, and if this Father Peyton had a message with suitable content, it would be easy to find a slot for him.

But that wasn't how it worked at all. Neither of us is clear about why, at the last moment, Tom decided that he himself would receive the visitor. He did, however, take the precaution to tell the adjutant that at the end of ten minutes, he should interrupt to remind the colonel that he had an urgent appointment, thereby assuring that an unnecessary interview would not waste too much of his time.

Tom tells the rest of the story much better than I do. With equal disregard for diplomacy and protocol, I plunged into my exposition. If I addressed him as Colonel when I was ushered in, the door had scarcely closed behind the adjutant when I was calling him by his first name. "I have come to Hollywood to harness the mass media for the glory of Our Lady," I told him. "The war is just about over, and the world is entering a state of readjustment. Families have been displaced and dismembered. Now they must be reunited, and the ties that bind the family together must be restored and strengthened. Unless we do this, winning the war will mean nothing. Our Christian civilization for which we fought will decline, and atheistic materialism will take its place. And this is where Hollywood comes in. It can be used positively. I want its facilities and its stars to project this message, to tell the world that family unity is the key to world peace, and that family prayer is the guarantee of family unity."

It was only much later that I learned all that was running through Colonel Lewis's mind. He was in the middle of his plans to get away from the desk at which I found him. He felt that he had done more than his share of public service. He was a young man, about my own age, with talent and ambition, and he realized that the next few years would be critical for his career. Advertising is hard-working, hard-hitting business, and the young man who wants to get ahead has no time for fooling around with grandiose but starry-eyed dreams, especially when their proponent, on his own admission, knows nothing about radio or about Hollywood and carries the handicap of a thick Irish brogue that marks him as a greenhorn straight out of the bog.

I didn't know all this, but I knew that my message wasn't getting through. I had an inspiration. "Don't answer right away, dear Tom," I said. "We'll kneel first and say a Memorare to Our Mother for guidance." I got on my knees and the colonel obediently followed me. No sooner had we finished the Memorare than I plunged into five decades of the Rosary. I knew that this was a turning point, that here I had a key to open the innermost recesses of Hollywood, and I knew my own poor words were inadequate to get that key into my hands. It was a job for Our Lady, and I besought her with all my soul. Poor Tom followed my lead mechanically, but all he could think was that the adjutant was going to open that door at any moment, and if the word got around that the unfortunate colonel had broken under the strain of his duties and was kneeling with a priest repeating some rigamarole at the top of his voice, then his next stop would not be an advertising desk, but a bed in a mental institution.

Our Lady took care of that, too, for we had just risen from our knees when the door opened. "Colonel, sir," the adjutant began. Tom told him he'd call him later. Then patiently and in detail he tried to explain to me the facts of Hollywood life. He had nothing but admiration for my project and for my enthusiasm, he said, but the job was impossibly ambitious. He would gladly help me, but frankly he didn't see how anybody could.

All I could hear was that he hadn't turned me down flat. He was willing to help me. There was still hope. "The first step is to reach the stars, the big stars," I said. "Can I ask you to introduce me to your wife? That would be pretty close to heaven." What I said was true, for Loretta Young was already at the apex of her fabulous career.

I met Loretta Young on August 4, 1945. I remember the day most clearly, because it was a Saturday, the eve of the feast of Our Lady of the Snows. Earlier that week Monsignor Cawley had introduced me to Monsignor Patrick Concannon, a priest from County Galway who was pastor of the Church of the Good Shepherd in Beverly Hills and who counted many stars among his parishioners. Monsignor Concannon had invited me to preach in his church on Our Lady's feast, and through Tom Lewis I saw Loretta the previous day to seek her advice as to how I might make best use of my opportunity to tell my story to so many of her associates and win them to my side.

Loretta had just given birth a few weeks earlier to her second son, Peter, and the infant was in a crib beside her. She was still weak, but she received me with the charm that never deserts this great lady, and she not only pledged her own co-operation but gave me excellent advice. "While you are preaching tomorrow," she said, "don't drop any hint of what help you are expecting from the stars. Just concentrate on doing a selling job for the family Rosary. Have

Monsignor Concannon down at the back of the church so that he can invite the various stars who have heard your sermon to come round to the sacristy to meet you. Then, when you get them one by one in the sacristy, close the sale."

It worked like a charm. Irene Dunne came to see me in the sacristy that day, and so did Charles Boyer and Maureen O'Sullivan and I believe Ethel Barrymore and five or six others, and every single one of them said yes. The first reaction of some of them was curious. "Oh, I could never play the part of the Blessed Virgin," Irene Dunne said. I feel she said it from a sense of humility, a consciousness of the dignity of Our Lady. In any case, I had to talk quite a bit to get across the idea that she wouldn't necessarily have to play the part of Our Lady, that there were many other ways she could help. And in the end she gave in, as every one of them did.

I don't think I was too explicit about just what I wanted them to do for me. In my own mind I was clear enough. I wanted to get a weekly program that would include the recitation of the Rosary each time, set in a beautiful framework similar to that of the Mother's Day program. But I was already conscious of the tremendous opposition to a program so specifically Catholic in its form and content, and I wanted to keep all doors open. I felt that if I could line up a real galaxy of great stars, I'd be able to persuade a network to buy my idea.

So I continued all through the following week, cheered by the success of my talk with Loretta and with the other stars I had met through Monsignor Concannon. My approach was very simple. I was staying at the cathedral rectory, thanks to the kindness of Monsignor Cawley. I'd make a list of names, get their unlisted telephone numbers through one of my contacts, and dial them one by one. "I'm Father Peyton, a priest at the cathedral residence," I would say, "and I'd like to come to talk with you." Almost always I'd get an appointment just with that opening, and when I explained what I wanted, I almost never got a refusal. I had heard and read so much about the kind of life these people lived—the glitter and the superficiality and the selfishness. I suppose there was plenty of this, but I found real human beings in Hollywood the same as every place else I've been in the world. It's hard to discover a man or a woman who lacks a sense of moral values, or one who is not happy to make a contribution to the well-being and the uplift of his fellows. And that goes even for some whose names are bywords. The world of acting is a strange world, and those who live in it cannot be judged by ordinary standards.

Meanwhile, I was also branching out through other contacts I made at the cathedral. The Sisters of the Immaculate Heart are a very important teaching order in Los Angeles. Monsignor Cawley took me out to the mother house one day to speak to a group of Sisters and meet Mother Eucharia, who was then mother general and who later became a dear friend and provided me with a permanent home in Hollywood. Tom Lewis did not take too active a part at this time, beyond introducing me to Loretta, but he was responsible for at least one other decisive introduction. He brought me to Louella Parsons, and Louella immediately became and always continued a sincere friend and ardent supporter. Her extraordinary influence in the entire world of the movies was of incalculable value.

Monsignor Devlin, the archbishop's representative for the film industry, also performed several significant services. He was very keen on promoting the devotion of the Holy Hour in his church, and he undertook to help me if I'd promise in return to fill his church for the Holy Hour each week. "How can I give you a promise like that?" I asked him. "What I can do is to assure you that if you help Our Lady, she will fill your church for you." This satisfied him, and he introduced me to Jane Wyatt. She was from New York, a wonderful wife and mother and a devout Catholic.

About the same time, I met Ruth Hussey, and that was another meeting with incalculable consequences. She was married to a Moravian, an extraordinarily fine man named Robert Longenecker. He was what I suppose one would call an impresario. He packaged shows, bringing together the writer, the producer, the stars, and financial backers. He was equally at home in the worlds of radio, of movies, and of the stage. He was to prove an essential cog in the machine I was laboriously building.

Monsignor Devlin was also instrumental in opening up for me the public-relations department of the Twentieth Century Fox studios. Robert Fennell was his parishioner, and through him I met his immediate superior, Clarence Hutson, who was the number-two man in the department. There was nothing that Clarence and Bob would not do for me. I would eat in the dining room in the studios along with the actors and actresses and technical workers. In a short time these two brought me to one of their associates, Doc Bishop. Doc was one of the founders of the March of Dimes, a man of imagination and drive. He was a convert to Catholicism, and he immediately bought my program to promote family prayer.

By now, a significant group of professionals was involved, and some of them quickly put the finger on a vital flaw in my method of procedure. I had verbal commitments from a significant and growing number of stars, but there wasn't a line in writing. No radio network would even talk to me unless I had signatures on the dotted line. I had to retrace all my steps. One of the people I had met, also through Monsignor Devlin, was a Hollywood writer named Fred Niblo, and Fred drew up a simple contract under which the signer pledged to contribute his services without charge on any free time I could succeed in getting from any radio network. Doc Bishop took a sheaf of copies and proceeded to collect signatures. Because of his position at Twentieth Century Fox, the stars wanted to be in his good graces. He would catch them in the dining room and tell them the publicity would be good for them, and I'm sure some of them didn't even read the contract. In no time, through his efforts and those of others, we had signed up thirty or more: Dick Haymes was one of them, and Pat O'Brien, Don Ameche, Maureen O'Sullivan, Maureen O'Hara, Jane Wyatt, Bing Crosby, Gregory Peck, Joe E. Brown, Ethel Barrymore, Shirley Temple, Jimmy Durante, and of course Loretta Young and Irene Dunne.

There was only one star from whom I had received a verbal commitment who never signed, and that wasn't her fault. It is something about which I have grieved ever since. The day I called Carmen Miranda, she insisted on finding out right there on the phone why I wanted to see her, so I had to change my regular practice and give her my full story over the telephone. Before I had finished talking, she was deeply moved at the thought that she might be allowed to help in a program to spread devotion to Our Blessed Mother, and with tears of joy she assured me that I could call on her anytime I wanted. When the time for getting the signatures came, one of my advisers—a layman—insisted that we cross Carmen off the list. "She is too well known as a pin-up girl for the soldiers," he said. "You will only hurt yourself by getting into that kind of company."

I followed his advice, but I never reconciled myself to it. Even if what he said was true, it was not the attitude of Christ to the sinner who turned to Him and offered to help Him. In any case, poor Carmen never did get on the program. But long years later I was working in Brazil, staying in the chaplain's quarters on the top floor of Our Lady of Mercy School run by the Felician Sisters in Rio de Janeiro, when somebody pointed out a cemetery just across the street and told me Carmen Miranda was buried there. It brought back memories of her generous response to my appeal, and I felt that if she had done nothing else to merit heaven, she was nevertheless safe under Our Lady's mantle. I never go to Rio without making a pilgrimage at least in my thoughts and my prayers to that cemetery and that grave.

The earthshaking events that occurred during those weeks I was in Los Angeles no doubt helped me by stirring in all minds a great awareness of the perilousness of our lives and the absolute need of God's kindly intervention in our affairs. The first was the explosion of the two atomic bombs over Hiroshima and Nagasaki. I must confess that I was so absorbed in my own concerns and preoccupied with my problems that I did not grasp right away the full meaning of the new nuclear power then disclosed publicly for the first time, or the awfulness of the holocaust which man's first use of it had wrought. But I was forced to see how those around me were affected, and I could sense that they not only were relieved that the war was ending but were also asking themselves what the new world we had produced would be like. It was a mood which opened their hearts to my message and my appeal. Then there occurred the relatively trivial yet significant disaster when a plane crashed into the Empire State Building killing all the occupants of the plane and several people at work in offices. And finally, on August 15, the feast of Our Lady's Assumption, Japan surrendered. It was still August 14 on our side of the international date line when the news came through. I was out at Maureen O'Hara's house that afternoon and got her signature. She drove me to the trolley car, and I rode downtown to the cathedral amid the fireworks and the throngs in the streets and all the gaiety of the national reaction to the happy news.

By the end of August I had done all that I felt could be done in Hollywood for the time being. The next step would be with the networks in New York, and I started back full of enthusiasm and confidence. Hollywood had opened wide its arms to me. It looked as if everything had conspired to launch the family Rosary movement. With the end of the war, there would be a tremendous expansion of the mass media. Already they were beginning down in Florida to build the base which was to become Cape Kennedy, a point from which man would reach out to the heavens, circling the earth with satellites that would carry instant knowledge to the most remote parts of the globe, bypassing iron curtains and bamboo curtains and all sorts of obstacles to the spread of knowledge. It seemed to me that I was in on the ground floor of this vast expansion, that I was going to be able to use the mass media to proclaim to the whole world the value of family prayer, so that there could never again be neutrality on this issue, that every individual would have the opportunity to decide, would be forced to decide, could never plead that he didn't know, that he hadn't been told. Little did I realize how high was the mountain I had still to climb.

The Peyton family in Ireland in 1921. A young Patrick stands at the right side of the first row.

The fourth and fifth grades of Bofield School in the west of Ireland. Patrick Peyton is on the far right of the first row.

Patrick Peyton was ordained, along with his brother Tom, at Notre Dame on June 15, 1941. Tom stands in the last row, third from left, with Patrick beside him, fourth from left.

Father Peyton, center, planned the first Rosary Crusade in Canada in 1948 with Rev. John T. Maloney, left, and Monsignor W. E. Dillon, right.

Father Peyton arrived by helicopter at the San Francisco rally on October 7, 1961.

The rally in Rio de Janeiro, Brazil, in 1962 drew an estimated 1.5 million participants.

Father Peyton had an audience with Pope Pius XII in 1955, after returning from his journey to Africa.

Pope John XXIII and Father Peyton.

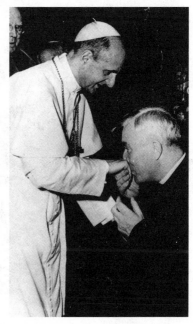

Pope Pius VI and Father Peyton.

Father Peyton discusses a script for a radio broadcast with a star-filled cast, including Ricardo Montalban, Maureen O'Sullivan, and Ethel Barrymore.

Father Peyton stands with Jack Benny and Lucille Ball.

Irene Dunne presents Father Peyton with an award for Family Theater.

Father Peyton stands with Jackie Kennedy. Photo by Henry Grossman.

In 1965 Father Peyton received the highest award the Church can give a member of a religious congregation, the Cross Pro Ecclesia et Pontifice.

Father Peyton prays the Rosary with Mother Teresa—now St. Teresa of Calcutta.

From his youth to the very end of his life, Father Patrick Peyton continued his devotion to the Blessed Mother and the Rosary.

Eight

"Family Theater of the Air" Takes Shape

I flew from Los Angeles back to New York at the end of August. It was my first long ride in an airplane, but I must confess I had so many things to occupy my thoughts that I was scarcely conscious of that fact. Everything seemed to be going just fine for me. At the same time, I recognized that I had reached a critical moment. One false step could spell disaster.

I felt pretty confident that, with the combination of the successful Mother's Day program and the signatures of the stars, I could walk into any network and virtually dictate my terms. I felt so strong, in fact, that I decided that I would shop around among the various networks before committing myself to one.

Accordingly, with only a brief halt in New York, I continued on to Albany to discuss the next steps with Father Woods and resume my interrupted program of triduums.

The triduum was not only my sole source of regular income. It was also the one concrete way I had developed to fulfill my commitment to devote my life to restoring the family Rosary in the Catholic homes of America. My schedule frequently took me to New York City or its vicinity, and over several months I exchanged ideas with radio executives whom I had already met or to whom I was steered by Tom Lewis and others. In this way I talked to many top-level people, both big shareholders and those engaged in operations. Many of them showed a positive interest. Yet it became increasingly evident, as the months passed, that they and I were still miles apart in our thinking. From the technical side, they wanted something far more specific than the signatures of a group of stars. They wanted a fully planned package, with samples, and a guarantee that I would be in a position to ensure continuity of delivery after I began. As to content, their idea was a program of entertainment with a minimum of religious content and a total absence of a specific denominational flavor.

In between the disappointments, little favorable events would occur, just enough to keep me from despairing altogether. Ruth Hussey came east to star in a play on Broadway. Both she and her husband, Bob Longenecker, had been wonderful to me from the Sunday night I knocked on their door in Hollywood and they invited me to stay for supper. While Ruth was tied up with the play, Bob did the rounds of New York as my leg man. He was well known in the radio industry, and his readiness to identify himself with me carried much weight, all the more because he was not a Catholic.

An important break resulted from a contact I made with William E. Cotter, a lawyer and also a graduate of Notre Dame. Bill was an executive of Union Carbide, and he was immediately able to provide me with office space and a telephone near Grand Central Station whenever I was in New York. That was already a big favor, but a far bigger one was ahead. Bill's wife, Evarista Agnes Brady, was a graduate of Saint Mary's, the women's college associated with Notre Dame, and she was a friend of Sister Madeleva, the poet and longtime head of that institution. In the spring of 1946, Evarista went to a reunion of alumnae at Saint Mary's, and she happened to mention to Sister Madeleva that she had met me in New York through her husband. Sister Madeleva was one of my most enthusiastic backers, and she asked avidly for news of my progress. In the course of the conversation, one of them recalled that Bill had been at Notre Dame with Ed Kobak, president of the Mutual network. That was before the First World War, and Notre Dame then had a residential grammar and high school, and the two of them had been "minims" there together. So Mrs. Cotter promised Sister Madeleva that when she got home, she would work on her husband to use his influence with Ed.

"I've been keeping away from that man for a year. I'm afraid he's going to end up by selling me the Empire State Building," was Ed's comment when Bill Cotter called him. But that call did the trick. He passed the word to his associates to work out a concrete proposal for me. The two men directly involved in the discussions were program manager Phillips Carlin, on behalf of Mutual, and Bob Longenecker on my behalf. The result was a formula offered me by Mutual, which I could accept or reject. It presented four conditions under which Mutual would provide free network time. I would undertake to supply a first-class program; it would be non-sectarian in content; it would present a major Hollywood star each time; and I would pay all production costs, including orchestra and writers.

The second condition caused me deep anguish. A non-sectarian program spelled the death of my hope to build it around the Rosary. In addition, at that time the Catholic authorities were still dead set against participation in any religious activity that might create the impression that one religion was as good as another. The ecumenical spirit of Pope John XXIII and the Vatican Council was still far in the future. I could see myself being shot down very soon under Mutual's proposed formula. At the same time, I had been driven reluctantly to the conclusion, as a result of many months of intensive activity by Bob Longenecker and myself, that no better opportunity, or even comparable opportunity, was likely to present itself. There was nothing sectarian about the concept of family prayer. The proposal would not prevent me from selling that basic idea.

I took my doubts and my hesitations to my provincial, Father Steiner. A wise man and a practical one, he advised me to get the reaction of three churchmen better located than he himself to sum up the pros and cons. The first was Archbishop Spellman of New York; the second, Bishop Michael Ready of Columbus, Ohio; the third, Monsignor (now Bishop) Fulton Sheen. Until a short time previously, Bishop Ready was secretary of the National Catholic Welfare Conference (NCWC) in Washington, DC, and closely associated with *The Catholic Hour*. Monsignor Sheen was more famous as a radio speaker than any other Catholic priest at that time.

When I went to call on Archbishop Spellman, I was met by his secretary, Monsignor Francis X. Shea. He had already been extremely helpful to me at the time of the Mother's Day program. "I can answer for the archbishop," he said when I explained my dilemma. "If Our Lady can't get a full loaf, she will take half; and if she is not even offered a half, she will take the crumbs." That was just about the conclusion to which I had by now come, and I was delighted to hear this confirmation. I rushed off right away to Ohio. Bishop Ready was noncommittal, but at least he didn't say no. My final stop was at Monsignor Sheen's. A short time previously he had received Clare Boothe Luce into the Church, and she happened to be visiting him when I arrived. "Take a good look at this young man," he said, as he introduced us. "You will be hearing more from him." His advice was that I'd be foolish not to try it. I reported back my three experiences to Father Steiner, and he agreed that I should continue.

To continue meant to go back once more to Hollywood, because that was the one place where we could assemble all the talent required to prepare and execute a first-class program. However, there was also the question of financing. Even with free stars, it was going to cost a lot of money to pay union scale to all performers, plus the other costs. Just how much we could only guess, but the experts were warning us of such astronomical possibilities as $1,000 to $2,000 per weekly half hour.

I had, however, been going far harder than I was supposed to in the light of my health record, and my friends finally insisted that I should take a break. Neither Tom nor

I had been back in Ireland since we had left eighteen years earlier. It was the custom at Holy Cross to allow its young priests to spend a vacation with their families immediately after ordination, but wartime conditions had prevented us from taking advantage. Agreement was now reached that the two of us would go home for the summer of 1946. Father Woods said he would come, too, and so did my sister Mary. Our passages were booked on a United States Lines ship, the SS *Washington*, scheduled to leave New York July 27 and reach Cóbh, Ireland, six days later. That seemingly casual arrangement was also fraught with incalculable consequences.

My numerous and widely scattered relations in the United States included three Neary girls, Celia, Mary, and Ann, in Philadelphia. Their mother was a Gillard, my mother's cousin. Ann was a maid in a big house in Philadelphia, and the people who owned it were friends of Basil Harris, president of United States Lines, and his wife, Mary. The Harrises were visiting there about a week before we were due to leave, and the hostess happened to mention to Mrs. Harris that the girl serving them at the table was a cousin of the Father Peyton who had been responsible for the widely praised Mother's Day radio program the previous year. Mrs. Harris spoke to the girl and learned from her that I was traveling to Ireland on the SS *Washington* the following week. "That's a coincidence," said Mrs. Harris, "because my husband and I will be on the same ship. I'll look out for him." My cousins happened to know my plans simply because I had been in Philadelphia preaching a triduum shortly before, and they had organized a benefit dance for my work among their Irish friends.

Mary Harris came to look for me as soon as we got on board the ship. With her was her daughter-in-law, Mrs. Basil Harris, whose maiden name was Marie Murray. She was a daughter of Thomas E. Murray, who later became Atomic Energy Commissioner. They both thought it would be a capital idea to say the Rosary on the deck every afternoon. Mary cleared it with her husband and they had an announcement made over the public-address system, so that each day we had a big turnout. One day Father Woods said the Rosary and I gave a little talk, and the following day we exchanged roles. By the time I reached Cobh, they were fully sold on my radio project, and I had a pledge of $4,000 for production costs from the Harrises and from friends who were traveling with them, William V. and Isabel Griffin. William worked in the Wall Street district and was a director of several companies. His wife and he remained true and generous friends as long as they lived.

Even more important than this substantial help arranged directly for me by Mary Harris was another opening which she then promised me and later provided. "When I get back to New York," she said one day during the trip, "I'll introduce you to a young man who will one day be one of the biggest businessmen in New York. His name is Peter Grace." I did not meet Peter immediately on my return, but as soon as I did, he befriended me. He took me to his home, which was then at Great Neck, Long Island, later at Westbury, and now at Manhasset. There I am made to feel one of the family both by his charming wife, Margie, and himself. My concerns are his. He is never too busy to spare time for me, never so committed to other causes as to refuse a request of mine.

In a somewhat lighter vein, though serious enough in its way, we re-enacted an old Irish custom on that trip. We made a match. There were two Marianite Sisters of Holy Cross from the French Hospital in New York, two sisters named Maloney, who were going back to visit their birthplace in County Westmeath. Like Tom and me, they had been away many years, and we were discussing the changes that had taken place in our absence. It turned out that the only one left on their farm was an unmarried brother, Michael, while down on our place in Carracastle were my eldest brother, also named Michael, and my sister Kitty. They were both unmarried, and there was little likelihood of any girl coming into our place as long as a sister of the owner remained there. So we decided that Kitty would make a wife for Michael Maloney. And when we brought them together, they agreed, and they are happily married and live with their two children, Patrick and Mary, in the village of Carrick, near Ballymore, County Westmeath. Kitty was not long gone until my brother Michael married a lovely girl from our own neighborhood, and now they have two teen-age boys. The older, my namesake, is now in the seminary on the way to the priesthood.

Things had improved greatly in Carracastle during the eighteen years since Tom and I had left. Michael had built himself a fine new house. He also had acquired additional land, so that the holding was about twice as big as that on which we had been raised. The availability of farm machinery and fertilizers, as well as improved strains of seeds and livestock, had taken much of the drudgery out of farming and guaranteed a better living. It was little short of miraculous, and we all enjoyed our visit to the little village of our birth, even if we were saddened that our parents were no longer there to welcome us and exchange around the turf fire the experiences of the intervening years.

Father Woods and I, in addition, had other things on our minds. We spent a considerable part of our time in Ireland contacting priests and laypeople who might advise and help us in our project. In Dublin we met Frank Duff, the founder of the Legion of Mary. He approved our plans from the first moment we explained them to him, and ever since, he and the members of his organization throughout the world have been with us. We also visited the shrine of Our Lady at Knock, County Mayo, and I had the great honor of being asked to preach there to a group of pilgrims on August 15, the feast of the Assumption. I also preached sermons and gave talks in various parts of the country, urging the people to retain the proud tradition of the family Rosary and asking their prayers for my efforts to spread the practice more widely on the other side of the Atlantic.

Our original intention was to spend about three months in Ireland, but Father Woods and I decided to head back to the United States after less than six weeks. We realized that we had to strike while the iron was hot, and that accordingly it was all-important for me to return to Hollywood with a minimum of delay. First, however, we wanted to create some kind of financial base for the operation. Our production costs alone were projected at between $50,000 and $100,000 a year. In addition, we would need an office and some staff, and we had to think of our own living and travel expenses. All we had as yet was a promise of $4,000 from Mary Harris and her friends. Our departure was propitious, for the ship sailed on Our Lady's birthday, September 8.

The moment I got back, I began to renew my contacts. I had earlier met John M. Haffert, author of many books on Our Lady. He was then lay director of the Scapular Apostolate and editor of *Scapular Magazine*, and he had started to work out the arrangements with the bishop of Fatima which resulted in the triumphal tour of the Pilgrim Virgin Statue in America in 1947, giving an opportunity to seven million persons to express their love for Our Lady. He later became national lay director of the Blue Army, an organization of more than a million devotees of Our Lady of Fatima. On my return to the East Coast from Los Angeles in the fall of 1945, John and I had attempted to implement an idea of his—namely, that all those engaged in promoting Marian devotion in the United States should come together in a single organization. We held three meetings, the first in New York in February 1946, the second in Washington, DC, in May, and the third in Philadelphia in September. Those who attended included Father Vincent Dominic Dolan, O.P., editor of *Rosary Magazine* and head of the Rosary Crusade; Father Joseph A. Skelly, C.M., of Germantown, Philadelphia, the man responsible so many years for spreading the Miraculous Medal devotion; Father James J. Galvin, C.Ss.R., editor of *Perpetual Help*; and Father Edmund J. Baumeister, S.M., a member of the Society of Mary, whose specific purpose is to honor Our Lady.

I was very excited by this possibility of all of us getting together, and I must confess that I was also terrified at the thought of having to carry singlehanded the financial burden of the radio project. So I offered to hand over to the proposed new organization the radio time which Mutual had promised me. The others all thought it was a magnificent opportunity, but they could not see any possibility of raising the huge sums that would be needed to keep it going. So they turned me down, and the whole idea of a common organization fell through. I often think that this also was providential. Perhaps an organization would have had less trouble with fund-raising, but its members would each have had a slightly different objective, and I think one of the great reasons for the success of the "Family Theater" is that it has stuck to the straight line of selling family prayer and nothing else. We were able to follow the practice of all successful advertising—namely, to keep the commercial simple.

The meetings were, nevertheless, valuable for me. All of the participants continued afterward to help me in many ways. Father Galvin, a dynamic young Redemptorist, was particularly enthused by the idea of using the radio regularly to sell family prayer, and when he went back home to Esopus, New York, he persuaded his provincial to contribute $8,000 toward helping me to get started. Father Seery, one of the Servite Fathers of the famous shrine to Our Sorrowful Mother in Chicago where I preached the family Rosary message many times, also convinced his provincial to pledge $8,000. This heartened me to return to Hollywood in late October or November 1946. I had found myself a writer in the person of Father Timothy J. Mulvey, O.M.I., a man with an established record as author of plays for *The Catholic Hour* on NBC and *The Hour of Faith* on ABC. When I reached the West Coast, I went to the Mutual station in Los Angeles, KHJ, and I tried to persuade its executives to develop a few trial shows, using Father Mulvey's scripts. They were most polite, and at first I thought that I was on my way. Gradually, however, it penetrated that the co-operation was only verbal. For one thing, we could not reach agreement on any of Father Mulvey's scripts. They claimed they were too religious. Personally, I think they couldn't appreciate them, because they were convinced that nobody who was not a member of their own fraternity could write for radio. I know that later we used these same Mulvey scripts and they were among our greatest success-es. But at this time all I was getting was the run-around. Months went by. The heads of Mutual back in New York were losing confidence. Once again it looked like the end of the road.

The Lewises had continued to treat me as a family friend, and I was out there one evening talking to Loretta while Tom was working upstairs. The report I had to give Loretta of my progress was totally negative, and she was grieving for my distress. "I've got an idea," she said sud-denly. "I'm going to get Tom to come down, and I'll lay it on the line for him. As you know, he's back with Young and Rubicam, and he is head of their entire West Coast opera-tion. They pay him fifty to sixty thousand dollars a year to do the kind of thing you're talking about. Let's draft him."

Up to that time Tom had not committed himself per-sonally. He had advised me. He had guided me. He had given me some introductions. Now we discussed the whole thing once more, and Tom agreed to what Loretta had pro-posed. "I'll get you on the air," he said. "I'll get my whole team involved and we'll put the package together. After that, you are on your own."

The following day Tom called Ed Kobak in New York. "I watched this operation all this time," he told Ed, "without committing myself. Now I'm committed." That was all that Kobak wanted to hear. "I had written it off," he replied, "but if you are in it, my confidence is restored." So Tom went to work, and he persuaded a group of his co-workers at Young and Rubicam to donate their time. Al Scalpone, one of the greatest copy writers in the history of advertising, was one of them. He put a professional stamp on our message from the outset, and he continues to be available as consultant and inspirer, ensuring that we never fall from the high standards he created for us. Martin Work was also on the team. He had been with Tom Lewis in the Armed Forces Radio Service and had broad previous experience in radio writing and production. He subsequently became, in 1950, executive director of the National Council of Catholic Men, a post he still occupies. He was a lay auditor at the Vatican Council, and he is a member of the Vatican's newly created Council on the Laity. And I must not overlook the contribution of Mary Harris, who is still with Young and Rubicam, now in the New York office.

This group of professionals started from the premise that if you were going to sell family prayer on the radio, you had to use the techniques which had proved successful in this medium for selling soap and automobiles and every other kind of product and service. That formula was the radio drama to gain an audience, followed by a commercial to sell the product or service. The drama would be presented in a family setting, so as to prepare the listeners for the message, but it had to be a legitimate drama, with a plot and its own internal development and excitement.

Al Scalpone wrote the commercials. He approached his job in his typical professional way. He would come to each strategy meeting with a long list of possible slogans and engage in a brain-storming session with his colleagues to refine his ideas. Every slogan was a winner, but it did not take us long to agree on three as the ones that would carry us to victory. All of them have stood the test of time and are today familiar in every corner of the globe. One was simply a quotation from Alfred Lord Tennyson: "More things are wrought by prayer than this world dreams of." The other two were original: "A world at prayer is a world at peace," and the all-time favorite, "The family that prays together, stays together."

"Family Theater of the Air," as the program was named, was heard over the Mutual network for the first time on February 13, 1947. The play was called *Flight from Home*, and it had three stars for good measure, Loretta Young, James Stewart, and Don Ameche. I was particularly happy to have James Stewart, a Protestant, as one of that original team, for it was a proclamation to Mutual that I was going to live up to my undertaking to make the program non-sectarian. I knew that some had been warning the Mutual executives that they had let the camel's nose into the tent, that I would go along for a while, but that very soon I'd sneak the Rosary into the program one way or another. I did in fact get time later from Mutual for the Rosary, as I shall explain, but I kept my promise regarding "Family Theater of the Air." The formula on which we had agreed has always been maintained.

Many of my Catholic friends throughout the country, who had been expecting something similar to the original Mother's Day broadcast, were disappointed. Monsignor Matthew J. Smith, managing editor of the *Denver Register*, had through a misunderstanding told his readers that it would be a Rosary program, and the following week he apologized to them for having urged them to tune in. In Albany the reaction was equally negative. After Father Woods had listened to the criticisms of some of the girls at the College of St. Rose, he telephoned me and said he wondered if we shouldn't call it quits then and there. But I remembered what Monsignor Shea had said about Our Lady being contented even with the crumbs, and I continued on. Gradually the reaction of the general public trickled in, and it was overwhelmingly favorable. One story was printed about a husband and wife who by chance tuned in the program as they were driving to Reno to get a divorce. They turned the car around and went home to have another try at it. Maybe the story was dreamed up by the publicity boys, but it expressed what many were thinking and saying. It was a good show, and it was creating an impact. Frank Burke, editor of *Radio Daily*, gave it his vote from the start. It showed how the new medium could be utilized to project the message of Christianity, he said. Each year he gave it a top listing when making the annual compilation of outstanding shows. Martin Quigley spoke in similar terms in his trade papers, and so did *Variety*, the bible of the entertainment industry.

Tom Lewis had hired Bob Longenecker at the outset as producer. Tom had made it clear that his volunteer team could carry on only long enough to show how the job could be done. The work involved was too great for them to perform indefinitely in their spare time. When they had proved their point and withdrew, the entire operation was left in Bob's hands. He continued in charge for some time, hiring the writers and other production talent, picking the stars, supervising the entire operation. The dramas were addressed to a very wide audience. The themes were moral rather than religious, and entertainment predominated over preaching. We continued to produce a show every week for almost ten years, the total number of productions being 482. At the peak of popularity, they were carried by 429 stations. By the middle of the 1950s, however, radio was taking a terrible beating from television, and we decided to cut costs by reairing our best shows. The reruns are still carried weekly by nearly 150 stations of the Mutual network in the United States. They are also used in Canada, Latin America, Spain, Mozambique, Australia, and the Philippines, and the Armed Forces Radio Service carries our message around the world.

I don't know how I raised the money to maintain production for ten years. I was in constant motion around the country, begging from everyone who would open his door to me. Mary Harris and her friends came through with the money they had pledged. She also set up the appointment for me to meet Peter Grace, as she had promised. It was early in 1947, about the time that "Family Theater" first went on the air. I remember quite distinctly that I was in the office of Frank Burke, and I said to him: "I'm lugging around this victrola because I'm going downtown to meet a young man called Peter Grace, and I want him to listen to the sample radio program that I have on these records. I'm going to be late, so would you please call his office and tell him to wait for me?"

Afterward, when I knew Peter better, I wondered how I ever passed that first test. Not only did I arrive late, but

I immediately took him for granted. "I have a record here that I want you to hear," I announced. "Where can we find an outlet for the victrola and a quiet place?" So he came with me and we went searching around until we found a place in the medical department on another floor, and he listened patiently. Then we went back to his office, and I told him straight out that I wanted money to pay for that program and an indefinite number of others like it. He didn't seem to mind. He accepted me immediately in his open, responsive, generous way.

"Get Gerry Carroll for me," he instructed his secretary. Gerry was administrator for a charitable foundation set up by Peter's brother Michael. "This is Father Peyton," Peter said to Gerry, when he came in. "He needs money for a family program on radio. I'll give him $4,000 if you match it." After some discussion Gerry agreed and said he was sure his directors would approve. And there, inside an hour, I had won a big breathing space, the first of many I would win from the same source.

Then Peter invited me to his home, where his wife, Margie, welcomed me. In due course I also met Peter's brothers, Michael and Charlie, both of whom at various times responded to my appeals. But it was Peter himself, and Margie, who always remained closest to me. When they moved to their present home in Manhasset, they provided a room and office space, always available to me whenever I visit New York. And Peter has been consistently lavish with his time and the administrative and financial talents which have made him the industrial leader that Mary Harris had foretold when she first mentioned his name to me. They were to prove of inestimable value when I decided to move into Latin America, a part of the world with which he is particularly familiar. Were it not for his guidance, I do not see how I could—humanly speaking—have accomplished many of the things which will be described in later chapters.

Yet even with the help of Peter and other generous friends, I never had money to pay the weekly bills for long. Production expenses were staggering. The regulations of the various trade unions were such that even the stars had to be paid the minimum wage in the same way as the supporting cast and the technicians. Usually, however, the star would send me back his check in the amount of the payment, and finally the Guild relented to the point of not insisting on payment to the stars. But even with this relaxation the weekly cost went as high as $2,000 one night when, in addition to Meredith Wilson's orchestra directed by Max Terr, we had an unusually big cast of supporting actors. And weekly bills ranging up to $1,000 were all too common.

Time and again I was at the end of my rope and ready to call it quits. But always something would happen to make me commit myself to a new effort. Sometimes it was money that appeared as though by magic. At other times it was an unexpected encouragement. I remember in particular arriving back at the French Hospital in New York, weary and tired from pounding the streets. Sister Magdalen, the superior, was waiting to intercept me when I arrived. "There's something upstairs for you worth a million dollars," she greeted me. "If there's anything up there worth a million dollars, it must be Our Lady herself," I thought as I dragged myself up the stairs. And though it wasn't Our Lady in person, the sister was surely right. For there waiting for me was a letter from Pope Pius XII addressed to his beloved son, Patrick Peyton, and in it he told me of his pleasure at learning about "Family Theater of the Air" and his delight that it was such a tremendous success through the length and breadth of the United States. How that letter came I had no idea. I had not suggested it, nor had any of my associates, to my knowledge. But a million dollars would not have been as welcome. For it was an assurance from Mary through her Son's vicar that I was doing what she wanted.

I was driven forward, also, by the obvious acceptance of the program. From the very outset, it was given all sorts of awards and citations, not only by Catholic organizations but by diverse groups of citizens and by the industry groups. Ed Kobak was consistently happy with the favorable image the program created for Mutual. He arranged an invitation for me to an annual convention of the radio industry at Atlantic City, where I was asked to the podium to address the experts and tell them what opportunities they were missing by neglecting the potentialities of religious broadcasting.

Emboldened by this success, I approached Ed Kobak with a proposal for a special program for Christmas, something completely separate from "Family Theater of the Air." It would run for an hour and would include the recitation of five decades of the Rosary. The title would be *The Joyful Hour*. It happened at this particular time that Ed was negotiating with Woolworth's for a Christmas program of an institutional nature, and he thought Woolworth's would agree to sponsor *The Joyful Hour*. So he told me to go ahead, and we developed a super-production, with eighteen stars including Ethel Barrymore. Perry Como sang "Ave Maria," and we had other famous singers for hymns to be sung between each of the five decades. Ethel Barrymore read appropriate selections from the Scriptures, and famous stars recited the Our Fathers and Hail Marys. The effort to get commercial sponsorship failed, but by then we had gone so far that Ed Kobak had to give us free time. The response was so excellent that he did not regret his decision. On the contrary, he not only authorized the repetition of *The Joyful Hour* as an annual feature of Mutual but cleared time for three more annual specials, *The Triumphant Hour* at Easter, and hour-long programs for Mother's Day and Thanksgiving. All of these included the recitation of five decades of the Rosary except the Thanksgiving program, which was entirely non-sectarian. And in this way Our Lady got considerably more than the crumbs with which it had seemed at first she would have to be satisfied.

And as a by-product, a most unexpected bonus, "Family Theater" was the means of leading me to the activity with which my name is most closely associated on every continent, the diocesan Family Rosary Crusade.

Nine

The Diocesan Crusade Is Born

It was in the fall of 1947 that the late Archbishop Alexandre Vachon of Ottawa organized a Marian Congress, bringing together the leading theologians from all over the world to discuss the latest developments in Marian theology and assembling the Catholic faithful with their leaders to pay tribute to the Mother of God. I asked for a booth at the Congress in order to make a presentation of "Family Theater of the Air" and explain its objectives.

Father Woods and Father Lawyer were with me at the Congress. One day, when I was absent, two priests from the diocese of London, Ontario, visited our booth, Fathers John T. Maloney and John McCormack. They listened to some of the "Family Theater" programs and talked to Fathers Woods and Lawyer. The upshot of the visit and the talk was that I received an invitation from Father Maloney to give a triduum in his parish, St. Mary's, in London, Ontario. In due course I arrived to fulfill the request, and I met Father Maloney for the first time. I took to him from that moment.

He was slightly older than me, about forty, medium height, outgoing, cheerful, and enthusiastic. He had a tremendous devotion to Mary and supreme confidence in the power of the Rosary to build and maintain his own faith and that of his parishioners.

I recall one discussion we had in which he said that Our Lady never stopped at herself but always led those who loved her to the feet of her Son. He then went on to explore the possibility of proving to the bishops of the world that the family Rosary could be restored to all Catholic homes in the twentieth century. "When the pastor gives leadership," he said, "the people follow. If the sheep are in the desert, it's because that is where the pastor brought them; if they are in green and rich pastures, the pastor deserves the credit." When he spoke in these terms, he was echoing my own deep conviction, and I in turn talked to him of my frustration that all I could do was to hit a parish here and a parish there with my triduums. "If only," I said, "there was some way to organize a whole diocese at one time."

It was at this point that Father Maloney came up with the thought that was to prove the catalyst. "We had a wonderful experience here in this diocese recently," he said. "We needed to raise several million dollars to build hospitals and schools. We called in a fund-raising outfit from Kansas City, headed by a man called Finn. His technique involved motivation combined with organization. Volunteers were enlisted in numbers sufficient to blanket the diocese. They went into every Catholic home and obtained a pledge for a certain amount. Why don't we use the same technique to obtain a pledge, not of money, but of the Rosary daily in every family?"

Once the proposal was formulated, it looked as inevitable as two and two making four. So we agreed that Father Maloney would invite Monsignor Andrew P. Mahoney, the vicar general, a close friend of his named Monsignor W. E. Dillon from Windsor, and four or five other influential pastors to the Holy Hour on the closing evening of the triduum. Afterward, they would come to the rectory, and we would submit the idea to them.

Their reaction was even stronger than mine. They had seen and benefited from the fund-raising operation. They agreed that its application to a spiritual pledge couldn't miss. Right away they agreed that next day three of them, Monsignor Mahoney, Monsignor Dillon, and Father Maloney, would submit the proposal to Bishop John T. Kidd that we test the idea right there in London. I had to leave in the morning to attend a Eucharistic Congress in Buffalo, but in the evening Father Maloney telephoned to report the outcome. The poor bishop—he was over eighty years old—was worried when he saw three of his senior priests coming up the driveway. He figured that they were going to drop some unpleasant problem in his lap. When he learned what they actually had in mind, however, he was overjoyed. For four hours he insisted on continuing to discuss the details with them. "The sky is the limit," he assured them. "I am ready to pay any price, if you undertake to restore the family Rosary to all our homes in the diocese before I die." Bishop John C. Cody, who was then coadjutor and who succeeded as bishop in 1950, was equally enthusiastic when informed.

A basic element of the fund-raising technique which we were copying, and this was an element which we found we could incorporate in its totality, was the mobilization of the internal dynamism of the diocese. The outsiders involved in the operation were kept to a minimum. They set up a small central office to supervise and co-ordinate. That was all. The central team transmitted its know-how, the motivation for wanting to join in the program, and the methods by which to implement it, to the first line of offense. This line passed it to the second, and so on, until the whole area was involved. Concretely, the first step is to assemble the pastor and two laymen picked by him from each parish for an indoctrination session. They select a district chairman for every hundred homes in the parish. The district chairman enlists five team captains, and each team captain recruits three men to join him in door-to-door visiting to collect the pledges. This means that one man is actively involved for every five families in the diocese.

Father Woods, Father Lawyer, and I went over this procedure and worked out what seemed to all of us the most logical adaptations at a preliminary meeting in London with Father Maloney and a few of the key priests of the diocese, in the early part of 1948. I remember the occasion very well. Fathers Woods and Lawyer had gone to London by train from Albany, but I was in Detroit on a typical trip which combined fund-raising for "Family Theater of the Air" with the preaching of a triduum or a talk to some religious community in order to promote the apostolate of the family Rosary. I was staying in the home of Fred Zeider, one of the founders and a top executive of General Motors, and Fred lent me a car to drive to London for the meeting. I hadn't driven for years, and I was terrified to find the road deep in ice and snow when I backed the car out of the garage in the dark of the morning. I had to drive at a snail's pace all the way, but finally I reached London safely and we got down to work.

We began the Crusade in February and ended it in May, Mary's month. The indoctrination session with the pastors and their lay helpers was to take place at a banquet, and we got the famous radio personality Don McNeill of the *Breakfast Club*, from Chicago, to be master of ceremonies.

Our conscious and concrete purpose in organizing the Crusade was to get each family of the diocese to commit itself by a written pledge to the daily recitation of the Rosary as a family in its home. But we realized that we would be accomplishing little or nothing by extracting signatures through high-pressure sales methods. What we needed was to motivate people by giving them an understanding of the Rosary and the benefits that flowed to the individuals and to the family group by their nightly assembly to honor God and His Blessed Mother. This understanding and enthusiasm had to be transmitted from our Crusade team to the pastors and their helpers, and then from group to group, all the way down, so that the two men assigned to visit a given family would be able to teach the lesson faithfully to that family and persuade them to sign for reasons that would ensure that the pledge would be honored.

Father John Maloney was the priest named by Bishop Kidd as his liaison with the Crusade team and the one primarily responsible for activating the internal dynamism of the diocese. He did this so effectively following the organization system we had adopted, that about seven thousand men were enlisted to go from door to door for the pledges, and they got a 90 percent response from those they approached. To inspire the men, he would tell them never to be annoyed or insulted if anyone treated them boorishly, simply to remind the person that they had come to ask a favor not for themselves but for the Mother of God. In that first Crusade the technique worked wonders, as it continues to do through the years. There was one man who had not attended to his religious duties for many years. When his home was visited, he repulsed the callers rudely. "Your words do not hurt us," one of them said gently. "We are here not for ourselves but for Our Lady." The soft answer continued to rankle after they had left, and all week it bored into the man's mind and his conscience. By Saturday he could stand it no longer. He went to the church he had not visited in so long, and he confessed his sins, especially the sin of having shut his door in the face of Our Lady's ambassadors.

As part of his program, Father Maloney arranged for me to preach in each parish of the diocese, and I covered them all in a month, preaching in three parishes every day. My sermon was always identical in its substance. I told them the same story that I told the audiences that had come to my triduums, the same story that I told the people on board the ship that carried me to Ireland, the same story that I tell the huge crowds at the monster rallies which are a feature of later Crusades. It is my personal testimony, my witness, my proclamation of the great things that Mary has done to me, her unworthy servant. They are the things that I am trying to describe in this book, the beautiful spiritual home and family into which I was born, the family love engendered and fostered by family prayer to the point that my mother and my sister were happy to give their lives so that I might live and perform my assigned task of proclaiming all over the earth the greatness of God and the sensitive love His Mother has for every one of Christ's brothers, her children.

More than once I have been urged by well-intentioned friends to polish up my rough-hewn talk. They suggest graceful sentences and profound concepts. But once I get up there in front of an audience, it always comes out the same. Beforehand, I am always terrified at the thought of the coming ordeal, and I accept with delight the offered help. But when I get on the platform or in the pulpit and join with my listeners in reciting a Hail Mary for guidance, then I realize that I am like the two men knocking at the door for the pledge. I am not there to seek for myself but only for her. My function is not to impress them with my oratory but to proclaim to them my experience, to have them understand the great things Mary has done to me and for me. And while what I say is always the same, in another sense it is new each time. It is like the devoutly recited Hail Mary, always the same greeting, yet constantly renewed by the spirit with which it is said. Every audience is the same, whether a dozen or a million. Each time I address one it is, for me, the first time, and I go through the kind of suffering which St. Paul so often describes himself as having experienced when facing tasks beyond his strength, to the point of giving up all hope of survival and of feeling deep in the soul the sentence of death hanging over, as he wrote to the Corinthians. But I remember with him that all this is necessary to remind us not to confide in ourselves but in God, who restores life to the dead. And in that way I find strength to force my unwilling steps to the pulpit or platform so that I can give witness to the power of God, who through His Blessed Mother restored my strength when man had despaired and who placed me on a road where I could continually give testimony to His mercy and to the sensitive love His Mother has for all of us.

There is an inspiring story about Father John Maloney that I want to record before I pass on. Enthused by the immense success of the Crusade and the massive signing of the pledges to recite the family Rosary daily in his parish and through the diocese, he decided to show the truth of his conviction that Our Lady did not keep for herself those who loved her, but that she led them to her Son. "We can get a far bigger attendance at daily Mass," he said, "because we have more people in the parish who pray the Rosary regularly." To motivate his parishioners, he arranged to get nine famous preachers to address them on nine consecutive Sundays, men of the level of Monsignor Fulton Sheen and Father Daniel Lord, S.J. I remember he contacted me at Albany to see if I could enlist Monsignor Ronald Knox, the famous English author and lecturer. I got on the telephone to England and finally tracked him down, but he had so many conflicting commitments that he could not oblige us. Nevertheless, Father Maloney did get an impressive list, and the series of sermons began. One Sunday came, however, when the scheduled preacher was forced by an unanticipated happening to cancel his commitment. So Father Maloney had no choice but to take over himself at a moment's notice. He preached at each of the morning Masses and again at the evening devotions. Then he had his supper and went to his room. The next morning they found him dead there.

Poor old Bishop Kidd also died suddenly in edifying circumstances. He was in the sacristy preparing to say Mass, and he fell over dead as he stooped to lift the vestments out of a drawer. And very soon there was a third death among those who had initiated the Family Rosary Crusade in London, Ontario, Monsignor Dillon, a young man in vigorous health. The memory of these three I carry with me every day, and I pray to them for their help in heaven for the continuance of the good work they began on earth.

It was not long until another bishop showed up who was ready to copy the formula we had developed in London. He was a close friend of Father John Maloney named Michael O'Neill, and he had served as a chaplain in the Canadian Army in Europe during the war. Upon demobilization, he was named archbishop of Regina. No doubt he was emotionally disturbed by his wartime experiences in Europe. In any case, no sooner did he learn of his new appointment than he fell into a deep depression, convinced that he was incapable of undertaking so vast an assignment. Trying to rebuild his self-confidence by showing concrete things a bishop could do for his people, Father Maloney described the great success of the Family Rosary Crusade in London. Archbishop O'Neill's response was immediate. "If you pull me through this emotional crisis," he told Our Lady, "so that I can force myself to go to Regina and be installed as archbishop, I won't stop until we have one of these Crusades." No sooner had he made this decision than his peace of mind was restored. In due course he took over the archdiocese, and he immediately invited all the bishops of the province of Saskatchewan to a meeting with Father Woods and myself. By this time Bishop Gibbons of Albany had released Father Woods to work full time with me, and Father Steiner, my provincial, had allocated two more Holy

Cross men, Father Albert Heinzer to replace Father Woods
in the various activities he had performed in Albany, and
Father Ray Finan to become a part of the Crusade team. In
time Father Heinzer was to become director of the "Family
Theater" office in Hollywood. This left Father Lawyer to
supervise the Albany office, by now a major contact and
fund-raising operation.

All the bishops went along with Archbishop O'Neill,
enabling the Crusade to achieve a further level of efficiency
by staggering the preparatory work. When Fathers Woods
and Finan had initiated the process in one diocese, they
would move on to the next. Meanwhile one of our secre-
taries from Albany maintained liaison with them in the
field through a central office at Regina. A further refinement was the introduction of the rally, held at one or several
central places in each diocese. The London experience of
preaching three times a day in different churches for thirty
consecutive days had almost killed me. Even my voice gave
out toward the end, so that I couldn't make myself heard.
So instead, we decided to bring as many people as possible
together in one place for a grand demonstration of faith and
a public commitment of the diocese to the service of God
and Mary. The first rally was organized at the Benedictine
Abbey of Our Lady of Mount Carmel by Abbot Severin
Gertken, and it stands out in my mind because of a very
good lesson given me by the abbot himself. Even after all my
years in the religious life, I had never succeeded in bringing
my Irish temper under full control. At a meeting during
the preparatory training, one of the lay leaders put up a
big argument against the visitation of the homes, which
was an essential element of the pledge campaign. I lost my

temper and caused a most embarrassing few minutes for everybody, including myself. The abbot, who was present, said nothing. Afterward, however, he came to me in private. "Always try to remember," he said, "that what is best must not be allowed to become the enemy of what is good." It is advice I constantly try to bear in mind.

From Saskatchewan the word of the Crusade spread through all western Canada, and finally a meeting was arranged at Calgary, Alberta, to discuss its extension to additional dioceses. At least a dozen bishops attended, and others sent representatives. They came from British Columbia, Manitoba, and Alaska, as well as from Alberta. The upshot of this meeting was that we blanketed the whole immense region of western Canada, all the way up to the Arctic Circle and beyond, to Hudson Bay, Whitehorse, and Mackenzie, using all kinds of conveyances from airplane to dog sled and experiencing all kinds of tribulations in conditions of climate and weather that for us were totally new.

I associate the Calgary meeting called to arrange this Crusade with the death of one who had helped me at a critical moment. As Father Woods and I were flying to it, he handed me a newspaper which carried a story of an air disaster in India. A pilot had flown a plane into the side of a mountain, and one of the passengers was Elsie Dick, the woman at the Mutual network who had approved the 1945 Mother's Day program. She was still breathing when the rescue party reached the spot, and her dying words were a request for water. "It was the water of Baptism she was begging," Father Woods said, for it was his custom to read a mystical meaning into every event. Whether or not he was right, I am sure the mercy of the Lord was ready to embrace one who served Him so well.

The endless empty spaces of western Canada gave me a sense of the vastness of our world such as I had never felt before. To communicate with the scattered inhabitants it was necessary to use to the full every one of the means of modern science available, the airplane, the telephone, the radio. "That is the secret of your Crusade, the harnessing of the air. That is why you are so successful," Archbishop William M. Duke of Vancouver said to me one day. We were already trying in our amateur way to get all the publicity we could win from the press and the radio wherever we went, so as to arouse faster and more fully the enthusiasm of each diocese. But what I was most conscious of was the inadequacy of our coordination. We had the other great activity of "Family Theater of the Air" moving along simultaneously in Los Angeles, and I was constantly commuting between the two operations. Each was being carried along its own road, each spreading the message of family prayer. What was needed was some way to tie them together, so that instead of two separate impacts, there would be a single cumulative impact. That would be gradually and progressively developed over the years, but the first seed had not yet even germinated. Archbishop Duke, nevertheless, had sown it in my mind, and in God's own time it would sprout and finally flower.

Before we had finished our work in western Canada, word of the success of the formula we had developed for the Family Rosary Crusade had spread through the United States, and I was hard at work trying to convince people that the same technique was valid for dioceses in the United

States. It was not long until I got an opportunity to test my theory. It came in the form of an invitation from Bishop William Hafey of Scranton. Although I had lived there only a relatively short time, I always regarded Scranton as my home in the United States, and even today Scranton is one of the places I love best in America.

We made no significant change from the methods we had developed in Canada. The one point about which there had been most discussion had resolved itself by experience in our favor. Many people had wondered why we didn't enlist women as well as men in our local organization to visit the homes and obtain the pledges. It was much easier to get women to do that kind of work, and they usually had more time available. That was true. We felt, nevertheless, that other arguments were more basic. As head of the house, the man represents God in the family, and it is his duty to provide spiritual leadership as well as material needs. Once you get the man of the house involved, you can be confident that the family Rosary is safe in the home. And finally, on a more practical level, the devout wife and mother was always delighted to find her husband being roped into a spiritual enterprise. Usually the priest either left everything to the women or drafted the men only for fund-raising or other material activities. It was a bad example for growing children, because it created the impression that religion was something for women, and that men should concentrate on more important things.

This we set our face against, and it has worked for us in all kinds of countries and cultures. We pick men from every social level, the rich, the middle class, and the workers, and we pick them from those who never set foot in church as well as from the daily communicants. Regardless of their standing, we welcome them as long as they are willing to work for Our Lady. The rest we leave to God and to her.

The bishop of Scranton was so pleased with the response in his diocese that he became a promoter of the Crusade among the neighboring bishops. So from Scranton we went to Baltimore and Washington, then up and down the eastern seaboard, as far north as Providence, Rhode Island, and south into Delaware, the two Carolinas, Virginia, Alabama, and Florida, then west to New Orleans and all the way north into Indiana. About the same time we covered eastern Canada, including the Maritime Provinces and Newfoundland and the English-speaking parts of Quebec. The Crusade was also preached in French-speaking Quebec by the Oblate priests from Cap-de-la-Madeleine. They had helped us in French-speaking areas in western Canada and there had learned how to organize the Crusade. I was not too happy at the creation of a unit not under our control. I was afraid we might run into problems of jurisdictional conflict, or that the concept of the Family Rosary Crusade might be so altered in the course of time as to lose its distinctive characteristics. The Oblate team, nevertheless, went ahead on its own. As soon as it had finished Quebec, however, it went out of business. So the issues I had feared never really arose. But today, in the changed circumstances I shall describe later, I am starting to think about a similar plan for Latin America. I can see the possibility of a training center in which bishops could send their own priests for a source of instruction followed by a period of practical experience on one of our teams. They could then return home and propagate the Crusade in their own countries.

The Crusades had been in progress in Canada and the United States for about two years when I made the first experimental foray overseas. Bishop Thomas E. Flynn of Lancaster, England, used to come periodically to lecture in the United States. On one of these trips, or through the superior of a Holy Cross foundation in his diocese, he learned about the Crusade and invited me over. The presence of Holy Cross priests in Lancaster made acceptance relatively easy, although we were wondering how our specifically American techniques would go down on the other side of the Atlantic. "There's only one way to find out," we said. Two Holy Cross priests, Fathers John Murphy and Joseph Quinn, had by now joined my team. Fathers Murphy and Woods went to Lancaster, accompanied by Patricia Spanbauer and Dorothy Kahl from Albany, leaving Father Quinn in the Albany office. Many of the Catholics in Lancaster were of Irish birth or extraction, and I suppose that made it easy, because they were already steeped in the tradition of the family Rosary. But whatever the reasons, the Crusade was a great success, and it was not long until we were invited back to England to cover eight more dioceses, ending up with a monster rally in Wembley Stadium, London. In between, however, we worked back in the United States, and it was during this interval that the Crusade was preached in Washington, DC, and fifteen other dioceses in the South and Southeast.

England in turn was the means of opening up the first approach toward what was to become, and what by all appearances is long destined to be, the primary field of action of the Family Rosary Crusade. Bishop Angel (later Cardinal) Herrera of Málaga, Spain, happened to be in

London while the Crusade was being organized there, and he attended the rally at Wembley Stadium. He was deeply impressed, and he urged us to come and organize a Crusade in his own diocese. He is a man of the most radiant personality, and he gave himself to me from that first moment of contact in a friendship that will perdure through all eternity. He is a brilliant intellectual, founder and longtime editor of one of Madrid's principal daily newspapers. He was fifty-four when he became a priest and in his upper sixties when I met him. But he was full of life and vigor, imbued with a deep apostolic and pastoral zeal. "You have here so many things we need in Spain," he would say to me. "You have a technique which we lack, and you have a message of love for Our Lady which the Spaniard will embrace the moment he is exposed to it."

The problem of communication seemed to me insuperable, but he insisted. "Very well," I said finally. "If you have patience with me and take me as your novice, so that I can learn your language and use it to penetrate the whole continent of Latin America, I will come." So he threw his arms around me in a fatherly embrace and kissed me. "You will come," he said, "and I will be the novice. You have more to teach us than we have to teach you."

By good fortune, a young Panamanian named Mark McGrath had recently been ordained a Holy Cross priest in the United States. He was a brilliant student, completely bilingual in English and Spanish. Before many years he was to become auxiliary to the archbishop of Panama City, and later bishop of Santiago de Veraguas in Panama, and he would become one of the major luminaries of the Vatican Council for his theological acumen and his pastoral dedication. He joined Father Woods, Father Murphy, and myself as interpreter and fellow worker in Málaga, where we began the Crusade about Christmas time of 1952. The mild climate permitted us to work efficiently at that time of the year.

The practical experience right there on the spot in Málaga made me realize just how big a problem the language barrier actually is. Father McGrath was wonderful, and so was Bishop Herrera. But communication through an interpreter is not like face-to-face and soul-to-soul speech. When Málaga was over, I had just about decided I had bitten off more than I could chew. I fought it out one day with Father Woods in—of all places—a barbershop. We hadn't even had time to get a haircut during the final weeks of the Crusade, and we had gone together to the barber before Father Woods started back to the United States to organize the diocese of Cleveland, to which Archbishop Edward F. Hoban had invited us. I wanted, right or wrong, to go with him. I argued that I couldn't afford the time to learn another language when there was still an indefinite load of work waiting for us in English. Deep down, however, I was rationalizing my fear and my reluctance. I didn't see how I could ever reach the point of being able to stand up before a crowd of Spaniards or Latin Americans and convince them in their own language. Father Woods, however, cut through all my talk. "It's now or never," he said. "You are today being offered the grace to invade a continent that needs our message more than any other. Latin America has tens of millions of people who believe in Christ and revere His Mother. But they have no priests. They are like the Irish in your grandparents' and great-grandparents' time. Why do you today have the faith? Because those great people clung to the Rosary when they had no other means to learn the truths of the faith and no other way to express their beliefs. That's the crossroad at which the whole Spanish-speaking world is standing today, and you have a chance to help, a chance that will never be repeated if you refuse it."

He was hitting me hard with his arguments, but I still was fighting back. We were speaking with the greatest frankness, confident that the barber didn't understand what we were saying. In this we were mistaken. He did speak English, and he finally decided to get into the discussion and point out the logic of Father Woods's arguments. I was so startled by this sudden turn of events that all pretenses were swept away and I was forced to recognize the justice of the position Father Woods had been espousing. I often shudder when I look back over my life and recognize the moments in which, in my weakness and fear, I have resisted grace. And that was surely one such moment. I don't know how I'd explain my failure on the day of judgment, if I had remained obstinate in my view and thrown away the extraordinary gift of God to Latin America that the Family Rosary Crusade has proved to be and promises to be in an even bigger way.

So Father Woods went to Cleveland, and I stayed on for several months. I worked at Spanish from early morning until late at night, with three teachers pacing each other. It was tough work after so long a separation from books. But I stuck at it, memorizing conjugations, building up a vocabulary. At least I learned how to say the Rosary in Spanish, and I made up a version of my rally talk which was translated into Spanish, and which for a time I read from the pulpit or platform. I never felt at ease, however, with a prepared text, and gradually I began to venture away from it a bit here and a bit there. I have no illusions about the quality of my Spanish, any more than about that of my English. When I stop to think, I'm ruined, and I come out with all kinds of mistakes that I have constantly to ask my friends to overlook. But when I have something really important to say, whether it's trying to enlist the co-operation of a group of priests in a diocese, or seeking to get across to a throng of people the message of the family Rosary, then somehow I forget myself and I am capable of flights of rhetoric that surprise nobody more than they surprise myself. I am told this is not an uncommon experience in a foreign language. One of the biggest emotional blocks is self-consciousness, which is so often a lack of humility, a fear of making a fool of oneself in public. And I have long ago learned that to make a fool of oneself is a small price to pay for anything that is worth doing.

While I was studying Spanish in Málaga, Father Woods and my other associates were hard at work in Cleveland, and there they attempted something which gave me an idea that ultimately revolutionized the Crusade by giving it a depth and a function far deeper than it had previously enjoyed. About a year earlier the Catholic Daughters of America had agreed to underwrite the cost of a series of fifteen half-hour radio programs, each dramatizing a Mystery of the Rosary. I had been in friendly contact with this organization, as with the St. Vincent de Paul Society and other Catholic groups, for many years. When Mary Duffy of South Orange, New Jersey, was president, she invited me to address many state conventions and even a national

convention. I was on equally friendly terms with Frances
Maher of Pennsylvania, her successor, and also with the
national chaplain, Bishop Vincent S. Waters of Raleigh,
North Carolina, in whose diocese I preached a Crusade in
1952. Frances arranged a meeting of the top leaders of the
Catholic Daughters at Atlantic City, and that was where
they agreed to sponsor the fifteen radio programs. They
were produced by our Hollywood office, and it had been
suggested that we should use them on fifteen consecutive
evenings in Cleveland as a build-up to the climax of the
Crusade. The radio stations in Cleveland, however, were
hard to convince. These are denominational programs, they
said, and we couldn't possibly give you all that free time
without an outcry from all the other denominations.

That was where we stood when I arrived from Spain.
Everyone was disappointed at the failure to get radio time,
but I refused to give in. "We have top-quality material here,"
I said, "and I have learned one lesson in dealing with radio
people. They respect quality. All we have to do is to get
across to them that we are doing something for them." We
managed to reach the director of one station and persuaded
him to listen to the first program, in which Bing Crosby
was the star. "What's the trouble?" he said when he heard it.
"This is great." He called his men and ordered them to clear
time at the peak hour every evening for fifteen evenings.

Now that was grand, but it was only the start of the new
enrichment of the Crusade. I sat in my room the first evening and listened to the story of the Annunciation coming
through the air by means of the great miracle of the radio,
and I knew that the same miracle was being re-enacted in
a thousand and a hundred thousand homes, that people

all over the area were hearing the good news of God's announcement through His angel to the humble maid of Nazareth that the promised time had been fulfilled and that His own Son waited only on her agreement to take on our human flesh and come to live always among us. The next evening I listened to the Visitation, and so on, Mystery after Mystery. And as I listened I rejoiced. For I knew that this sublime teaching was reaching many minds and hearts for the first time, reaching out to people who had never attended a catechism class and who never darkened the door of a church. Yet this great happiness did not entirely fill my mind. On the contrary, each day another thought intruded itself with mounting force. "There is one thing still missing," I kept repeating to myself. "They should be able to see as well as hear."

Before we had completed the transmission of the fifteen radio programs for the first time there in Cleveland, my mind was made up. My next project would be fifteen half-hour films, each re-enacting a Mystery of the Rosary. They would have to be fully professional and in color, so that all the senses of the viewer would be fully involved, so that any man in any part of the world could see and understand, so that whether he was a Hindu, a Confucian, a Muslim, a Jew, or a Christian, they would give him an understanding and an appreciation of the greatness of God and the beauty of the Mother greeted by the angel as full of grace.

I could hardly wait for the end of the Cleveland Crusade, so anxious was I to get started on this new enrichment. Archbishop Hoban had a great friend across the lake at the mother house of the Sisters of St. Dominic in Adrian, Michigan. She was the superior general, Mother Gerald

Barry, a member of a family from County Clare, Ireland, which had made a significant contribution to the growth of the Church in the United States. One brother had been bishop of St. Augustine, Florida, for eighteen years up to his death in 1940. Another, my good friend and longtime dean of the same diocese, Monsignor William Barry, was the founder and first editor of *The Florida Catholic*, and subsequently pastor of St. Patrick's, Miami Beach. I had promised Archbishop Hoban that I would go from Cleveland to Adrian to speak to Mother Gerald's community. The day was July 1, a broiling summer day, but the heat outside was nothing to the fire that was burning in my heart. I could think of nothing but how to make a reality of my dream of the fifteen films. That was what filled my mind while I addressed the five hundred or more sisters who thronged the auditorium. They were from schools scattered all over the diocese and had come to Adrian to pass the summer vacation together. While I was talking, I realized what I was going to do. I would throw myself on the mercy of the orders of nuns around the world, and I would get them to make the sacrifices that would be involved in paying for this project.

After I had finished, I called Mother Gerald aside and I told her about the terrific idea I had. "Tomorrow is the feast of the Visitation, Mother," I said, "and I'm asking you to sponsor the Visitation film and get your nuns to find the money." "How much is it going to cost?" she asked. As yet I had no real idea, but we had some experience already of Hollywood costs, even for people like myself who could get so much free. "I'm guessing that it won't be less than $20,000," I told her, "but think what a worldwide sermon for Our Lady you will be getting for that $20,000." She pondered for a while. "It's a big decision," she said. "Give me till tomorrow."

The next day she called me out into the open space in front of the convent. She was a strong woman, strong willed, outspoken, a leader. "Look at that big building," she said. "It still has to be paid for. Look at all those nuns that thronged the auditorium yesterday. They have to be fed and clothed. I couldn't give you the kind of money you are asking for. Your technique is wrong. Instead of asking a lot from a few, ask a little from many. That way you have a chance. And to start off, I'll give you a thousand dollars." I was deeply disappointed. I had been counting on a dramatic sign on this feast of Our Lady, an assurance that I was on the right track. Still, I had no choice but to thank Mother Gerald for her generosity and take off for Detroit. It was still early in the day, and I had no intention of giving up yet. My reason for picking Detroit was that Mother Teresa, mother general of the Immaculate Heart Sisters of Monroe, Michigan, was visiting one of her convents. For years she had stood out in my memory as one of the great champions of the Family Rosary Crusade, and a champion she continued right up to her death in 1967. Every visitation she made to the schools conducted by her nuns, she talked to the children about the family Rosary and urged them to become apostles in their own homes. Through her efforts, I believe that as many as seventy thousand families undertook to say the Rosary in common every evening. So I went to Mother Teresa and I told her what I had planned and how I had started out unsuccessfully. "I've just been refused," I said, "but I'm not giving up. This is still the feast of the Visitation, and now

Mary is giving you the privilege to sponsor the film on the Visitation." She didn't hesitate for a moment. "I'll do it," she said. "I'll have to consult my Council, and it may take a month or more before I can give you an official answer. But have no fear. The answer will be yes."

So there I was, filled with elation and thinking to myself how shameful it was that I had thought even for a minute that Mary would let that day go by without a sign of her favor. Little did I realize how prodigal of favors Mary was planning to be that blessed day. As I was thanking Mother Teresa for her faith and generosity, I happened to inquire about a member of her community whose family had been extremely kind to me on various occasions. "I'm sorry to say," Mother Teresa replied, "that both she and all her family are in deep distress. Her sister-in-law is critically ill." I immediately canceled a flight I was about to take to Chicago and went to the hospital, where I met the girl's husband and father. They were indeed in deep distress. We went to the sickbed, and together we recited the Memorare to Our Lady, calling on her with all the fervor of our souls to hear our petition and restore this young wife and mother to her husband and family. I consoled them as best I could, and I then went with some of the nuns in charge of the hospital to have a cup of tea. While I was still drinking the tea, the father-in-law rushed in very excitedly. "She's cured," he said. "She's going to be all right. Just now she whispered to me that Our Lady herself had come and promised her she would get well." All I could think was that surely Mary was showing her gratitude to Mother Teresa and the community that had been praying for this sick woman, because of their generosity in agreeing to sponsor the Visitation

Mystery. And the girl did get well rapidly, and since that time her husband and she have been blessed with several more children.

The day was not yet over. I was able to get a later plane to Chicago, and I went to stay the night at the Hilton Hotel. Several years earlier, I had met Bob Quain, then hotel manager and now senior vice-president of Hilton Hotels, at a businessmen's luncheon held to raise funds for my work, and he had told me the Hilton would always be my home in Chicago. It was no empty rhetoric. Not only have I ever since been welcome, but often I am embarrassed by being ushered into the Royal Suite. Once, when I was about to take off for a Crusade in Spain, they put me in the Spanish Suite. In any case, I had left word when setting out that morning that I would spend the night at the Hilton in Chicago, and when I arrived, a message awaited. "Please call Mother Gerald at Adrian, Michigan," it read. "I've changed my mind," she announced, when I got her on the telephone. "I'm going to sponsor one of the Mysteries, and I'd like to take the Nativity." That was better, because the Visitation was taken care of. So I thanked her, and I thanked Our Lady for having made up so unexpectedly for the inadequacy of my pleadings.

No sooner had I got off the phone to Adrian than I telephoned Milwaukee. I had conceived an outrageous idea, and I was determined to put it to the test right away. The American headquarters of the School Sisters of Notre Dame was in Milwaukee, and I had met the superior, Mother Andrina, through the Dominican Sisters of the Perpetual Rosary, whose convent is not far away. "I have an awful favor to ask of you, Mother Andrina," I told her. "I want to discuss a very important project, but it must be tonight, because I'm taking off for a long series of Crusades in Australia. It's going to be near midnight when I get to Milwaukee, and what I'm asking is that you alert the members of your Council so that we can all meet the moment I arrive." It was an extraordinary demand, because back in those days it was unthinkable to break the solid routine of convent life in such a way. Mother Andrina responded heroically. "We'll be waiting for you," she said.

Before boarding the train I called Harry John in Milwaukee, told him my arrival time, and asked him to be at the station with his car. Harry was a graduate of Notre Dame. His mother was a Miller, a member of the brewery family, and he was a stockholder in the company and a man of considerable wealth. His big interest was the promotion of the contemplative life in the United States, and through the DeRance Foundation, of which he is the president, he has helped many enclosed monasteries and convents. Through the same foundation he has also helped the Family Rosary Crusade on many occasions, especially since it started to work in Latin America, a region in which Harry is profoundly interested.

Harry John met me, drove me to the convent, and waited while I talked to the nuns. My prayers were answered, my hopes fulfilled. They said yes. "This is the money we had accumulated to build an infirmary for our old and feeble Sisters," said the letter which reached me later with their check, "but they are willing to wait, because we all know that you are offering us a better investment."

Few days of my life were as filled with emotion and elation as that feast of the Visitation in 1953. In the morning, I had nothing but a starry-eyed dream. Before I went to bed, I had pledges for $60,000 toward its realization. And I also had the formula to get the rest. I would offer the Mysteries one by one to the nuns of the world and the nuns would come through. They would contribute the major part of the production costs, but I am also eternally grateful to those other friends, bishops, religious superiors of men, and laypeople, whose substantial contributions also helped to make the fifteen films on the Mysteries of the Rosary possible. They would never have been made without the faith and the sacrifice and the prayers of those valiant people around the world.

Ten

Rosary Crusade Girdles the Earth

From the first invitation to Spain by Bishop Herrera, Father Woods and I knew that our Family Rosary Crusade was being called to Latin America. Father Woods's insistence that I remain in Spain after the Crusade there in order to get some fluency in the Spanish language sealed our commitment. It would be several years, from 1953 to 1959, before we actually started to work in what has since been and what promises long to be the principal area of our activity. Yet this delay was almost providential, for it enabled us to reach Latin America with two elements not earlier available, elements which were essential for success in the environment of that continent. These were the fifteen films on the Mysteries of the Rosary and a strengthening of our teams by the addition of helpers belonging to a Spanish secular institute of women, the Instituto de Misioneras Seculares.

My first meeting with one of the Misioneras was in early 1954 at the home of Bishop Herrera of Málaga, where I stayed for my crash course in Spanish after the Crusade preached in his diocese. The Misioneras engage in a wide range of professional and secretarial activities, always on behalf of an apostolic activity and with the approval of the bishop of the diocese in which the work is conducted. The girl who came to see me was a journalist and a member of a distinguished newspaper family. She was María Luisa Luca de Tena, and her father owned the internationally best known and one of the most important of Madrid's dailies, *A.B.C.*

The Málaga Crusade had developed some controversy in Spain. Most Catholics agreed with Bishop Herrera that we had introduced a technique and a spirit beneficial to the Church and the community. A minority, however, felt that it was undignified for Catholic Spain to look to materialistic America for religious guidance, and doubly ridiculous for the homeland of St. Dominic to be told how to say the Rosary. María Luisa's assignment was to interview me and evaluate the issue on the basis of her observation.

The moment I met her, I recognized a cultured and sophisticated young lady. I said a quick interior prayer to Mary, and I found the way to disarm her. "I want you to pray with me before we talk," I said. We knelt together. After that we had no problem. We had a very friendly chat, and her subsequent evaluation for her newspaper was all I could ask for.

In the course of the conversation, I learned that her father owned *A.B.C.* "Tell him," I said, "that I want him to give me four pages of the paper to do justice to the Family

Rosary Crusade and to explain to the Spanish people what it can do for them." "I could never make such a request," she said. "He'd think I had gone stark crazy. *A.B.C.* is not a devotional paper. It's a regular newspaper for a sophisticated public." I cut her explanation short. "Just tell your father," I said, "that Our Lady will be very grateful if he does it." And we parted on that note.

It was a family custom for all the members of the Luca de Tena family to eat with their father once a week at his home. María Luisa was very silent during the meal the first time she was in Madrid after our conversation. She listened to the sparkling conversation about national and international affairs in which her brothers and sisters joined with her parents. The more she listened, the more incongruous the message I had given her sounded. But she felt committed. "When I was in Málaga," she finally blurted out to her father, "I met this Father Peyton who is preaching the Family Rosary Crusade all around the world, and he says you are to give him four pages in *A.B.C.* to present his story to Spain." As she had anticipated, her father began to laugh and the others joined in. "He told me to tell you," she added quietly, "that if you say yes, Our Lady will thank you." The laughter stopped. In a minute her father put his hand in his pocket, took out a visiting card, and wrote briefly on it. "Tell Father Peyton to give this to Luis Calvo, the editor, when he comes to Madrid."

If I didn't get four pages, I got enough space to make a dignified and adequate presentation, and the exposure in *A.B.C.* helped to prepare the way for Latin America, where the paper is universally known and widely respected. During a Crusade the following year, I stayed at a convent in Zalla near Bilbao. The Sisters there are known as the Irish Nuns because their foundations in Spain were originally made from Ireland and because many of the Sisters are Irish born. One of them, Sister Madeleine, had copies of the *A.B.C.* story about the Crusade reproduced and distributed to all the hundreds of bishops of Latin America.

When we got to Bilbao, María Luisa happened to be working there, and through her we met several of her companions. As a result of these contacts, we asked the Instituto in 1956 to lend us some of its members for the Crusades then being prepared for the five dioceses of Galicia. The first two assigned were Magdalena Rene Bach and Carolina Zubiria. The work in Galicia was extremely trying, and Carolina's health gave out in a short time, so that she had to be replaced by Begoña Díaz. Magdalena stuck with us through thick and thin. She now works in our regional office in Madrid. After Galicia, Begoña and she went to Ireland and England to learn English. Begoña also stayed with us for many years, and she played a big part in developing the formula for the *misión popular*, a technique for incorporating the Rosary films into the format of the Crusade, and in implementing the formula in Latin America. She was later called back to join the administration of the Instituto and is now a member of the general council in Salamanca, Spain.

Another of our longtime associates is Margarita de Lecea. When she was only twelve years old in her native Bilbao, Margarita read one day about a priest in Hollywood who was persuading the film stars to help him promote family prayer, and she was so delighted that she wrote him a letter of encouragement and congratulation. Little did she then think that she would years later be assigned by her superiors to work with him in the same apostolate. She first joined us in the Philippine Islands and later worked in Latin America and Spain.

Our relations with the Misioneras developed rapidly during the long process of production of the fifteen Rosary films in Spain. We finally decided to make them there for a combination of reasons. When the scripts for the first films had been prepared by our Hollywood staff, it quickly became apparent that my initial estimate of $20,000 per unit was way short of actual costs. The first revisions were up to $25,000, then to $30,000, amounts which reached astronomical proportions when multiplied by fifteen. Yet even at $30,000, we could not get the level of quality we needed.

That was the time when American producers were going to European studios for much of their work, in part because of lower wage structures, in part because they had blocked funds which they could spend abroad but could not transfer to the United States. Several companies with which we were dealing were in this category, and they pointed out that they could do much better for us in Europe than in Hollywood. Madrid was one of the places in which excellent studio facilities were available. Spain had the technical advantage for the producer that landscapes and physical conditions similar to those of the Holy Land are commonplace and that, particularly in the Andalusian southland, there is considerable Arab admixture of race from the long centuries of Arab domination of Spain. In consequence, it would be easy to find the extras and crowds with facial characteristics similar to those of Palestine. From our viewpoint, there was the added dimension that movies made in Spain by predominantly Spanish casts would provide more identification for the prospective viewers in Latin America than would films made in Hollywood.

While this tedious and often frustrating process continued, I was constantly on the move, not only from country to country but from continent to continent, in a path that seemed to have little logic or consistency but which gradually wove a pattern of Rosaries all over the globe and carried to more and more millions the message of family prayer. At an earlier stage, in 1951, I had paid a quick visit to Melbourne, Australia. One day, to my great surprise and delight, I had a telephone call from Archbishop Mannix's secretary, all the way from Melbourne to Albany, inviting me to visit Australia and be the guest of His Grace. Few names carried more magic when I was a boy back in Ireland. Mannix was a fearless and tireless exponent of the Irish cause during the years of our bitter struggle to win independence. I can remember many a time reading stories of his pronouncements from the daily paper for old people in the village who from lack of schooling or poor eyesight could not read for themselves. We had found the incisiveness of his satire irresistible. A typical comment was one he made to the press when put ashore in the south of England in 1919 or 1920 from a British submarine. He had been on a liner coming from Australia with the announced intention of landing in his native Ireland and expressing before Irish audiences his well-known views on their right to be free. The British government had decided they already had enough problems in Ireland, intercepted the liner on the high seas, and forced the archbishop to accompany them to England. "The greatest British naval victory since Jutland," he summed up the experience on landing. The details of the biggest sea engagement of the recently ended First World War were fresh in the memory, so that there was no need for him to recall the indecisive outcome of that clash.

More than thirty years later, the man who welcomed me and took me to his hearth and his heart was still the same Mannix. Though in his seventies, he was physically as sound as a bell, and my recollection is that it was his practice to walk several miles daily from his home to his office. He had an ascetic face, a commanding manner, a smile that one knew lingered inside even when his features were in repose, and an elfin sense of humor. His commitment to the cause of the family Rosary was total, as was his personal hospitality and warmth. I knew that here I had the key to unlock for me the entire continent, and I was not deceived.

It was not until two years later that we were in a position to execute the Australian program, but we were then able to do it in a thoroughly organized way, starting in Queensland, on to New South Wales, Victoria, Tasmania, South Australia, the Northern Territory, and Western Australia, a total of twenty-six dioceses. We had long since seen that this kind of planned progression permitted the most efficient utilization of the personnel, but it has seldom proved possible to develop in practice a whole region as methodically as we were able in Australia.

Many wonderful things happened in Australia during the months that followed my arrival there on August 15, 1953, feast of the Assumption. Father Woods and I made the first contacts in each diocese, starting in Brisbane where we were welcomed by a grand old Irishman who had been a bishop for fifty years but was still vigorous and in full command of his archdiocese, Archbishop James Duhig. Father

John Murphy followed us to supervise all the detailed organizing and the training of the hundreds of volunteers who
would visit every Catholic home to explain the meaning
of the family Rosary and ask each family to pledge to say
the Rosary daily. Then Father Woods and I would move
on to another diocese, and I would come back at an agreed
time for a central rally or a series of regional rallies in the
diocese depending on distances, transportation, and other
factors. We achieved a tempo that perhaps had never previously been reached. An entire continent set progressively
in motion, section by section, rallies at nighttime, or weekdays, or Sundays.

It was like a whirlwind. Yet I could never for a moment
forget the Rosary films and the good they would one day
accomplish. Wherever I went I talked about this dream,
looked for people to help make it a reality. Four communities of Sisters listened to me and each pledged to contribute
$20,000, the Good Shepherd nuns, the Sisters of Mercy,
the Brown Sisters of St. Joseph, and the Presentation Sisters. The Cardinal Archbishop of Sydney, Norman Thomas
Gilroy, added $20,000 to bring Australia's contribution to
$100,000.

Money, however, was not the only thing I needed for the
films. I was firmly convinced that two prices would have
to be paid: one price to men to obtain the ideas, the skills,
the product, and the labor that would go onto celluloid; the
other and bigger price to God to win His blessing and His
grace so that the spiritual fruits would follow our planting
and watering. And contributors to this spiritual price I also
found in abundance. I recall in particular an incident in
Tasmania. I had reached this remote part of the continent

with much emotion, for I felt I was treading on ground made holy by the sweat and exile tears of the many Irish patriots who had been shipped to the infamous penal colony of Van Diemen's Land, as it was formerly called. I was in the little town of Longford, and I was talking to a community of cloistered Carmelite nuns, so strict in their withdrawal from the world that the curtain hiding them was not drawn back even for the priest who addressed them. I told them about the films and begged for their prayers and sacrifices.

"Have no fear for their response," the mother superior said to me later. "What I will have to watch is that they don't kill themselves in their enthusiasm." She promised that she would write me in Melbourne, where I would be staying with Archbishop Mannix, to report what concrete action they would decide to take. The letter reached me there on December 7, 1953, and its contents filled me with joy. The Marian Year was scheduled to begin the next day, the feast of Mary's Immaculate Conception, and I was promised a daily recitation for the whole year of special prayers by the entire community. In addition, the mother superior had authorized each sister to choose a particular sacrifice, and one in particular I recall from the list of wonderful undertakings. "I will fast on bread and water for the success of your films for one day every week during the Marian Year," that great Sister's letter read. "We're in," I said to myself. "With that kind of support, nobody or nothing can stop us."

From Australia Father Woods went to Papua in New Guinea and held Crusades in the two vicariates apostolic just before Christmas 1953, then he and I went south to New Zealand's four dioceses in the first months of 1954. In South Island I had an extraordinary stroke of luck. I came across a priest, Father Francis Bennett, who combined a special knowledge of the Holy Land in Biblical times with an artistic sense. His bishop released him to work with our Hollywood team for more than a year, and he became our adviser on costumes and various other technical aspects of the production of the fifteen films.

We finished in New Zealand just about St. Patrick's Day and headed off immediately for St. Patrick's island, halfway round the globe. Some considerable time earlier, the bishops of the West of Ireland had issued me a joint invitation to come and preach Crusades in their dioceses. It was for me a moment of great pleasure, a moment also in which I got a new understanding of the infinitely more profound love, awareness, and concern for us that God and Mary have than we have ourselves. I looked back to my departure from Ireland as a penniless and uneducated emigrant a quarter of a century earlier. At that time, I thought of myself and the place and people I was leaving as poor and backward. I looked forward to the land of opportunity where I would make a fortune and return in triumph to delight my friends and impress those who had failed to recognize my true talents.

Now I was being invited back in triumph indeed, and I was and am human and need human encouragement to continue the incessant struggle which is my life. But it was a form of triumph so far more meaningful and satisfying than what I conceived or could conceive that it stirred in me a new understanding of how much God's mind exceeds ours and how infinitely God's love for us exceeds our love for ourselves. God was enabling me to triumph by allowing me to repay a small part of the debt that I now knew I owed, the debt of having been raised in a family and in a society which worshiped Him and which expressed that worship in devotion to His Mother and faithfulness to the recitation of the family Rosary. I was being allowed to come to these people, my people, to thank them for what they had done for me, to tell them what it had meant to me, to remind them that in our age it was important to continue the holy practice they had received from their forebears.

I have to tell an amusing incident about the Crusades in Ireland. When the invitation came from the Irish bishops, many other Crusades were lined up, in Spain, in the United States, in Australia and New Zealand. I knew that considerable time would have to elapse before I could fulfill the undertaking. At the same time, I wanted to firm up the understanding right away, because I had learned from bitter experience how quickly an opportunity slips away if it is not seized. It hangs on a silk thread, and you must grasp it before the thread snaps. So while the Cleveland Crusade was in progress in the middle of 1953, I found myself one day in New York. Conrad Hilton had invited me, as well as two planeloads of his friends, including movie and television personalities, writers, columnists, and publicity people, to attend the opening of the Hilton Hotel in Madrid. I was happy to go in order to cultivate still more the friendship and support Spain was beginning to give the Crusade. Many Spanish dioceses were interested in repeating the experience of Málaga by holding a Crusade. Father Woods came down from Albany to exchange some ideas with me in New York, as I was passing through. We were outside the hotel, waiting to board the buses, when an inspiration struck me. I went over to Mr. Hilton. "Conrad," I said, "is there any chance that you could smuggle my friend, Father Woods, aboard one of the planes as far as Madrid? From there, it will be a short hop for him to Shannon. If you do it, you will save Ireland." Conrad began to laugh. All I had in mind was that he would save the projected Crusades from falling through, but he knew nothing about that matter and thought it very funny that it should suddenly fall to him to save Ireland. He was so tickled that he smuggled Father Woods aboard, and we carried him off to Madrid with only the clothes he stood up in and a hair comb, a toothbrush, and a razor. But he saved Ireland!

The Irish Crusades were wonderful. Everywhere there was a welcome and a warmness. I was conscious of one curious barrier that I had to pierce. The Irish love and have always loved Americans. They never forget what the United States meant as a haven for them in their days of need, what a land of liberty it was when they lacked freedom. But they have a resistance to what is known as the "returned Yank," the person of Irish birth who goes back home with fine clothes, a synthetic accent, and a readiness to boast about his adventures and his exploits. Had I returned in the frame of mind in which I had left home, I would undoubtedly have fallen into this category. Instead, I was coming in humility, for I had at least learned that what I had to offer was not my own. Nevertheless, I had to be careful to avoid any appearance of arrogance, and I quickly found a way to achieve this and get right to the hearts of my listeners. "I am your neighbor from the bogs of County Mayo," I would tell them. "When I left for America, I brought one priceless treasure with me, the tradition of the family Rosary, which is Ireland's most abiding tradition. But it was only when I

went out into the world and found places where that tradition is unknown or weak, that I realized its full value, its
incalculable worth. That is all I have come here to tell you.
I come to plead with you to hold fast to that tradition and
pass it to your children, for your own sake, for their sake,
and for the sake of the example that we Irish give to the
world by our devotion to the Mother of God."

It was a tremendous satisfaction to be able to offer this
message to the good people of County Galway, where the
first Crusades were held, and later to the people of my own
townland and neighborhood and to see how they accepted and endorsed my poor words. All through Ireland, the
response was the same. In Roscommon the heavens opened
and the rain came down in torrents, yet not a single person thought of leaving until the rally ended. Generally,
the crowds were not as big as in other parts of the world.
Because of transport problems, several regional rallies were
held in each diocese. But nobody stayed away who could
come, and in the towns we had substantial numbers. The
gathering in Belfast was estimated at a hundred thousand.

In Ireland I continued to search for money for the Rosary films, and here again the good Sisters did not refuse me.
The amounts they could afford were usually small, though
substantial in relation to their resources. The joint contributions of the mother superiors of several orders provided the $30,000 needed to sponsor the film on Our Lady's
Assumption.

Our big project to follow Ireland was India, and I was
particularly happy about this, because it enabled me to
attend the Marian Congress organized by Valerian Cardinal Gracias of Bombay to coincide with the closing of the

Marian Year on December 8. On December 7, at the opening session of the Congress, I was approached by a nun who
identified herself as from Ireland. She said she was Mother
Fidelis, of the Sisters of Jesus and Mary, and that she was
in Bombay with her mother general from Rome, a Spanish
woman named Mother Rosario. She had looked for me,
she added, because Mother Rosario wanted to talk to me.
I went immediately to meet her, and I found ready communication and understanding between us from the first
moment. When I explained the plan I had for making the
Rosary films and told her that the Hollywood people were
now saying that they would cost $25,000, she did not bat
an eye. "I'll sponsor one," she said, "and I'm confident that
my Sisters will find ways to pay for it." So she sat down and
wrote to all her convents, urging them to do without dessert
on Saturdays as a concrete way to help save the money. I had
suggested the following September 8, Our Lady's birthday,
as an appropriate date for delivering the money, and we
parted with that understanding. Both of us, however, were
staying for some time in India, she to visit her convents in
that country, and I to preach the Crusade in thirty-three
Indian dioceses and in thirteen dioceses of Burma, Mala-
ya, Thailand, Ceylon, and Pakistan. So some time later I
met Mother Rosario in New Delhi. "I have bad news," I
said. "The latest calculation is that each film is going to cost
$30,000." She smiled. "It could be worse," she said, and from
the way she said it I knew I could count on her. And I was
right. Early the following September a letter reached the
Family Rosary Crusade offices in Albany with a request not
to open it until September 8. Inside was a check for $30,000
to pay for the film of the Annunciation.

Six months before that letter arrived, in mid-March, I had completed the first big operation in Asia, an experience wholly different from anything in my previous life. I was profoundly impressed by the mysticism of the people, by a concrete presence of holiness and a social respect for holy men, qualities observable not only in the Christian community but also among Muslims and Hindus and all the other non-Christians who form the vast majority of the inhabitants of that region. Even where the poverty and degradation are great, there is always this extraordinary counterweight of the spiritual, giving a dignity and meaning to otherwise wretched lives. It gave me deep satisfaction to mingle with such people and pray with them. But nowhere was I more moved than in Bengal, the place where I had planned and hoped to spend my life as a Holy Cross missionary. Providence had decided otherwise, yet I felt it was a mother's consideration on the part of Our Lady that had arranged for me to offer at least a token fulfillment of my youthful longing.

While I was in India and Pakistan, other members of my team were opening up the continent of Africa, and I set out for South Africa from Karachi about St. Patrick's Day, stopping briefly in Nairobi, Kenya, on the way, to meet Archbishop John J. McCarthy of Nairobi and three or four other Irishmen in charge of neighboring dioceses. From Nairobi, I went direct to Johannesburg, which was to be my headquarters for several months while we preached the Rosary Crusade in twenty-three dioceses of South Africa, Southwest Africa, and Basutoland. People of every race and condition attended the rallies, and it filled me with joy to be privileged to address the downtrodden black Africans and assure them that they and I had the same Mother in heaven who held each of us in equal esteem as a human being redeemed by the life of her own Son.

Those who have lived a long time in the tropics continually warn the newcomer that he must slow down. But it is hard for him to believe it, especially if he is in as great a hurry as I was. I refused to believe that I had to adjust. The heat and the humidity in India and Pakistan had been unpleasant, but I had never found them unbearable. Now, with my additional experience of several months in Africa, I felt I was fully acclimated and could scoff at the warnings. I was to be brought up with a sudden jolt.

I had returned to Nairobi to start a series of Crusades which would take us to twenty-four dioceses in Kenya, Tanganyika, and Uganda. Nairobi is very close to the equator, but it is at an elevation of five to six thousand feet, so that it cools off at night. It is a beautiful climate, but it does get extremely hot during the day, and that was the point I was overlooking. The big rally was held in the open under a blazing sun, yet I insisted on preaching without wearing a hat or other protection. It was a tremendous sight in the brilliant light, and I was so deeply moved to see people of all races joining together to praise God and honor His Mother, that I lost all thought of myself, and I was racing around afterward arranging photographs and greeting people and filling myself with the wonder of it all.

That same night I began to pay for it. An awful weakness descended on me, accompanied by an incredible depression of my spirit. It was quickly diagnosed as acute sunstroke. For two weeks I couldn't crawl out of bed. I didn't want to eat. I didn't want to drink. Some days I wasn't even able to open my mouth to swallow the Holy Eucharist. I felt sure I was finished, that I would never get on my feet and face a crowd again.

All that time Father Woods stayed constantly at my side, nursing me night and day, encouraging me, trying to get some spirit back into me. As the time came for our next commitment, in the diocese of Moshi at the foot of Kilimanjaro, he pleaded with me and fought me. "You have to come," he said, "or the whole image we have laboriously built up will be destroyed. Everything is planned, and the people are expecting you." So he forced me against my will to get out of bed and get on the plane, and once I arrived and got my heart back into the work, my energy was gradually restored. Our host, Bishop Joseph Byrne, played a big part in getting me out of my depression. "Look at me," he would say. "When I was a youngster back in County Tipperary, the Christian Brother who taught me geography asked me one day where is Kilimanjaro. I didn't know, so he gave me three or four whacks with his cane, and I said to myself: 'They can keep their Kilimanjaro.' But I was doubly wrong, because that is where I ended up, and I have to admit it is one of the most beautiful places in the world." And so it was, that majestic snow-capped peak towering above the African plain. With stories like that, the hearty laugh and lavish gestures pointing the moral, Bishop Byrne helped me put my troubles into perspective, so that I grew reconciled as I understood that even my dark clouds must have their silver linings.

Behind his jolly exterior Bishop Byrne was a very spiritual man. They made me rest as much as possible while I was in Moshi, so I had opportunity to listen to him in

serious mood as well as gay. He summed up his whole attitude toward life in three brief sentences. "Only God gives
grace," he would say. "Only God saves souls. Our only real
enemy is the devil." As I pondered them over, I realized
that they expressed perfectly my own view of life, especially
the first two. They gave me a clearer realization than ever
before that I was a simple instrument in the hands of God, a
human instrument, but nonetheless an instrument. It mat-
tered little what I did or didn't do, whether I got sunstroke
or fever or anything else. It was for me to be as obedient
as our little donkey back home, not to kick or bite, but to
accept the harness and the load, to go forward, to stop, to
turn left or right without questioning, always remembering
that the responsibility for saving or restoring family life
was not ultimately mine but the driver's. This thought also
helped greatly to restore my peace of mind.

Those were politically very troubled times in East Africa. The Mau Mau outbreak of violence and terrorism had
passed its peak, but large numbers of members and suspected members were in concentration camps. One big compound in the Kenya highlands held twenty thousand prisoners behind twenty-five-foot-high stockades. We decided
that these unfortunates were more entitled to our message
of encouragement than anyone else, and arrangements
were made for me to go and talk to them. When Father
Edward Colleton, Father Joseph Quinn, and I arrived in a
jeep, one could sense the tension. Sentries stood all around
at the alert, submachine guns cradled in their arms. The
men were assembled, with 1,800 of the maximum-security
prisoners off to one side dressed in distinctive orange-col-
ored shorts with T-shirts. Machine guns all around, most

of them directed at this group. I spoke to them in English, with a Protestant minister translating into Kikuyu, and I got a most edifying response. The prisoners were forbidden to break ranks, but I went around among them and shook hands with many of them after I finished my talk. I then invited all who wished to do so to join me in reciting the Rosary, and great numbers followed me to another location in the compound and sank reverently to their knees. We had hardly started, however, when sirens began to blare and the loud-speakers announced that four of the maximum-security prisoners had escaped. There was tremendous agitation for a considerable time, until the four men were found. They had slipped away from their group and followed me to a small chapel on the other side of the prison compound. They were on their knees praying.

That day's excitement was not yet over. By making a small detour on our way home, some of the guards told us, we could drive through one of the finest game preserves in the world. It was indeed a most impressive sight: herds of elephants, rhinoceroses, hippopotamuses, lions, zebra, wildebeests, monkeys, many varieties of gazelles, and a dozen other species. At one point we stopped to admire a small group of delicate giraffes silhouetted against the sky. It proved a mistake, for the jeep refused to start again. As the driver became alarmed, I had an idea. "Let's say the Joyful Mysteries of the Rosary," I suggested. When we had finished he tried again, and his second failure spread the alarm to the entire group. It was fine in a game preserve during the day, but how would we fare when the rapidly approaching night fell and the lions started out to forage for their families? "Don't give up yet," I said. "Let's try the

Sorrowful Mysteries." That did it. The motor started up, and we said the Glorious Mysteries in thanksgiving as we completed our journey without further incident.

From East Africa we carried the Crusade to nine dioceses in Rhodesia and Nyasaland (now Malawi), then completed our African tour with three vicariates in the Sudan, Khartoum, Bahr el Gebel, and Bahr el Ghazal. The Blue Nile coming down out of the mountains of Ethiopia joins the White Nile at Khartoum, and at sunset the scene is one of unspeakable beauty with the copper-colored sands of the desert imparting to the skies all the burning colors of the rainbow and the swirling waters blazing with the reflected radiance. I would stand by the banks and picture in my imagination a young woman with a pail to carry water balanced on her head, or a bundle of clothing to wash, approaching this very same river. Though humbly dressed, she radiated a dignity and glory, and the child whose hand she grasped was not only her son but the Son of God. For this was the same Nile beside which Jesus, Mary, and Joseph could have lived during their years of exile in Egypt.

Christians constitute only a tiny minority in the predominantly Muslim Sudan, and we were able to observe the start of the movement which has subsequently driven nearly all the Christian missionaries out of that country and brought death or exile to many of the members of the Christian community. Our activities were severely limited to avoid any suggestion of proselytism. Nevertheless, it was gratifying to find a response not only among Christians, but also on the part of Muslims. Islam gives a place of high honor to Our Blessed Mother, even though it recognizes her Son as merely a great prophet and not the only-begotten of

God. My experience both in the Sudan and in other Muslim regions in which I have worked convinces me that our common devotion to Mary is our most logical and promising starting point for an approach to the members of a religious body which through the centuries has proved extraordinarily resistant to the teachings of our faith.

Whenever I think of this first great contact with the continent of Africa, the sufferings and the consolations, I always recall with special pleasure the letter which Pope Pius XII addressed to me on November 2, 1955, soon after the African Crusades. His earlier letter of January 14, 1948, the letter I had agreed was worth a million dollars, had referred directly to the radio apostolate of "Family Theater" in the United States. The 1955 letter dwelt on the "encouraging spiritual results" that had flowed from the Family Rosary Crusade both in the United States and in distant lands.

> As the building depends for its soundness on the foundation, so does civil society on its primary and essential cell—the Family, which draws, in turn, from the illuminated norms of Christianity, not only its greatest strength but also its highest sanction and perfection. To the end, therefore, of re-inforcing the sacred unity of the domestic circle and of sanctifying the individual members through communal prayer and the fostering of a fervent love for the Blessed Mother of God, we have, on the occasion of the Marian Year, drawn upon the treasury of the Church to enrich with further indulgences the pious Catholic practice of the family recitation of the holy Rosary. Consoling indeed has been the response, throughout the Catholic world, to our appeal for the ever wider extension of this devotion, so particularly

adapted to serve as an antidote to the secularistic
spirit of the present day. We renew our words of
paternal encouragement to the Ordinaries who
are lending their zealous support to this most
praiseworthy effort, and in like manner to you,
beloved son, in your collaboration, when called
upon by the episcopal shepherds of the Flock
of Christ, to assist them in the conduct of the
Family Rosary Crusade. In pledge of abundant
celestial favors, we cordially impart to you our
apostolic blessing.

By the time this wonderful letter reached me and swept
away any lingering residues of the cruel depression I had
suffered in Nairobi, I was back in Kansas City, Missouri. The
initial program for Africa had been completed, and it was
now essential that I should keep close to important sources
of revenue in the United States in order to meet the staggering financial costs of production of the Rosary films. For
the next three years, while this enormous task was being
completed, I would confine the activities of the Crusade to
the United States, where I was begging for money, and to
Europe, where production, dubbing, and developing of the
films was concentrated. I made one brief trip to Canada in
1956 for a renewal Crusade at the birthplace of the movement, London, Ontario. And in 1957 I took a little time off
from my other activities for Crusades to the small Catholic
communities in three dioceses in Greece.

All the time I was in Africa I never had far from my
thoughts the project of the Rosary films. There was no question of raising any substantial amounts there, though I did
get generous contributions from the Good Shepherd nuns
and some others in South Africa. But those who had little

material treasure more than compensated by their spirit of sacrifice. I remember going to the superior of a convent in Nyasaland and asking her help. "We don't have enough money to live here," she said, "but I'll tell you what I'll do. I'll have the Sisters work during their recreation time every day for a year at embroidery and other African handicrafts. All the products will be sent to you in Europe or America to sell or raffle off, and whatever money you make will be our contribution to the films."

A short time later I said Mass in another convent not far away. "I'd like to eat breakfast with you," I said to the superior after Mass. She hesitated, and I tried to reassure her by saying all I needed was a cup of coffee. "I'm sorry," she said, "but we have no coffee." "Tea is all the same to me," I said. "We have no tea either." "No coffee or tea," I said. "What do you drink?" "Water," she said, "except on feast days, when we serve tea or coffee when we have any." "I'll eat with you anyway," I said. One of the Sisters ran over to the bishop's house, which was not far away, and got a loaf of bread for me. The Sisters ate a dish of boiled rice seasoned with goat meat. We all drank water. I found the experience edifying beyond description. If nuns who live in such poverty are willing to make additional sacrifices in order to help in the production of the Rosary films, then there will be no limit to the good those films will accomplish.

Father Lawyer was then in charge of the Hollywood office of "Family Theater," and he kept me constantly informed of the way things were progressing. He had got Joseph Breen Jr., son of the Joseph Breen who was for many years administrator of the motion picture code of morality, to become director of the Rosary films. Joe and Father

Lawyer had gone to Spain to cast the actors, and everything was going along fine with one important exception. They had tested five hundred professional and nonprofessional aspirants to the role of Our Blessed Mother, and not one measured up to their expectations. It was a real crisis, and we would not be ready to start production at the agreed time.

I was visiting a convent of Holy Cross Sisters in Aliwal North, South Africa, when the news reached me. This is not one of the congregations of Sisters associated with our Congregation of Holy Cross, but a Swiss group of the same name. Mother Pascalina, who was secretary to Pope Pius XII, is one of them. Their mother provincial, a warmhearted lady, had made me at home and assembled the entire community, the old and infirm, the healthy, the novices, and postulants. I told them of my preoccupation with the Madrid problem. "The girl exists somewhere whom Christ Himself would pick, if He were choosing the person to play the part of His Mother in these films," I told them, "and I count on your prayers and sacrifices to find that girl for us." After I finished, a nun in her fifties came to me in the yard outside and introduced herself as Sister Enda. "I am gravely ill," she said, "and I don't think I have long to live. I gladly offer my sufferings and my death for your intention."

When I find such faith and such generosity, I know Our Lady always responds. I was accordingly not surprised when I had another letter shortly afterward from Madrid to say the problem was solved. The same Sisters, popularly known as the Irish Nuns, with whom I had earlier stayed near Bilbao, have a convent in Madrid in which there was always a welcome and hospitality for my colleagues and myself. Father Lawyer said Mass and had breakfast here each morning. On one such visit he was talking about his problem, and a Spanish nun, who came from Murcia in the southeast of the country, said that she knew a girl there who looked exactly as she imagined Our Lady had looked when she was young. "As a child, she used to come frequently to our home to sew for my mother, and she had a face so beautiful that I always asked myself why God had given so much beauty to a little peasant girl who was surely destined to live out her life in that remote village." That was not her destiny at all. Father Lawyer sent for her. She had never acted, never been in a big city in her life. Mother Concepcíon, the superior at the convent, took charge of her, coached her, taught her to speak the English lines required by her part. And in a short time Dolores Cantabella was ready to go before the cameras. She was perfect for the part in every way. The most polished actors who have seen her performance agree that she yielded to none in the part of Mary in the Joyful Mysteries.

Fourteen of the fifteen scenarios were completed to everyone's satisfaction, but the writers back in Hollywood were still having endless trouble with the final one, the Crowning of Our Lady in Heaven. Several approaches had been tried, but none of them seemed to come off. I was staying close to Lake Victoria when Father Lawyer wrote to me about this complication. It is the third biggest lake in the world, and I find it hard to believe that any other is so beautiful. It lies astride the equator, bordering on Uganda, Kenya, and Tanganyika (now Tanzania), and it is the source of the White Nile which starts its course by cascading over great waterfalls at its northern end. I believe I must have been in Mwanza, the diocese of Bishop Joseph Blomjous, who later played a big part in mobilizing the thinking and in expressing the mission needs of the bishops of Africa during the Second Vatican Council.

As I was pondering on the problem of the script, I went for a walk by the lake and found a rocky place where I could sit and enjoy the great natural beauty surrounding me, the deep blues and vivid greens and reddish browns which dominate the landscape, and the tireless lapping of the water on the beaches. And while my eyes feasted on all this loveliness, there came to my mind with extraordinary vividness a very different scene. It was an idea based on some medieval legends which the novelist, Ted Bonnet, had once given me.

The setting, as I now reformulated it, was a bleak, cold, wintry day, the kind of day to which I had been accustomed in my youth in Ireland. There was a big field with a dilapidated cow barn at one end. Rain was pouring down in torrents, leaking through holes in the barn roof, dripping down on seven men squatting among the dirty straw and dung inside. The men were poorly dressed in a kind of sackcloth or denim, but their faces were those of honest and intelligent men with qualities of leadership. Among them, they represented the various occupations and professions. One was a farmer, one a storekeeper, one a knight, one a priest, and so on. The farmer, more outspoken than the others, was complaining of the misery in which they were living, and particularly of the discomfort of the endless rain. One, who was obviously their leader, reproved him. "We are princes," he said, "and our mother is a queen. We must be ready to sacrifice for her, be worthy of her; and if we understand this, we will cease to complain." So he ordered them to keep silent and meditate on the qualities of the queen who was their mother. They obeyed for a long time, but toward evening the farmer spoke up again. Then the leader recalled that he was Giovanni di Bernadone, known as Francis, and that he had rejected the rich clothes and wealth showered on him by his father, a merchant of Assisi, because he preferred to follow Christ and—like St. Paul— esteem as valuable what the world despised and value what the world rejected.

When the leader revealed himself as Francis, the audience was made to realize that the others were his companions and that he was engaged in developing his own spirit in them. They asked him what he wanted them to do, and he directed them to meditate further on their mother who was a queen. This they did for a time, but again the farmer became restless. "Tell me," said Francis, "what is the result of your meditation? How do you see your queen?" By this time it had become clear that he was referring to the Blessed Virgin Mary. The farmer began to describe a scene of great magnificence, a golden stairway leading into a vast hall, a sparkling crown, earrings, ornaments of solid gold. Francis indicated his dissatisfaction with the attempt and went to each in turn. They tried to outdo each other in the lavishness of their description, but the more they struggled, the less they pleased Francis. They were amazed and asked what was wrong.

"What is wrong," Francis replied, "is that you retain the same values you had before. You count wealth still in worldly terms, but what the world loves, God regards as rubbish."

"Tell us then how you see our queen," they demanded. "With pleasure," he replied. "I see our queen as going
before her judge to be judged like every one of her children." The priest was outraged. "That is scandalous," he
said. "There can be no judgment in the case of our queen,
who was without sin, who is free of every blemish." Francis
smiled as he replied: "Is it not better to get one's reward
by justice than gratuitously?" With that, the trial began,
Mary coming before the judge. The judge presented the first
accusation against her. When she was selected as Mother of the Redeemer and accepted that honor, he said, she
did not shut herself away from other people and keep far
from what might contaminate her, but on the contrary went
immediately out across the country on a visit to friends.
She admitted the charge and justified her action with one
brief sentence. "Elizabeth needed me." The judge approved
the answer, then went on to formulate a new charge. She
had started her Son on His public life before He was ready,
thus hastening His Passion and Death, by her action at the
wedding feast at Cana. Again her justification was brief. "I
was embarrassed for the young couple." Again the judge was
pleased, but not yet fully satisfied. This time his charge was
that even when Judas had betrayed Christ, she was sorry for
him and wanted to help him. To this she merely remarked:
"Poor Judas, if only he had listened." The judge ended the
hearing and announced his verdict. "I could not entrust
to you the distribution of justice," he said, "but I proclaim
you Queen of Mercy and entrust to you the distribution of
mercy." Then he led her to a window to show who were to
be the recipients of her mercy. Spread out in a valley was the
whole human race, the liars appealing to her as the model

of truth, the thieves greeting her as exemplar of honesty, the adulterers hailing her chastity, the sinners of every age and race, all who need mercy, all crying to her, as their queen, to exercise her prerogative of mercy.

I immediately sketched out this whole idea and rushed it off to Hollywood hoping that they would develop it into a script for the final decade of the Rosary, a script that would interpret the Queenship of Mary in terms more meaningful than any attempt to set her on a throne as one to be venerated from a distance. I'm sorry to say that the professionals turned thumbs down. The film they finally made left much to be desired. I think most viewers agree that it is less satisfying than the others. And I still hope that one day somebody will try to reinterpret the Queenship of Mary in a film along the lines of the idea that flashed into my mind by Lake Victoria.

Eleven

Rosary Films Create a New Dimension

All through the 1950s I was growing progressively more frustrated at my failure to bring the message of the family Rosary to Latin America. This continent was the most Catholic of all and the most devoted to Our Blessed Mother. Because of its extreme shortage of priests, it was also the one which most needed the consoling and faith-preserving message. As early as 1949 I made my first actual visit. I went to Buenos Aires at the invitation of a group of ladies who wanted me to take charge of a shrine of Our Lady of Fatima and set up Family Rosary Crusade headquarters there for all Latin America. The project didn't work out, and I'm glad it didn't. We were not then ready for the kind of problems we would meet when we finally entered the region. Besides, I think we would have been cramped by the commitments involved in promoting pilgrimages to one particular shrine.

I didn't then know it, but in that same year of 1949, I began to weave a web of personal relationships in Europe which were providentially to provide the key to open Latin America at a much later date and in circumstances that made success possible. The first of these was a Portuguese Jew who was then living in New England but who enjoyed influential contacts in his own country. José Bensaude listened to one of the "Family Theater" programs on the Mutual network. It was the special Mother's Day program in 1949, entitled *The World's Greatest Mother*. It starred Loretta Young, Anne Jamison, and Charles Boyer, and it told the story of the appearance of Our Blessed Mother to three little shepherd children at Fatima six times in 1917 to deliver a simple message: "Pray the Rosary always."

The story so impressed José Bensaude that he contacted a priest with whom he was friendly in New England and got the priest to write to "Family Theater," offering to send me on a trip to Fatima. I had never been on the continent of Europe. Some time earlier, Fulton Oursler had graciously offered to pay for a visit to Lourdes, which he was most anxious for me to see, but other commitments had prevented me from accepting. So it was now arranged that I would visit Fatima, Rome, and Lourdes on this trip.

José Bensaude not only paid the expenses but also alerted the Catholic Church authorities so that I was met at the Lisbon airport and taken to the home of Archbishop Manuel Largo do Mitelo. He welcomed me and himself accompanied me to Fatima, then made arrangements with a priest there to take me back to Lisbon the next day. My first experience at Fatima was disillusioning. Before leaving my hotel room to visit the shrine, I debated with myself whether to leave my wallet containing money and passport under the pillow or to carry it. I decided to carry it and keep a firm grip on my pocket. But the crowd was so dense and I was pushed so vigorously hither and thither that my thoughts were distracted from the wallet. I reached the sanctuary and sat to await my turn to say Mass, then put my hand in my pocket to find the wallet was gone. Later, when I reported the matter, the Portuguese government was embarrassed and refunded the money. My friends also arranged to get me a new passport, so the incident was less serious than it looked at first.

Apart from that, I was profoundly impressed by the visit and felt myself on hallowed soil while I prayed and said my Mass at the spot where Mary showed herself to the three unsophisticated children. I was enthralled by the spirit of prayer and sacrifice visible among the hosts of pilgrims, the women on their knees, the processions, the hymns, the visits to the shrine all day and far into the night. I felt enriched by the company of so many devout lovers of God and Mary.

I had another unpleasant experience on my way back to Lisbon. The priest assigned to drive me apparently had little understanding of the way of automobiles. Like many European drivers, he seemed to think he had a monopoly of the road and the duty to scare pedestrians out of his path. He drove along at a breakneck speed, sounding the horn constantly both in the country and while sweeping through the towns on our way. I had my heart in my mouth, and with good reason. Suddenly we saw in front of us a peasant driving a flock of sheep. Instead of slowing down, my driver speeded up wildly, and before I could even utter a prayer, man and sheep were scattered in all directions. I was sure the poor fellow was killed, and when we stopped the car and got out, I was relieved to find him struggling to his feet. They must come of tough stock in the Portuguese countryside, for neither the shepherd nor his sheep were seriously hurt, and they continued on their way as though nothing had happened. As for me, I thought what a horrible nightmare I would carry for the rest of my life, if we had killed the poor man, and all the way home I prayed the Rosary in thanksgiving to Our Lady of Fatima.

Rome was my next stop. The previous year, January 14, 1948, Pope Pius XII had written to "our dear son Patrick Peyton, priest of the Congregation of Holy Cross," expressing his pleasure at what the "Family Theater" was doing to ensure that the new homes which parents were building for their children and the family of nations were "modelled on the prayer, labor and sacrifice of the holy home of Nazareth." His Holiness had further assured me of his continued encouragement and prayerful support of this work, so that it was with a sense of extreme confidence combined with a deep-felt need to express my thanks in person that I approached the See of Peter for the first time.

My way had been prepared by a friend of long standing who was then, as he is still, procurator general in Rome of the Congregation of Holy Cross, Father Edward L. Heston. One of the closest of his many friends was the Pope's secretary, Mother Pascalina, and he took me first to meet her. She was already informed about the Family Rosary Crusade and assured me that I could count on her support for all my efforts. I am sure she spoke to the Pope and briefed him before my audience with him. Both his words and attitude expressed the deepest interest and lifted me up to the highest heaven. "The vicar of Christ has repeated his blessing of the cause of family prayer and of the family Rosary," I told myself as I left. His words continued to sing in my ears afterward in good times and in bad, always reminding me not to swerve or be deflected.

Mary Harris, the wife of the president of United States Lines, wrote several letters of introduction to important people in Rome. She also had three young ladies, American friends of hers who were visiting Rome, look after me. They showed me around the city, so that in addition to St. Peter's, I visited St. Mary Major, St. Paul's Outside the Walls, and the Redemptorist church which contains the original painting of Our Lady of Perpetual Help. But I must confess that the splendors of Rome left me rather cold, even the religious splendors. Places generally move me little. I am interested mostly in people. I will make an exception for a few places I visited in the Holy Land, the Church of the Crucifixion where I said Mass, Bethlehem, and the place where tradition says Mary was born. I will also make an exception for Lourdes, where I always get riches of faith, love, and companionship, so that I can hardly bear to tear myself away from the grotto. But generally my pleasure in travel is in meeting new people and getting new ideas from them. And in that respect my first trip to Rome was rich, for I was privileged to make friends among the people in the high echelons of the administration of the Church. Probably the most decisive one in relation to my determination to reach Latin America one day with the Crusade was Count Enrico Galeazzi, governor of Vatican City. But it was not until years later that his importance on this score would emerge.

How that came about was as follows. I was back and forward to Madrid from the United States and the other places in which Crusades were being held from the start of production of the films in 1955 until their delivery in 1957. Among the many people whom I came to know in that time was Father Xavier Echenique, secretary to the Spanish national director of the Society for the Propagation of the Faith. He is a very brilliant man, a great intellectual, and well known throughout Spain, and he has done much to promote the Family Rosary Crusade in Spain and world-wide. One day in 1957 he happened to talk to me about the significance of the decision made some time previously by the Vatican to participate in the Brussels World's Fair scheduled to open the following year. "It will create a mag-nificent public-relations image for the Church all over the world and especially in the most advanced countries of Europe," he said.

The comment set me to thinking that this would be the ideal place and occasion to present the Rosary films to an international public for the first time. We had really done a magnificent job, fifteen half-hour programs in Eastman Color for projection on a panoramic screen, with top-lev-el producers, script writers, and musicians. Our special-ists included not only Joe Breen Jr. but his distinguished father, and such men as Sam Taylor, Tom Blackburn, James O'Hanlon, R. H. O'Sullivan, Eugene Ling, J. Kelley, and Adele Comandini. Fathers W. Robinson, C.S.C., Bennett, and Echenique were responsible for the Biblical side and theological control. All the major roles, with the one excep-tion of Our Blessed Mother as a girl, were acted by Spain's leading professionals, and Dolores Cantabella, our great find from a village in Murcia, had proved as professional as the best. Maruchi Fresno played Our Lady in the Sorrowful and Glorious Mysteries. Antonio Vilar doubled in the parts of Pilate and St. Peter. Virgilio Teixeira was St. John. The top-rank actors numbered at least thirty, with 120 other actors for secondary roles and many hundreds of extras for the crowd scenes. After much discussion and many differences of opinion, we had hit on a reverent and extremely satisfactory way of dealing with the central figure of Jesus. The camera was always located in such a way as not to show his face on the screen, only his back, or the back of his head with just a little of the side face. The effect of this, coupled with the total impact of the professional production, left me no doubt about the ability of these films to win the acclaim of the kind of audiences one could expect at the World's Fair.

Without wasting any time, I took a plane to Rome and went to see Count Galeazzi. Thanks to our now long-standing friendship, I had no difficulty in winning his approval. He immediately wrote me a letter of introduction to Paul Heymans, a former minister of finance of Belgium who had been named the Vatican's commissioner general in Brussels and charged with the creation of the Vatican Pavilion at the World's Fair. It was already August 1957, with only eight months left to opening day, and I knew that plans were far advanced. I accordingly set out immediately for Brussels with my letter and an album of color stills from the movies. Mr. Heymans was hesitant. The time was short, and plans were already fully developed and in large part executed. He had never heard of the Family Rosary Crusade or "Family Theater," and he asked himself if the kind of films he suspected a priest would make would fit into the twentieth-century concept of the Vatican Pavilion as he had planned it.

Fortunately, the priest who had been named as ecclesiastical adviser for the Pavilion knew me. He was a Father Jan Joos, a member of the Immaculate Heart of Mary Mission Society, commonly known as the Scheut Fathers because they were founded at Scheut, Belgium. A former missionary in China, Father Joos had long been active in the apostolate of the mass media, and he had once visited the Hollywood headquarters of "Family Theater" and been present at one of our network broadcasts. Father Joos quickly persuaded Mr. Heymans that this was a serious proposition. That, combined with Count Galeazzi's letter, won me a lunch appointment and the opportunity to present my proposal in detail to Mr. Heymans and his assistant, Count de Monceau de Bergendal, with Father Joos also present.

That was all I needed. I gave them a full description of what we had done, stressing the seriousness and professional quality of the films. This, I told them, was a true life of Jesus, a reconstruction according to the best historical knowledge of the atmosphere and facts of the central event of Christianity nineteen hundred years earlier, eliminating imaginary or fictitious elements. The production in Spain had already taken a year and a half since started in April 1956, and it would not be completed until December. Altogether, forty thousand feet of color negative and more than a hundred thousand feet of sound track would then have been shot. Forty reconstructions had already been made, including such elaborate buildings as Pilate's palace and the Temple of Jerusalem. The total cost had risen from my original guess of $20,000 per film to more than $66,000, or a million dollars for the entire fifteen. This, however, included such additional costs as that of making versions in several languages. Although the actors were Spanish speaking, the original was in English. To ensure perfect synchronization of the lips, they had all learned to speak their words in English. Hollywood professional speakers then made sound tracks to fit their speech. Afterward, the sound was to be dubbed for Spanish, Portuguese, French, German, and other languages.

Mr. Heymans was more than persuaded. He became full of enthusiasm, and he instructed the architects to figure out what could be done. Their report was that the building as planned did not have a suitable room for projection, and construction was too far advanced to permit alteration of the structures. One thing, however, was possible, and that was to excavate and provide a cinema at a lower level, but as an integral part of the Vatican Pavilion, at a cost of $30,000. They did not have that kind of money left in their budget. If I wished to proceed, I would have to find it.

I made my decision on the spot. It was a unique opportunity. "I'll provide the money," I promised them, "and I'll have my team and the films here in time for the opening of the Pavilion." I kept my word. When I explained my need to Harry John, he supplied the $30,000 without a moment's hesitation. I assembled my team in Spain to plan our participation. Father Peter F. Mueller, a colleague of Holy Cross, had recently come from the United States, primarily to recruit members for the Congregation but also to help in the Crusade. He and Father Lawyer got together with Begoña Díaz and two other Misioneras to prepare leaflets and other informational materials both about the films and about the work of "Family Theater" and the Family Rosary Crusade. This was translated into several languages. They also got supplies of rosary beads both for exhibition and for sale in the vestibule. In due course they transferred to Brussels and set up the equipment, so that all was on hand for the world premiere, May 1, 1958. The Vatican Pavilion had opened a few weeks earlier, but all of the elements we wanted for our three-hundred-seat theater had not been completed, and besides I was happy to delay the official unveiling of our million-dollar effort in honor of Our Lady until the first day of the month dedicated to her.

Success was not long in coming. Each show lasted an hour and consisted of two films. To prevent performances from being disturbed by the continual coming and going of casual passersby, an entry charge was established, although the contrary was the practice both in the rest of the Vatican Pavilion and in the other exhibits. Nevertheless, it was a common sight to see lines of people waiting their turn patiently. The first audiences consisted largely of women and children, but as news about the quality of the films got around, men began to predominate. In the five months that the showings continued, 250,000 persons saw two or more of the films.

My interest, of course, was not in the spectacle but in the impact. And while that was usually hidden in the soul of the viewer to be revealed only to God, enough evidence came to light to satisfy me that all the effort had been worthwhile. Priests were constantly at hand in another part of the Pavilion to hear confessions, and I heard many authenticated stories of Catholics who had long neglected their duties going from cinema to the confessional. Visitors who were not Catholics were equally impressed. "This is the right way to present the beauties of our Christian faith," one Anglican minister commented. "It is performances of this kind that bring us nearer each other. Continue with your fine work." An American marine, nominally a Protestant but one with little instruction in his religion, said he had never learned so much in so short a time.

Auxiliary Bishop Leo Josef (later Cardinal) Suenens of Brussels was one of the many bishops who saw the films and were conquered. He was then relatively unknown outside his own country but destined later to acquire world fame for his theological and pastoral leadership at the Vatican Council. Veronica O'Brien, envoy of the Legion of Mary in Europe and the Near East, had advised me to be on the lookout for him, and I made his acquaintance one day early in the Fair, when he came to visit the Vatican Pavilion. He was enthusiastic about the films, and the Assumption film made a particularly deep impression. Years later, when he received an honorary doctorate from the University of Notre Dame, he recalled the scene where St. Peter knelt by the bedside of Mary as she was dying and asked her to tell the Lord that he loved Him. "He knows already," Mary said. "Yes," replied Peter, "but it's better when it comes through your lips."

Bishop Suenens liked the films, but he did not give me an automatic endorsement. He invited me to his home, and there he put me through a grilling which reminded me of the experience I had in 1945 at the Maryland vacation house of the Holy Cross seminarians when Paul Bailey insisted on a reasoned argument for family prayer rather than individual prayer. Bishop Suenens had obviously heard different versions of my activities, and he wanted to determine for himself if he was dealing with a fanatic or a crazy man. Under his cross-examination I formulated for the first time the distinction between the will of Our Lady and her personal honor. As far as the Family Rosary Crusade is concerned, I said, the personal honor, recognition, and advancement of Our Blessed Mother are secondary. What is primary is the execution of her will, which is to get men to recognize her Son and to draw close to Him. When I said this, I was thinking of the emphatic affirmation by Father John Maloney of London, Ontario, that Our Lady did not keep for herself those who loved her, but that she led them to her Son. So while I confessed to Bishop Suenens my own deep and unshakable love for Mary as a living mother, I assured him that my labors and sacrifices were to advance her holy will regarding the family and its worship of her Son.

The bishop was completely satisfied, and from that time he has been an enthusiastic supporter of the Crusade and a sincere and loving friend. He wanted to arrange a Crusade in Brussels right away, but his archbishop, Cardinal van Roey, was not willing to underwrite the substantial cost that would have been involved in organizing a diocese of more than two million inhabitants, almost all of them Catholics. Bishop Suenens was disappointed, but he did the next best thing. He introduced me to his colleague and friend, Bishop Emile Josef de Smedt of Bruges, another who would acquire a world reputation for his leadership during the Council. Bruges is also a very big diocese, more than a million Catholics, but when Bishop de Smedt saw the films and heard Bishop Suenens's evaluation of the Crusade, he did not hesitate. We put a team to work as soon as possible, and a Crusade was held during April, May, and June 1959. It proved an overwhelming success in this sophisticated and highly industrialized region.

A significant part of the credit must go to a Belgian nun, Sister Marie Eymard, who was our interpreter both at the meetings of the priests and their lay helpers during the preparatory stages, and at the rallies. In those pre-Council days there was some resistance to having a woman interpret for a priest when preaching a sermon or even giving a talk. One priest in fact insisted on substituting two men as interpreters at a meeting of pastors, but they failed completely and he had to accept her. Sister Marie was not only an excellent interpreter. She was a woman of profound culture. She worked as an inspector in the Catholic school system, and she was trained in pedagogy. She knew that one of our main purposes in making the films was to utilize them as Crusade aids. She accordingly made an analysis of the films and prepared a manual for teachers to enable them to build an integral course of religious instruction around them in the schools. We were subsequently able to utilize much of her work in the manuals we made for the lay leaders when we built the films into the *misión popular*, the mission for the masses, which we were shortly to incorporate into the basic program of the Family Rosary Crusade.

Bishop de Smedt made what was probably the most profound analysis to date of the impact of the Crusade on a diocese. It is recorded in a *monitum ad clerum*, a recommendation to the clergy of his diocese dated July 20, 1959. This five-thousand-word letter opened with thanks and congratulations to the parish clergy, nearly all of whom had put into action with docility and generosity the campaign plan presented by the Crusade team. He then quoted some statistics. Most parishes had found without difficulty the two laymen needed to visit each ten families even in some towns where difficulties had been anticipated, so that a total of 35,000 visitors had been recruited and families representing 800,000 of the diocese's 1,050,000 inhabitants had pledged to join each day in family prayer.

At the beginning and in the course of the Crusade, the bishop continued, it was evident that, on human evaluation, there was no prospect of success, because the influence of materialism had caused family prayer to disappear in large part, so that most families were totally indifferent or even opposed to it.

> The facts having contradicted notoriously these well-founded human considerations, it is evident that we may recognize here an extraordinary intervention of divine grace. It is manifest that the Holy Spirit, by the intercession of the Mother of God, has poured upon the members of Christ's Mystical Body special graces of light and strength. During the five weeks of the campaign, He has admirably intensified Christian life in our diocese, so that we hear it said continually: "The Rosary action is the most beautiful and precious grace our diocese ever received."

Bishop de Smedt attributed this result in the first place to the faith with which the diocese had prayed for the success of the Crusade. Most of the priests had made a daily hour of adoration before the Blessed Sacrament, many of them in common, "and very soon the fervent parishioners, struck by the example of their priests, came spontaneously to kneel down and pray with them." Each parish had offered a Mass every day for the Crusade's success. The priests had visited the sick and won pledges from them to offer their suffering for the same object. The school children had been enlisted and had co-operated enthusiastically. In a word, "there was a general mobilization of all spiritual forces of the diocese."

The next point singled out was the recruitment of the laity and especially of the men, and the willingness of the priests to entrust to them the responsibility to which they are entitled but often denied in the Church. The Holy Spirit, he said, had crushed "with a sledgehammer blow" the widespread prejudice that it is impossible to find men willing to co-operate and capable of co-operating in a purely religious apostolate. "Father Peyton was right when he drew attention to the important role the man has to fulfill in the family and in the neighborhood. To carry on religious propaganda is primarily a matter for men. One must avoid considering prayer and religion as something for women and children."

The third point singled out by Bishop de Smedt was the mobilization of public opinion by articles in the daily and weekly newspapers, by radio and television, by the showing of the Rosary films, by sermons on the Rosary in every church on five consecutive Sundays. All of this, he said, gave the Crusade a social dimension.

> Christian life is not solely a personal and intimate contact with Christ. The Christian is placed by the Lord in an ecclesiastical community, that he may be sustained by his brothers in his spiritual uplifting; thence the apostolic importance of the

climate in which the Christian lives. The apostolate must see to it that the Christian never has the impression of being isolated, but that on the contrary he lives his religion in communion with his brothers. Father Peyton made us understand the importance of external factors. He made such good use of them that at the end of the Crusade there was not a single family in the diocese which was not aware of what was going on.

Bishop de Smedt put the rally in perfect perspective as an element in the formation of a proper public opinion.

It is not without reason that Father Peyton attaches so much importance to the rallies. He seeks to put in action the psychology of the masses for the benefit of the cause that he defends. Everyone has been able to see clearly that there was no question of excitement or demogogy. Father Peyton was always on the watch in order to keep the rallies in a very serene and deep religious atmosphere. It was touching to see how very humbly he put the influence radiating from his person in the service of Jesus and Mary, never giving the least importance to his own person.

The bishop next turned to the most important and most debated aspect of the Crusade, the depth and permanence of its impact on the diocese. Among the devout members of the community, he said, the results were evident: a new enthusiasm, few homes without a crucifix, a well-rooted devotion to Mary being given a concrete expression in the daily recitation of the Rosary. But even among the many Catholics who did not practice their religion regularly, he insisted, a new positive factor had been introduced. Many were flattered by the fact that they had been visited, and even "some notorious non-practitioners" were hurt because they were passed over. The fact that most non-practitioners who were approached signed the pledge showed that they still had the faith. Even if many of them did not live up to their promise, an opening had at least been effected, a situation created in which men and women of every parish could profitably undertake the apostolate of the neighborhood. "The hour of grace has struck. The parochial clergy has the serious duty to profit by this moment of 'the Lord's passage' to build up systematically the apostolate of the neighborhood."

In the final section of his letter, Bishop de Smedt elaborated on the need for continuing machinery in the diocese to ensure the perpetuation of the fruits wrought by the Crusade. This was a joint task, he suggested, for the priests and for the existing organizations of the faithful. Priests should remind people of their commitment, in the confessional, in the pulpit, and in their visits to the homes of their parishioners. "A very favorable opportunity is the pre-nuptial interrogation of the betrothed; in that moment they are generally well-disposed to take the resolution to pray together, so that they may remain truly united in conjugal love. Would it not be fruitful to suggest that they sign the family pledge in the course of the first month of their marriage, and then go together to deposit it at the feet of Our Lady?"

Additional concrete proposals were that a layman should lead the recital of a decade of the Rosary at all meetings of Catholic organizations, that a family Rosary poster be prepared each year to announce October as the month of the Rosary, and that the weekly religious broadcast be

used regularly to promote family prayer and recite part of
the Rosary.

> It is obvious that in our diocese the parochial
> apostolate, Catholic Action, and the social works
> have not scattered their seed in vain. The laymen
> willing to help us are numerous and adequately
> trained. All the people of the diocese are open to
> the voice of religion. We assert without hesita-
> tion that, with some years of effort, it is possible
> to convert those who have strayed and to place
> the religious life of the diocese on a remarkably
> sound basis. If this prospect is not realized, it will
> be because of a lack of faith and courage on the
> part of the priests.

I have quoted at length from this document because of
the great help it gave me in evaluating the strengths and
weaknesses of the Crusade. The whole approach had started
by what I can only call the providential accident of meeting Father John Maloney back in 1947 and the resultant
invitation to make a concerted onslaught on the diocese
of London, Ontario. From that time, we had pragmatically
added one feature after another. In the mission territories
of Asia and Africa, where many were illiterate and had only
infrequent contact with priests because of great distances,
we had come to see how valuable visual aids would be for
getting our story across. Now we had superb visual aids
in the Rosary films, and Sister Marie Eymard had shown
us ways to incorporate them into our existing structures.
Bishop de Smedt's letter clarified further the respective part
to be played by priests and people. It also put the finger on
what we already knew was a missing element, the structures
needed to ensure the permanence of the benefits brought

to a diocese by the Crusade. We knew that element was missing, but we also knew that we did not have and were unlikely ever to have the facilities to take care of it. Bishop de Smedt clarified that such was not our function. If we planted the seed, it was up to the diocese to water and ultimately harvest.

The point has become more critical as we have become deeply involved in areas in which the dioceses seldom have the organization to continue the work after we leave. But the principle enunciated by Bishop de Smedt continues to be valid. Our current efforts are not to assume responsibility for post-Crusade activities but to provide the men and means required by each diocese to organize and train its own resources within the framework of its overall pastoral program. And whenever a bishop or a diocesan director of Catholic Action questions the value of such an effort, I find that Bishop de Smedt's letter quickly sets him straight.

While the World's Fair was in operation, I tried to spend as much of my time in Brussels as possible. The Vatican Pavilion naturally acted as a magnet to bring church leaders from many parts of the world, and many archbishops and bishops presented in person their requests to have the Family Rosary Crusade come to their dioceses. Nevertheless, I tried to keep a team constantly busy, and it so happened that our major center of Crusade operations that year was in the northwestern United States, so that I had to commute frequently across the Atlantic to address rallies in thirteen dioceses. Our field teams had by this time acquired considerable expertise in servicing the newspapers and other publicity media in order to get the maximum publicity benefit. The media, for their part, were quick to recognize news when it was shown to them. The *Minneapolis Star*, for example, broke pioneer ground in photo journalism in October 1958. The day after the rally, it ran a 140-degree sweep photograph in full color across sixteen columns, the entire top of the front and back pages of the paper, just under the masthead. The caption noted that the crowd, estimated at 224,000, was the biggest gathering of people in the entire history of the Upper Midwest. The one depressing element on that joyous occasion was the news from Rome. Pope Pius XII was in his agony. He died four days later.

The World's Fair brought another invitation, the effects of which still continue. Archbishop Rufino J. (later Cardinal) Santos of Manila, whom I had first met some years earlier, asked for a Crusade. I told him he could count on us immediately after Bruges. Father Quinn was the first to arrive in Manila in August 1959, and he was shortly joined by two Misioneras, Tere Aguinaco and Margarita de Lecea from Spain, and an Irish girl, Terry Fellowes of Dublin, who worked with us for several years. Things were humming when I followed them in mid-October, and after a successful press conference, we got a practically 100 percent attendance of pastors, each with two lay helpers, at the planning meetings. The pastors agreed to a daily Holy Hour for the forty days of the Crusade, from November 1 to December 10, to preach on five consecutive Sundays on the Rosary, to visit the sick and obtain pledges from them to offer their sufferings for the success of the project, to build an army of one hundred thousand door-to-door visitors to call on every family in a diocese of 2.5 million, and to organize four rallies, with a target of a million people for the main Manila rally. Father Bienvenido López was chosen by the archbishop to represent him. He is now auxiliary bishop of Manila and head of the Family Rosary Crusade office in that city.

We won extraordinary co-operation on the part of the press, radio, motion picture theaters, schools, and churches. Vans patrolled the city with loud-speakers. Posters placarded the best locations. An airplane with "Rosary Rally" in easily legible neon lights on its wings droned overhead. The day after the big rally, I wrote a report to my colleagues. "The Manila rally is over," I told them, "and I feel that the Family Rosary Crusade in yesterday's rally has reached the highest peak, that never again in any country in the world will it be duplicated, not only from the number of people attending, but from the thousand handicaps that they surmounted in order to let their bodies and souls cry out to heaven and earth their response to Our Blessed Mother's holy will regarding all that is implied in the sentence: 'The family that prays together, stays together.'"

Up to the very last moment, the holding of the rally was in doubt. The several preceding days were filled with rain and oppressive heat, and shortly after three o'clock on the Sunday afternoon of the rally, with a quarter of a million persons already assembled, the heavens opened in a torrential downpour such as occurs only in the tropics. Father Quinn came to me and said we would have to cancel. With extreme reluctance I agreed, and I went to a telephone to notify Cardinal Santos. When I reached his residence, however, I was informed that the cardinal was on his way. Father Bienvenido López, the cardinal's liaison with the Crusade team, went to the loud-speaker and began to recite the Rosary. The crowd standing in the torrential rain responded, the sound swelling as more and more joined the original throng. By four-thirty, when the ceremony was scheduled to begin, the sun was shining. Pressed shoulder to shoulder throughout the vast expanse of Luneta Park, the crowd extended right down to the shores of Manila Bay, with Bataan and the island of Corregidor forming an emotion-laden backdrop offshore. The numbers were greater than for the Marian Congress of 1954 or the Eucharistic Congress of 1957, more even than for the inauguration of President Ramón Magsaysay, who had assembled the biggest crowd to that time. The estimate put it at a million and a half. But what moved me more than the numbers was the devotion which persuaded them to stand for several hours in mud and water. It was a demonstration of faith one had to see to believe.

Other archbishops and bishops of the Philippines understandably wanted to repeat the experience of Manila, and we promised to come back as soon as possible, a promise that was fulfilled in 1962. But something even more important was arranged on the spot. Cardinal Santos decided on the feast of the Immaculate Conception to set up a permanent office of the Family Rosary Crusade in the Pope Pius XII building in Manila and to name Father López as its full-time director. It was an expression both of his appreciation of what the Crusade had done for his diocese and of the extent to which he agreed with Bishop de Smedt on the importance of an organization to maintain the dynamic thrust afterward. The agreement provided that this office would be a subsidiary of the worldwide Family Rosary Crusade and that it would promote the movement throughout the whole of the Far East.

After his consecration as auxiliary bishop of Manila in January 1967, Bishop Bienvenido López continued to head the Manila office. This office has responsibility for arranging Crusades in the Philippines and other parts of the Far East. It distributes the "Family Theater" films in theaters and nontheatrical outlets. It promotes family prayer on radio and television, an activity that will be intensified with the completion of Radio Veritas, a powerful system of radio transmitters which Cardinal Santos is creating to blanket the entire region. And it has been responsible, as I shall describe in a later chapter, for adding a new and important dimension to the popular mission.

Before the Crusade had started in the Philippine Islands, the final pieces had fallen into place for our long-anticipated move into Latin America. I was in fact in Santiago, Chile, when Father Quinn notified me in October 1959 that they were waiting for me in Manila. At Brussels, during the World's Fair, the deciding event had taken place. Peter Grace had arrived one day, on his way back to the United States from an economic conference in Germany with the Rockefellers and other international businessmen and financiers on the recovery of postwar Europe. "My schedule is absolutely impossible," he said to me. "I have only five minutes to see a snatch of one of the films." It must have been a Friday, because that was the day we showed the Crucifixion, and he saw the part where the centurion allows Our Lady to come forward from the crowd and stand under the cross. It immediately moved him to tears. Afterward he explained his emotion. "I had an idea," he said, "that I was reasonably well instructed in my faith. And I suppose

I was, at the intellectual level. But what I never understood before was how Our Lady had suffered for me on Calvary."

He immediately reshuffled his program and spent three hours in the theater the following day, so that he could get a proper idea of the total impact of the group of films. When he came out, he summed up his reaction. "You must saturate Latin America with these films," he said. "You have here the answer to the shortage of priests and catechists." They were, of course, the words I wanted to hear, and I never let him rest until we had worked out the concrete implementation. We decided to start in Chile, where Father Mark McGrath, the Holy Cross colleague from Panama who had earlier been my interpreter and helper in Spain, was on the staff of St. George's College. I flew down to Chile and received a hospitable welcome and a quick approval from Auxiliary Bishop Emilio Tagle Covarrubias, who was in temporary charge of the archdiocese in Santiago until a successor to the recently deceased Cardinal Archbishop José María Caro Rodríguez would be named. It was agreed that we would create a base in Santiago from which we would cover the country's twenty-three dioceses.

Meanwhile Begoña Díaz and some of her colleagues in the Misioneras took the instructional manual on the use of the films prepared by Sister Marie Eymard in Belgium and adapted it to Latin American conditions so as to integrate the films fully into the Crusade by devising what soon became known as the *misión popular* (popular mission). What emerged was a new structure that comes into play early in a Crusade. The diocese is divided into sectors, in each of which in turn the fifteen Rosary films are exhibited for the entire population, thereby ensuring that as a preliminary to the Crusade, the entire diocese has a basic course of instruction in Christian doctrine.

The films are not shown in commercial cinemas, since that would restrict attendance to those able and willing to pay. Neither are they shown primarily in parish cinemas or schools, because that would discourage those who were not regular churchgoers. Instead we choose stadiums, market-places, or big public squares, picking locations in shanty-towns and slums as well as in the middle-class districts. The entire operation is placed in the hands of local volunteers in each area, classes being given by members of the Crusade team and others trained by them. The classes are of two kinds, one for the technicians who erect the screens and operate the projectors, the other for the speakers who give a simple commentary at the end of each Mystery. The speak-ers are provided with ideas to develop, but the expression is in their own words and in a context meaningful to their neighbors. To parallel the teams of men who will later go from door to door to collect pledges, teams of women are enlisted to promote knowledge among their neighbors of the upcoming film showings, and they similarly make blan-ket house-to-house visitations. This is particularly useful in poor neighborhoods into which the normal media of mass communications do not always penetrate fully.

Such is the popular mission as it gradually evolved and as it is operated today. Two films are shown each evening for a week, starting with the first Joyful Mystery and going through the entire fifteen. On the last evening, as only one film remains, the ceremony is concluded by a Mass, the recitation of the Rosary, or a procession to a sanctuary of Our Lady. The films are also shown in hospitals, barracks, and prisons. The result is that everyone in the diocese is exposed, many for the first time in their lives, to a quick course of Christian doctrine. Within the framework of the Rosary and of devotion to Mary, they get an understanding of the meaning of Christ's life and the purpose of His Death and Resurrection. If the impact was striking on the sophisticated audiences who saw the films at the Brussels World's Fair and in Bruges, it is ten times greater with the simple people of Latin America for whom the magic screen is still a miracle that seldom enters their lives.

To get this operation on the road involved an immense monetary outlay. The first trial in Chile required the use of between forty and fifty projectors and screens and an even bigger number of copies of the film dubbed in Spanish, as well as four jeeps to move the equipment from place to place. Many people helped, especially Cardinal Cushing of Boston, Peter Grace, Ignatius O'Shaughnessy of St. Paul, Harry John of Milwaukee, Eleanor O'Brien of Chicago, James and Mary McArdle of Pittsburgh, and Father Cecil Nally, O.F.M. Cap., head of the Seraphic Mass Association. James F. McCloud, president of the Kaiser operations in Argentina, was instrumental in getting us three jeeps built in that country. If Conrad Hilton can claim to have saved Ireland, then I think these generous friends deserve a like honor for having saved Latin America.

Twelve

I Finally Reach Latin America

Chile was probably the best country in Latin America in which to begin the Family Rosary Crusade. Although a great part of the population lives in ignorance and poverty unlike anything we know in the United States, the cultural standards and the level of religious practice are better than in many of the other Latin American countries in which we have subsequently worked. The proportion of priests, while distressingly low, is high for that part of the world, one for each three thousand Catholics, as compared with an average of one for close to six thousand for the entire region. In consequence, the change from the conditions to which we were accustomed was less abrupt than if we had started in a country like Bolivia or Guatemala.

One of the things that we did learn quickly was how vast are the distances involved in relation to the population. Latin America is about two and a half times the size of the continental United States, and in 1960 it had about the same population. Because the rate of population increase is the world's highest, its population today is significantly greater than ours. Although a big and growing proportion is concentrated in and around great cities, about half is still scattered in the countryside. Communications with remote villages are so poor that many of them see a priest only once a year. In this respect Chile is better than most of its neighbors, because about two-thirds of the people live in cities. Still, we also had to try to reach the rural population of the twenty dioceses during the 1960 series of Crusades. A measure of the difficulty can be gauged from the fact that, although the entire population was just eight million, the distance from one end of the country to the other is greater than that from New York to Los Angeles.

Another fact of life we had to learn fast was the concentration of the decision-making process in the hands of a small group. It is, practically speaking, impossible to do anything without the approval of the bosses, if I may use an American word to cover a wide range of situations. Everything depends on the right connections. It is easy to oversimplify this fact or take it out of its context. Some of those in control take advantage, human nature being what it is. Others use their authority with admirable benevolence. What is a universal fact is a widespread paternalism, which has deep historical and social roots. To recognize its existence is neither to approve nor disapprove. If we wanted to carry out a clearly defined activity in this society, as we did, we simply had to work within the system we found, just as everyone else does.

We were not long in Chile until I had a concrete experience which illustrates this situation. I started the preparatory work there in August 1959 with María Luisa Luca de Tena, Begoña Díaz, Carmen Amann, and Fuensanta González. They remained on when I left for Manila in October, and they were joined about Christmas by Father Quinn, Margarita de Lecea, Tere Aguinaco, and Terry Fellowes. Father Quinn was subsequently joined by two other Holy Cross priests, Father William Belyea, a Canadian, and Father Philip Higgins, and these three have been the principal supervisors of all the Family Rosary Crusade activities in the whole of Latin America. The girls were all Misioneras, except for the Irish lay missionary Terry Fellowes.

When I returned to Santiago on March 8, Father Quinn had divided the country into three areas, selected to ensure the most suitable weather for the Crusades in each. We were to start in the center, which includes Santiago, Valparaíso, and other big cities, then go north into the tropical region in the midwinter months of July and August, and finally cover the far south at the end of the rains and approach of summer in October and November. My first trip out of Santiago was to the neighboring diocese of San Felipe, and on our way back we stopped at the fundo or estate of Pedro Ibanez. The bishop had advised us to make this call and arranged that we should receive a formal invitation from Mrs. Ibanez. It did not take long to discover the importance of this courtesy visit. Pedro Ibanez was president of the State Bank. His brother-in-law was head of the company which published the five most influential and popular magazines in the country. Adlai Stevenson had been their guest a short time earlier. Mrs. Ibanez had welcomed President Eisenhower when he came to Chile. We showed them a film of the Manila rally and a documentary built up from footage shot during Crusades in many parts of the world. Their reaction was excellent, and Mrs. Ibanez assured Father Quinn that she would see that her brother gave every possible exposure to our work in his magazines. He in fact came to see Father Quinn and me a few days later.

Like Argentina and Uruguay to the east, Chile has a higher proportion of European blood than most Latin American countries, and the Irish have been far from the least important of the races who built the nation. As the Spanish administration came to an end, Ambrose O'Higgins, born at Ballinary, County Sligo, not many miles from my own home, was governor of Chile and viceroy of Peru between 1789 and 1801. His son Bernardo was born at Chillán in Chile, a diocese in which we held a Crusade, and at Talca in 1818 he proclaimed the independence of Chile and was named the country's first president. I suppose accordingly I should not have been as surprised as I was the first night I stayed in Talca, when the bishop regaled me with an excellent rendition of "Galway Bay." He was a prince of a man, Bishop Manuel Larraín of Talca, a gentle, holy, soft-spoken priest full of pastoral zeal and totally dedicated to the uplift of the poor and to basic reform of the outmoded social institutions of Latin America. His constant call was for land reform. "Communism rides on the shoulders of a discontented peasantry," he would say. "If every man is a property owner, it will lose its appeal." But for him land reform was not simply division of the big estates. It involved education, health, sanitation, a sense of dignity, and working capital. He was consequently an ardent supporter of a voluntary organization called the Institutes of Rural Education, which sought to educate the young people of the land and develop their internal dynamism.

Bishop Larraín was a vice-president of the Latin American Bishops Secretariat (CELAM) when I visited him. He was delighted with the impact the Crusade quickly made in Chile, and he became a staunch supporter. "The Family Rosary Crusade has been like a great explosion of dormant faith—the awakening of which has enabled so many straying souls to find God again," was how he expressed it. "It is a great victory of Mary who has always loved these Latin American lands in a special way, and who by means of this Crusade has once again manifested her love. Today in my diocese and in ten other dioceses of Chile, there are numerous men attending Mass who before did not do so. A great number of families have returned to the traditional devotion of the family Rosary and a great number of apostolic vocations have been awakened. It is the triumph of Christ through Mary and it is the fruit of the Family Rosary Crusade." Bishop Larraín's support became all the more valuable when in 1965 his fellow bishops from all over Latin America chose him to become president of CELAM. His death in an automobile accident in 1966 was a cruel shock for millions of others as well as for me.

It was while we were in Talca that Chile experienced the national tragedy of a series of major earthquakes that killed hundreds and left a million homeless. The entire economy of the country was shattered and took years to rebuild. Talca was on the fringe of the tremors. Damage to property was not great, and no lives were lost. But it was a terrifying experience, and we never knew what moment our turn might come. The earth began to tremble as the people were assembling for the rally, yet nobody got frightened or ran away, and a total of forty thousand persons turned out. Later, when we moved farther south, we saw indescribable scenes of destruction, towns in which the churches, the schools, and other important buildings were flattened. One bishop who saw the efforts of twenty years destroyed in an hour lost heart and resigned. But he was an exception. Bishops, priests, and people stood together with Christian fortitude, and even as we went the new was rising on the ashes of the old. When we saw their courage, we were heartened to continue our own unending struggle.

Great numbers of families living in urban or rural slums in Chile do not possess a set of rosary beads to help them count the decades, nor can they afford to buy them at commercial prices. We realized we would be faced with the same situation elsewhere in Latin America, and that it would handicap our efforts to teach these people to say the Rosary. While we were still in Chile, a providential solution, at least partial, presented itself. I met two Canadian priests, Father Robert J. Ogle and Father Al Pich, who had been sent down by their bishops on an inspection tour to suggest ways in which Canada could help the Church in Latin America. When they returned home they suggested to Miss Marguerite Burns, then national president of the Catholic Women's League of Canada, to raise $50,000 among the members to pay for a million sets of Rosaries. Both Miss Burns and her successor, Mrs. Hermon Stevens, promoted the project with such enthusiasm that the target was exceeded. Through friends in Ireland, a source of supply was secured to ship the Rosaries at an extraordinarily low cost, and the Canadian fund-raising initiative has encouraged other organizations to help maintain a flow of Rosary beads to impoverished families throughout Latin America, Asia, and Africa.

Long before we were finished in Chile, negotiations for the Crusade had begun with bishops on other parts of the continent. Several things happened in the late 1950s and early 1960s to dramatize the need for a concentration of help in Latin America and in particular to revitalize the Church there. One big event was the formation in Rome toward the end of the pontificate of Pope Pius XII of a papal commission to work with the Secretariat of the Latin American bishops. It issued a series of statements stressing the urgent need for co-operation by the Catholics of North America and Europe, the most specific being an appeal to all religious orders of men and women in the United States and Canada to send 10 percent of their personnel to work in Latin America within ten years.

The superiors of the Congregation of Holy Cross took this appeal with the seriousness with which it was intended. They immediately began to plan substantial expansion of various mission activities already in existence in Latin America, and they gave official recognition to the fact that the work then being initiated in Latin America by the Family Rosary Crusade was itself part of the response of Holy Cross to the papal appeal. Father Christopher O'Toole as superior general wrote a circular letter to all members of the Congregation. "All the Provinces of Priests and Brothers," it said, "should recognize the pressing need to assist in the widespread and important apostolate of the Family Rosary throughout Latin America in the immediate future, by making every effort to provide the manpower needed at once to make possible the multiple Crusades already planned." Father Germain-Marie Lalande, who succeeded as superior general in 1962, repeated this recommendation the following year, because of "the immense contribution which the Family Rosary Crusade has made and is still making in Latin America," and because "it can be regarded as one of the most effective means of preventing the peoples of Latin America from sinking rapidly into materialism and becoming the prey of communism." Father George DePrizio, who as provincial of the Eastern US Province was my immediate superior, reacted in the same way, treating the Crusade as a major part of his province's response to Rome's appeal.

Shortly before he died, Pope Pius XII honored me once more with a special letter dated April 4, 1958. The occasion was the completion of the fifteen Rosary films, which he was one of the first to see, and which he described in the letter as "a massive undertaking that has been achieved with distinction." I had only to show that letter to a bishop and tell him that the films were now an integral part of the Crusade program in order to win his approval and enthusiasm for a Crusade in his diocese. "These films have an apostolic character and value quite beyond their technical and artistic perfection," it read.

> They open up the book of God's revelation to man; they turn the pages of a divine love story for those to read who will, and reading to understand the infinite yearning of God for the creature of His omnipotence. Nazareth, Bethlehem, the towns of the Jordan Valley, and dear, unhappy Jerusalem, all play their part in portraying the successive phases of the redemptive work of the Incarnate Son of God. As the scenes of that

life pass before the eyes, contemplation becomes more fervent, love glows more ardently, allegiance is firmer. And who will follow the tragic sequence of Christ's Passion, enacted so vividly, with such blind fury and with all due reverence, and not weep for his sins? Blessed will the faithful be who have the good fortune, let us rather say the precious grace, to see these films. We sincerely hope their number will be legion.

Pope Pius died on October 9 of that year, and Angelo Giuseppe Roncalli succeeded as Pope John XXIII on October 28. The new Pope took me to his generous heart with the effusive love and generosity which endeared him to all men. Pope John was intensely concerned with the problems and needs of Latin America, and he lost no time in confirming the approval accorded the Crusade by his predecessor. He not only did this in personal conversation but picked the earliest appropriate occasion to put his views on record. The letter he wrote me dated May 1, 1959, is rather long. But it is so characteristic of Pope John's spirit and also expresses so precisely my own motivations and aspirations that I must quote in full.

We have been informed that you are beginning a new stage in the apostolate which has so characteristically distinguished your life. With the technical help of motion pictures to show the meaning, value and excellency of the Mysteries of the Rosary, you wish to increase devotion to the holy Rosary in the nations of Latin America.

The undertaking of such a step has given us paternal joy. Everything which tends to increase devotion to the Mother of God and at the same time makes more devout the faithful, re-echoes in our soul feelings of joy.

You are carrying out this work on a continent where cathedrals, churches and shrines preserve the nation's deep love of the Blessed Virgin sculptured in stone. One day long ago there arrived in that continent a ship named "Mary" (Christopher Columbus' flagship, the Santa Maria); "Mary"— the same name which missionaries were to spread on the mountain tops, in the plains and in the jungles. Our spontaneous wish is that your mission today—wherever the bishops will call you—may in like manner penetrate the depths of hearts and the intimate circle of families and leave many lasting fruits of salvation.

Individuals, whatever their spiritual status may be, will undoubtedly find in the fervent recitation of the holy Rosary, an invitation to regulate their lives in conformity with Christian principles. They will, in truth, find the Rosary a spring of most abundant graces to help them in fulfilling faithfully their duties in life.

Souls lacking in faith and wavering for want of courage are in need of maternal help to overcome discouragement in their sad plight. This maternal help they can receive through devotion to the Blessed Virgin who has given a Redeeming God to the world. She has at her disposition an overflowing abundance of treasures of mercy for all those who have recourse to her with fervor and confidence. She is the Mother of Divine Grace, the Refuge of Sinners, the Health of the Sick. She wishes always to live up to these titles and she does so for those who, aware of their need, invoke her aid.

There are other souls with high ideals for self-immolation. These souls wish to be associated with the redeeming work of Christ. Meditating on the Sorrowful Mysteries they will be able to assimilate all that, from Gethsemane to Calvary, was exacted from the hearts of Jesus and Mary—and therefore all that is expected from one who considers himself united to the Man of Sorrows and who proposes to live like a son of the Queen of Martyrs.

A most practical and easy way of enriching individual lives in a Christianlike manner is to imitate and follow the lessons contained in each Mystery of the Rosary. By this means a Christian is working, as he must, for those rewarding riches which the Mother of God is already enjoying in heaven and which Our Lord has promised to His faithful servants.

If the Rosary is such an efficacious and convenient way for individuals to communicate with God and win such an abundance of graces through the invaluable intercession of the Blessed Virgin, we are persuaded that families will receive from this salutary form of prayer a guarantee of heavenly blessings, while at the same time they will find in the Rosary a school in which to form themselves in virtue.

When parents and children gather together at the end of the day in the recitation of the Rosary, together they meditate on the example of work, obedience, and charity which shone in the house of Nazareth; together they learn from the Mother of God to suffer serenely; to accept with dignity and courage the difficulties of life and to acquire the proper attitude to the daily events of

life. It is certain that they will meet with greater
facility the problems of family life. Homes will
thereby be converted into sanctuaries of peace.
Torrents of divine favors will come to them, even
the inestimable favor of a priestly or religious
vocation.

As Supreme Pontiff, our gaze certainly fixes
itself on these great spectacles of faith and love
of the Virgin Mary—such spectacles so often
in themselves landmarks of the history of Latin
America and a testimony that for civilization to
be genuine it must be in contact with spiritual
and eternal values. And how our heart would
expand if, reviewing those noble nations so dear
to us, we would discover rising from the intimacy of family circles scattered throughout lands so
distant among themselves, the very words of the
Ave Maria—rising repetitiously in honor of the
Queen of America as a proof of spiritual unity
and a message of calmness and peace.

Most ardently we beg the Lord from our
heart that souls, families and nations may derive
abundant fruit from the holy Rosary and that
Our Lord may assist you, beloved son, with His
grace in your enterprise. As a pledge of such
favors, we are pleased to impart to you our apostolic blessing which we joyfully extend to all who
aid you in these labors and to all who in their
homes honor the Queen of Heaven and of Earth
with the laudable practice of the family Rosary.

At the very same time that the Catholic Church was
growing conscious of the plight of souls in Latin America, the United States was acquiring an awareness of the
problems and needs of the countries to the south and of

the intimate way in which our national safety and well-being were bound up with events there. During 1958 we had watched with sympathy as a small band of bearded revolutionaries expelled an unprincipled tyrant from Cuba, then recoiled during 1959 in shocked horror as they proceeded to implant a more ruthless tyranny and to form a public alliance with Soviet communism. We all welcomed in March 1961 the formulation by President Kennedy of a new common approach to hemisphere development in the Alliance for Progress. It was a total emotional climate in which the Family Rosary Crusade had everything going for it in Latin America, and we did our best to grasp the opportunity.

There was never any shortage of requests for Crusades. On the contrary, my constant embarrassment has been to have to postpone time and again the most insistent invitations. I have to make difficult judgments because of the smallness of my group of helpers, the eternal shortage of resources which may permit acceptance in one set of circumstances and force refusal in circumstances that are only slightly different. I may say yes because I feel that one area is more troubled than another and consequently needs more urgently the blessings that come when the people pray daily to their common Mother. I may say no because of the difficulty of getting an import permit for the projectors, transformers, mobile generators, and cans of film, the seventeen tons of equipment without which I cannot take the first step. Sometimes, when I see how urgent the need is everywhere and how vast the still unplowed field, my spirit fails me. To recover hope, I have to look at the slowly lengthening list of the places already visited and recall the beautiful experiences that have happened to me at the least expected moments.

Venezuela follows Chile on the list, then Colombia, Brazil, the Dominican Republic, Panama, and Ecuador. Little as the figures mean, they at least indicate some awakening of a sense of the spiritual in great masses of people who all too often go from one end of the year to the other without entering a church, kneeling in prayer, or recalling the purpose of their lives. The estimated attendance at the rallies was 250,000 in Panama City, 600,000 in Caracas, a million in Bogotá, a million and a half in Rio de Janeiro, two million in São Paulo.

Victor Riesel happened to be in Panama the day the rally was held. He is Jewish, and he is a man who has devoted his life to the promotion of the well-being of the working man, regardless of creed, class, race, or nationality. A fearless and outspoken man, he has known how to suffer with dignity for his beliefs. He was totally and permanently blinded by goons set on him in New York by racketeers whose activities he had exposed. I can be forgiven if I am moved each time I read what such a man wrote in his syndicated column about what he experienced that day in Panama City.

"This is gospel, not gossip," he began.

> When Communist Party operatives and their labor allies and youth movement here attempted to raise a mass march against the United States embassy to protest against America's moves in Santo Domingo, they were able to raise all of fifty-seven "outraged" demonstrators.
>
> But the other Sunday, when a crusading priest, as Irish as a field of shamrock, called on working people here to come and pray with him

in the streets of the old city, . . . men, women and youngsters came out into the broiling sun.

They jammed the old railroad yards. They filled the Fifth of May Plaza. They rippled through the slum streets and the main thorough-fare, Central Avenue. They squeezed onto stoops, roofs and tiny balconies.

Wherever possible, all eyes were on Father Patrick Peyton, who has carried his prayer cru-sade through forty-six countries and now is in Ecuador. Though his South American activities are not widely known in the United States, Father Peyton is making a powerful moral as well as religious force of his theme, "The family that prays together, stays together."

There was religious fervor. You could hear that in the prayers of the multitude—the larg-est demonstration ever held in any Central or South American country. But there was national fervor too. After the prayers, there was a strong outburst of emotion as the strains of the Pana-manian national anthem . . . billowed against the ancient houses and churches.

Diocese by diocese and country by country, it became more apparent that a Crusade in Latin America calls for a longer and more intense period of preparation than was necessary in the United States or in most of the places in which we had previously worked. I can best illustrate this by an example. In Brazil, a country as big as the United States and with a population of more than eighty million, of whom 95 percent are nominal Catholics, it is common to find a parish with forty to fifty thousand people served by a single priest and an average attendance at Sunday Mass of three to four hundred.

In a situation like this, the people lack not only religious instruction but general education. Their economic condition is usually such as to be beyond the comprehension of the average North American. Hunger and malnutrition are their constant companions. Vast numbers live in mud huts, or in huts made from wooden boxes and scraps of metal salvaged from junk heaps. Some of these are erected by squatters in swamps. Others are near garbage disposal areas, and the people rake over the garbage each day to find scraps they can eat. Rats abound and the incidence of disease is unbelievable. The combination of religious neglect and the horrible living conditions results in a low level of moral life. Promiscuity is often the norm rather than the exception, and stealing and destruction of property is prevalent. One Apostolic Nuncio reported that he baptized four hundred children on a Sunday afternoon, only one of whom was legitimate. An estimated 11 percent of births among the million slum dwellers of one big city result from incestuous unions.

Church structures in such circumstances are weak or non-existent, and so are social structures. We have to begin from the very beginning and give the first lessons in self-help and cooperative help. Yet everywhere I have found a great love for the family, an intense sense of family, and it is on this foundation I build. The whole problem is to reach out to them, to get them to listen just once so as to touch their hearts, and that is where the technique we have developed in the Crusade is so marvelous. When we go into a diocese, the priests simply refuse to believe that we can get the men to co-operate. I remember one pastor in Rio de Janeiro who was particularly pessimistic. "Do you realize," he asked me, "that often only four or five men come to Mass here on Sunday? We have more than twenty thousand people in the parish—that is to say, more than five thousand families—and you tell me you want a man for every five families. That means more than a thousand volunteers. The army couldn't do it." I laughed. "Maybe the army couldn't do it, but let us see what Our Lady can do." So we went to work, and in due course I met him again. "You didn't quite make it," he told me. "The number of volunteers was only 882. Still it was a miracle. I have architects, doctors, engineers, skilled workers, unskilled laborers, and they are all working together like brothers."

The miracle, of course, is the work of the Blessed Mother, but like all true miracles it occurs because the human instruments played their part energetically and with dedication. I want, accordingly, to sketch the plan of action which we learned to apply in the big cities of Latin America. The first step was the formation of a team of specialists, who very quickly became known by the name of Our Lady's gypsies, because they lived out of suitcases, constantly flitting from place to place. The basic team consisted of two priests backed up by five of the Misioneras who were doubly useful because Spanish was their mother tongue. The high level of their education, combined with the similarity of the Spanish and Portuguese languages, enabled them to work in Brazil almost as efficiently as in the Spanish-speaking countries.

A Crusade is planned in phases: the popular mission, the hospitals, armed forces, prisons, the school campaign, the universities, the parish campaign, publicity and public-relations activities—all of them culminating in the rally and the collection of pledges. Two local priests are assigned full time by the bishop to participate in all the planning, one as diocesan director for the Crusade, and the other as director of the popular mission. They become the liaison between the Chancery and the Crusade office. They know the priests and people, the local customs and prejudices.

The popular mission is designed to ensure that every Catholic in the city, but particularly the illiterate and un-instructed masses of the poor quarters, will get a basic course in Christian doctrine in a way they are capable of understanding—namely, by the projection of the fifteen Rosary films. Through them they are shown the life of Christ in a context which stresses its relevancy to the problems they encounter in their lives and in their own families. To achieve the desired saturation coverage, the Crusade team begins with an intensive on-the-ground reconnaissance of the entire city, plotting on a large map the individual parishes and the best sites in each parish for outdoor film showings. In most Latin American cities the climate is suitable for outdoor projection and viewing at night. Since most of the people seldom have the money to go to a movie, the free show is a novelty that quickly generates its own publicity.

It is up to the parish priest to find four men for each projection site, two to operate the film projector and two to give commentary and instruction at the end of each film. The men must belong to the neighborhood and represent the social class or classes who compose it. This ensures that they will achieve complete identification with the audience and express themselves in language meaningful to their neighbors. Courses lasting about two weeks are organized by the Misioneras. The projectionists are taught to handle film and run the machines. The commentators study a manual which explains the significance of each of the films and suggests points on which they can base their talks. They then practice in class and criticize each other. This, however, is not carried to the point of developing set talks to be repeated by rote. Experience has shown that the greatest impact is made on an audience when one closely identified with it comments on the scene to which they have all just been exposed in informal language. At the end of the course each man gets a diploma and identification card.

Two films a night are shown for a week, making a program that runs for a little more than an hour, depending on the length of the commentaries. Only one film remains for the last night, but the program is completed by a Mass preceded by confessions. At that point, the impact of the popular mission becomes evident. For those who have worked so hard, it is a great satisfaction to see the long lines waiting with bowed heads to approach the confessor and to see the unusual numbers who receive Holy Communion. The joy is increased when the local priests report later on the high proportion of men who had long been neglecting their religious duties. In Santiago, Chile, the confessions in some parishes were not completed until one in the morning, even though additional priests had been called in to help those of the parish.

The program for the sick in the hospitals, for prisoners, and for the armed forces follows the same procedure. Instructors and operators are chosen from among those who worked in the parishes. What is interesting is to see how readily the men offer themselves for the additional work, men who never before spent an hour working for the Church. They have seen the palpable evidence of the effect of their contribution, and now they take a pride in being part of Our Lady's team. The sick and those in jail are asked to offer their hardships for the success of the Crusade and for the renewal of family life in their country, and nearly all of them gladly go on record by signing a pledge to this effect.

The school campaign is designed to reach the parents through the children, encouraging each child to become an apostle of family prayer in his own home. The first step is to divide school districts into zones, with a zone chief for each. The bishop sends individual invitations to all teachers, religious and lay, men and women, to attend a meeting in a suitable auditorium or theater. At the meeting I explain the meaning of the Crusade, and each teacher is given a manual outlining the activities he can promote. Arrangements are made to show the films to school children at appropriate times in city theaters. A poster contest is organized on the theme: "The Family That Prays Together, Stays Together." Prizes are given in various age categories, and an exhibition of the best posters is held. Homework assignments are given which require the help of the parents, thus drawing the entire family emotionally into the program.

I have always insisted on involving the universities to as great an extent as possible, since the students are the future leaders of their countries. I must confess, however, that the results so far have been mixed. We start with small committees of professors and students in each college and try through them to reach as many students as possible.

They arrange film showings, organize discussions on the importance of the family and the social function of family prayer, and encourage those with artistic or literary ambitions to design posters or write articles for publication. In a few cases the results have been good, but in general we do not seem to have found the formula to draw the same response in university circles as among the general public. Part of the reason undoubtedly is that many Latin American universities are seething with discontent and heavily influenced by leftist ideologies. This has even expressed itself occasionally in organized demonstrations against the Crusade. But, more generally, the university situation requires special techniques. The student needs a personal approach. He is more individualistic, less likely to respond to the message of the mass media. The nature of his life, with staggered classes and laboratory assignments, makes it harder to reach him or arrange a program for him. But I am confident that the re-evaluation of the Crusade now in progress to attune it more fully to the updating begun by the Second Vatican Council will add this essential additional dimension.

The next two steps, the parish and publicity campaigns, start about five weeks before the rally and are conducted simultaneously. The parish campaign opens with a general assembly of all the priests and members of religious orders of men in the diocese, as well as two laymen from each parish. The program is explained in detail, and the instruction manuals are distributed. The priests get outlines for sermons to be preached on the following five Sundays, on the family, family prayer, and the Rosary. A timetable is set up for visiting the sick, distributing publicity materials, and arranging for Masses and Holy Hours for the success of the operation. Each pastor and his lay helpers make a parish census, something that most parishes had never done or never thought possible. The parish is divided into districts of one hundred families each, with a district chairman in charge of five teams of four members each. The men visit the homes in pairs, each pair being allotted ten homes. The visits are scheduled for the final Sunday, one week after the rally, and their purpose is to get the families to pledge that they will join in the family Rosary every day.

The publicity campaign starts with a press conference, to which I invite the owners and directors of radio and television transmitters, newspaper proprietors and editors, and representatives of the major advertisers. I had always been acutely conscious of the value of the mass media, but it was one day in Rio that I realized that I was missing one big opportunity, and that was how the publicity campaign as it now functions began. I knew that we were reaching only a small proportion of the people by sermons in the churches. We got a bigger group through the movies shown in public places, through the school children, and so on. But others were escaping our nets, and they could all be caught if only we could project our message in every medium of communication used by advertisers to sell their goods. It should jump out at the man who bought a paper to read on the bus on his way to work. It should shout from the billboards to those walking down the street. It should answer back from the store window to the man or woman whose eye was caught by a beautiful display. It should come over the radio in taxis, in automobiles, in the home. It should flash on the screen the moment the television was switched on.

But what would that cost, and where would the money come from? Such were the invariable questions when I mentioned my dream. The interesting thing is that this is the kind of saturation exposure the Crusade now gets and that it costs next to nothing. Just as soon as I got the idea in Rio, I made the round of the newspaper offices and asked the proprietors to give us free a full-page advertisement every Sunday for the six weeks that remained before the date fixed for the rally. There were thirteen papers in all, and I was getting yes from one after another. Finally, however, I ran into trouble with a small sensational newspaper that had a tremendous circulation among the poor. It was the one I needed most of all, but the proprietor said it was out of the question. "These other papers have twenty-four or thirty pages. One page makes little difference to them. I have only eight, so you are asking far more from me proportionately." It was shortly before Christmas, and the office was in the shopping district. "Look out the window," I said to him, "at all those crowds. In your business, you know how many of those people are involved in bad marriages, how many of the wives have adulterous husbands, how many of the children are growing up to become hoodlums because of broken homes. This Crusade is from God to help stop the rot, to help the disintegrating homes of today to become sound again. And you can help. Nobody in Rio can do as much as you to help." He threw up his hands. "I'm licked," he said. "You can have your full page. It will come back to me." And it did.

From that beginning, we developed the press conference, at which we get all the people involved in the communications media to pledge so much free space or so much free time during the Crusade. Some of it comes from the newspapers and the radio and television stations themselves. More comes from the advertisers who pay for the advertisements but substitute our message for their own. We have worked out a series of professional advertisements for newspapers, posters for billboards, radio spots, television spots, and all kinds of stickers and throw-aways. The result is that wherever people go, in the bars, in the restaurants, on the streets, in a telephone booth, in their own homes, always the message of the Crusade is calling to them. The grace of God is knocking at their hearts.

From time to time, all this publicity starts people asking questions. It does not seem possible to them that we could get so much advertising free or without strings attached. And I am talking about really big amounts. To buy the donated time and space we have got in many cities would cost as much as a quarter of a million dollars per Crusade. "Do all the people who co-operate do so from religious or altruistic motives?" I am frequently asked. That is a question I cannot answer. I don't suppose there is an answer to it. I have often been asked a similar question about some of the film stars who have so generously helped "Family Theater of the Air," and a long time ago I learned how to answer. The question runs something like this: "Is So-and-So a good Catholic?" And my answer: "If So-and-So were to ask me if you are a good Catholic, what answer could I give him? I could only say I don't know."

It would certainly be much easier for me if I had the quarter million dollars in my pocket each time to buy the publicity at commercial rates. I wouldn't have to go around with hat in hand like a beggarman, and I could be sure that nobody was taking a ride on my coattails. But I don't have those quarter millions. So I take my chances for Our Blessed Mother's sake, knowing that she will in the final analysis ensure that those who deserve reward are rewarded, and that even those whose motives may have been less than pure will surely get some crumbs of grace and mercy for having promoted her cause.

Thirteen

Vatican Council Endorses Family Prayer

The massing of the main effort of the Family Rosary Crusade in Latin America since 1960 most definitely does not mean that I have lessened my hope and determination to bring its message to the rest of the world. It is simply a question of priorities and techniques. Actually, we have held Crusades in many places during the 1960s, in San Francisco and Sacramento in the United States in 1961, in nine dioceses in the Philippine Islands in 1962, in Madrid in 1964, and in several dioceses of Spain and the adjoining islands in 1966. In addition, our permanent offices in Manila, Madrid, and other places have been constantly engaged in utilizing the radio programs, the Rosary films, and other films we have made, and a growing mass of publicity materials to maintain the message of the Crusade in the dioceses in which it has been preached. This post-Crusade work is steadily growing in importance. I shall return to it later.

I was particularly stirred by the experience in San Francisco and Sacramento. It had been several years since we had given any Crusades in the United States. Some people were saying that the technique was outmoded for this country, particularly for a sophisticated city like San Francisco. Though I knew they were wrong, their negative thinking clouded the early period of the preparations. Authorities suggested a large auditorium, the Cow Palace, I believe, for the rally. When I opposed this they suggested a stadium that would hold some fifty thousand. I appreciated their intention. They wanted to avoid the hurt I'd feel if only a small crowd showed up in a big stadium. "But I'm not thinking about myself," I insisted. "I'm thinking about Our Blessed Mother, and she won't be satisfied with less than half a million." So they named a place that would hold a hundred thousand. I refused to give in, and after the greatest effort, I succeeded in getting Golden Gate Park's polo field. It holds half a million.

Our Lady was not disappointed. The *San Francisco Chronicle* and the *San Francisco Examiner* of the day following the rally both spread an aerial picture across their front pages. The *Examiner* reported that the crowd, estimated at more than five hundred thousand, "filled the huge oval yesterday and spilled beyond its confines." The first arrivals checked in at seven-thirty in the morning, six hours before the scheduled time. I was able to get the full impact of the vast throng of families united to honor Mary as I arrived at 1 p.m. by helicopter with Auxiliary Bishops Merlin Guilfoyle and Hugh Donohue, San Francisco's Mayor George Christopher, and California's Governor Edmund G. Brown. The sight is impressed on my memory as indelibly as that breathtaking day in Manila. One curious statistic was drawn to my attention later. There have been many great assemblies in our country since man first began to live in what is now the United States. But no person or event ever drew so many people to one place at the same time as assembled in San Francisco's Golden Gate Park on October 7, 1961, to honor the Mother of God.

What I do recognize is that the techniques we have developed in Latin America are intended specifically for places in which there is a high incidence of illiteracy and a low level of religious instruction. That means that they are good for some two-thirds or three-quarters of the world for the foreseeable future, but it would make no sense to project the Rosary films in parks or squares in the United States, as we do in Caracas or Lima. San Francisco demonstrated again, however, if demonstration was necessary, that in the United States the same recognition of the value of family prayer and the same desire to venerate the Mother of God can be found and can be developed. Each year, in addition, I find new evidence that these attitudes exist outside the Catholic community as well as inside it. Protestant theology and devotion are rediscovering and re-emphasizing the dignity of Mary. And both Catholics and Protestants find a quick understanding and ready response in Jewish tradition when they speak of family prayer. For it is in the intimacy of his own home and in the company of his family that the worshiping Jew has always celebrated many of the most significant of his acts of adoration of Jehovah.

I have, accordingly, by no means abandoned the goal I set for myself twenty-five years ago: to preach family prayer and promote veneration of the Mother of God, especially through the practice of the family Rosary, in the United

States. I have expanded my goals, not altered them. But it does now seem to me that I must develop techniques geared as specifically to our conditions here as are those of the present Family Rosary Crusade to those of Latin America. More concretely, I think this means a concentration on the media of mass communications and particularly on television. My first great break-through in the United States was on radio, which at that time was the dominant medium. It is still important, just as the newspaper is still important. But the future is with television, at least until something still unimagined replaces it. For technical and financial reasons, I was not able to follow through automatically in the 1950s on a massive scale from radio to television. But I have not given up hope or effort. I believe there is a way to do anything that has to be done. And this is something that has to be done.

Before I attempt to evaluate the possibilities further, however, I think I ought to say something about the other big new factor in the equation, the Second Vatican Council. Between the opening of that assembly in October 1962 and its closing in December 1965, deep changes occurred in the thinking of many Catholics, making it evident to the willing and the unwilling alike that all of us would have to reassess our attitudes and practices.

I know quite a number of people who were afraid that this might spell the end of the Family Rosary Crusade. They thought or perhaps feared that the spirit of renewal and updating breathed into the Church by Pope John and formalized in the Council decrees was going to bring to the surface new attitudes which would make the Rosary cease to be significant for many and possibly most Catholics. I never had any such qualms. I knew Pope John. His love for Our Lady and his devotion to her Rosary contributed an essential element to his spiritual growth and stature. His letter to me of May 1959, which I quoted earlier, was followed by another dated May 6, 1961.

"At the beginning of this month, dedicated in a special way to the honor of the Blessed Virgin," he wrote,

> it is specially pleasing to us to renew our sentiments of affection, which continue encouraging you in the already prolonged labor which your zealous priestly ministry has undertaken in spreading devotion to Mary. . . . We are convinced that authentic devotion to Mary, among whose practices the Rosary takes precedence, besides contributing to intensify the religious life of the faithful, can and ought to make them (as your characteristic method of preaching teaches, and your experience proves) efficacious instruments of collaboration in the different organizations of the apostolate.

It became clear quite early in the first session that we were going to have a Council in the spirit of the Pope who had convoked it, and I tried to explain this to any who expressed to me their worries. But I also tried to explain to them something even more basic, and that is that they were creating an issue that could never be other than artificial. I had dedicated my life to preaching family prayer and specifically the family Rosary because the immemorial tradition of the Catholic Church supported this preaching, and because my experience as boy and man proved to me that we had here a formula that worked. But if the Church in Council should decide that the changed times and manners had made the Rosary obsolete as a form of devotion for Catholics, it wouldn't cause me to lose a single night's sleep. One of my dearest friends, Father Arthur McCormack, the Council expert on problems of world hunger, once said of me: "Pat has an obsession but he is not obsessed." I think that describes very well the way I feel. I have a total commitment to what I am doing, but I have not the slightest temptation to put my judgment before that of the Church as expressed by the Council or the Pope or even my own superiors.

Actually, however, the total impulse of the stimulation of Catholic life produced by Pope John XXIII, the Vatican Council, and Pope Paul VI has been to create a new sense of the importance of family prayer and of the Rosary as a form of family prayer appropriate to our times and to the times ahead of us as far as it is possible for us to peer into the future. Discussions and exchanges with various bishops and theologians quickly confirmed my initial conviction— namely, that the Council was not a danger to be guarded against but a blessed opportunity to be grasped and utilized. After a considerable amount of impassioned debate during the second session of the Council, it became clear that there was no question of de-emphasizing the role of Mary in the Church and in the work of our salvation but simply a clarification of that role. Once that became understood on all sides, the acrimony gave way to a spirit of co-operation and conciliation, leading through a series of drafts to the magnificent chapter incorporated in the Constitution on the Nature of the Church promulgated on November 21, 1964.

"This union of the Mother with the Son in the work of salvation is made manifest from the time of Christ's virginal conception up to His death," the document read in part.

> This maternity of Mary in the order of grace began with the consent which she gave in faith at the Annunciation and which she sustained without wavering beneath the cross, and lasts until the eternal fulfillment of all the elect. Taken up to heaven she did not lay aside this salvific duty, but by her constant intercession continued to bring us the gifts of eternal salvation. By her maternal charity, she cares for the brethren of her Son, who still journey on earth surrounded by dangers and difficulties, until they are led into the happiness of their true home.

Later in the same statement, in a clear reference to the Rosary, the Council Fathers urged that "the cult, especially the liturgical cult, of the Blessed Virgin be generously fostered, and the practices and exercises of piety recommended by the magisterium of the Church towards her in the course of centuries be made of great moment."

I was not surprised but I was delighted by these statements and by the entire framework of theological evaluation of Mary's unique place in the Church in which they were presented. It seemed to me that Pope Paul's decision, announced in the same speech in which he promulgated this decree, to proclaim Our Lady as Mother of the Church was a logical outflow from the Council's own action. It clarified that Mary is the Mother of the family of God, the Mother of the members of Christ, the Mother of the Mystical Body. Her honored and indispensable role in the Family of God is thus the same as that of the mother in any family who pours herself out in selfless love for her children. The title solemnly conferred by the Pope is neither more nor less than the Council's affirmation that Mary in maternal charity cares for all her children, all the brethren of her Son "who still journey on earth surrounded by dangers and difficulties."

I cannot pretend to any part in the honor paid to Mary by the Council in the Constitution on the Nature of the Church or by Pope Paul in proclaiming her Mother of the Church. I can, however, claim a modest role in a movement which culminated in statements in two Council documents on the efficacy of family prayer. Pope John had insisted from the outset that what he wanted was a pastoral Council, one that would stress elements calculated to strengthen or restore Christian living, and Pope Paul had repeated the same theme insistently. All over the world there were bishops who had experienced for themselves the pastoral benefits produced by an increase of family prayer through the Family Rosary Crusade. I had no difficulty in finding volunteers to promote the idea of a formal statement in a Council document.

A thing of this kind, nevertheless, takes careful and complicated planning. Here, the advice of my former associate, now Bishop Mark McGrath, was invaluable. He was a member of many drafting commissions, admired for his knowledge, respected for his dedication, loved for his selflessness. After long discussions, we worked out a procedure which included two essential elements. First we drew up appropriate statements to be inserted in the Decree on the Apostolate of the Laity and the Pastoral Constitution on the Church in the Modern World. Then we found speakers to explain to the Fathers in St. Peter's the importance of a statement along the proposed lines.

The first speaker was Cardinal Suenens. In the course of a debate on marriage and the family, on September 29, 1965, he presented the argument that "in order to strengthen the sense of God in the intimacy of the family, prayer by which all its members together in faith and love worship God and receive His most fruitful blessings is especially advantageous." The following day, Coadjutor Bishop Herbert Bednorz of Katowice, Poland, elaborated in still more specific terms. "Family prayer—which in our times Father Peyton of the Congregation of Holy Cross stresses with such insistence in his Crusades—so intrinsically unites the family that the children most willingly turn to it."

The result was a ready acceptance by the Fathers of the statements on family prayer when the time to vote on them arrived. The reference in the Constitution on the Church in the Modern World occurs in the first chapter of the second part, a chapter which discusses ways of fostering the nobility of marriage and the family. Husbands and wives who fulfill their conjugal and family obligations, it points out, are penetrated with the spirit of Christ to perfect their own personalities and promote their mutual sanctification. "As a result, with their parents leading the way by example and family prayer, children and indeed everyone gathered around the family hearth will find a readier path to human maturity, salvation and holiness."

The idea is further spelled out in the third chapter of the Decree on the Apostolate of the Laity, where the decree discusses the various fields of the apostolate. "Christian husbands and wives," it says, are cooperators in grace and witnesses of faith for each other, their children, and all others in their household. They are the first to communicate the faith to their children and to educate them by word and example for the Christian and apostolic life. They prudently help them in the choice of their vocation and carefully promote any sacred vocation which they may discern in them. . . . This mission—to be the first and vital cell of society—the family has received from God. It will fulfill this mission if it appears as the domestic sanctuary of the Church by reason of the mutual affection of its members and the prayer that they offer to God in common, if the whole family makes itself a part of the liturgical worship of the Church, and if it provides active hospitality and promotes justice and other good works for the service of all the brethren in need.

Both before and after these Council statements, Pope Paul VI has frequently confirmed for me the approvals expressed by Pius XII and John XXIII. I do not want to bore by repetition, so I shall quote just one short and typical statement from a letter to me dated March 12, 1964.

The unity and sanctity of the family, today so gravely and so universally threatened and attacked, will find their sure defence and unfailing protection in the practice of family prayer. As the motto of the Family Rosary Crusade succinctly asserts: "The family that prays together, stays together"; and this unity will be a holy one, founded on the raising of the mind and heart to God in the meditation of the mysteries of the life, death and resurrection of Our Divine Redeemer and the life of His Immaculate Mother. We therefore warmly recommend the Family Rosary Crusade, which inculcates the practice of daily prayer, of family prayer, and of prayer by means of the Rosary, in which, "meditating upon those mysteries . . . we may both imitate what they contain and obtain what they promise" (Collect, Feast of the Most Holy Rosary). We exhort all Catholic families to introduce this devotion into their lives, and to encourage its propagation.

The Council sessions were also extraordinarily rich for the Family Rosary Crusade and for me personally in countless other ways. They provided a unique opportunity to meet not only individual bishops and small groups at a time, but to meet entire national hierarchies and to discuss with them the spiritual and pastoral benefits they expected from the Crusade, this at the very moment when they were discussing among themselves their long-term plans for their dioceses and regions.

My talks with leading Brazilian bishops were particularly valuable. We had had a number of extraordinarily successful Crusades in some of the biggest dioceses in Brazil: Recife and Rio de Janeiro in 1962, Salvador, Belo Horizonte, and Pôrto Alegre in 1963, and São Paulo and Curitiba in 1964. These seven dioceses have a combined population of some fourteen million Catholics, and they represent a broad cross section of the social, economic, and religious conditions of the entire country. The impact of the Crusade had been studied with the greatest interest not only by their own bishops but by the other bishops of Brazil. Thanks in large part to the impact of the Council, the approximately two hundred bishops of Brazil had become acutely conscious of the extreme seriousness of the religious situation in the country, and they were anxiously seeking new techniques to achieve a national renewal. It was natural that they should ask if and to what extent the Family Rosary Crusade might fit into their plans.

At a series of meetings in Rome in October 1964, I was able to obtain a better over-all view of the situation in Brazil than I ever had before. I had just come from São Paulo, where we had experienced the greatest triumph of the Crusades to that time. The number of attendances at the showings of the Rosary films had been well in excess of four million. Forty thousand lay leaders had attended several indoctrination sessions and had made personal calls on their neighbors to urge them to undertake to pray in their own families every day. An estimated two million attended the rally. It was a moment in which I had no difficulty in getting the bishops of Brazil, apostolic men truly anxious to do everything in their power to uplift their flocks, to listen to what I had to offer them.

My first call was on Archbishop Hélder Câmara, whom I had met two years earlier during the Crusade in Rio de Janeiro. He had been and still was auxiliary to the Cardinal Archbishop of Rio. Subsequently he has become archbishop of Olinda and Recife in Brazil's northeastern region. Dom Hélder, as the Brazilians affectionately call him, was one of the most energetic leaders of renewal among the Latin American bishops, and when I visited him at Domus Mariae, I found with him another great leader and my longtime friend, Bishop Manuel Larraín of Talca, Chile. I had a most enjoyable meeting with them, though I was sorry to learn that Dom Hélder had been replaced as secretary general of the Central Committee of the Brazilian Hierarchy (CNBB)

at the elections held a short time earlier and was consequently no longer able to discuss my plans in an official
capacity. I was relieved, however, when he told me who had
replaced him. The new secretary general was Bishop José
Goncalves, also an auxiliary of Rio. We had all known him
well during the Rio Crusade, and he had been a particular
friend and helper of Father Quinn.

Over the course of about two weeks, I had the opportunity to have talks with at least a dozen Brazilian bishops,
and I was also invited to address a general meeting attended
by all of the bishops available in Rome on that particular
day. At that time, the Brazilian hierarchy was engaged in
discussions of an over-all pastoral program for the country.
It is a highly ambitious plan which takes into account all
the most modern techniques of sociology, and it seeks to
achieve the most efficient utilization of the small number
of priests and the limited resources of the Church by the
development of teams of experts and the establishment of
short-term and long-term priorities. Both the bishops and
I saw the mutual benefit that would result from a correla-
tion of the efforts of the Family Rosary Crusade with the
pastoral plan.

The two members of the hierarchy most directly concerned were Archbishop Fernando Gomes dos Santos of
Goiânia, national secretary for Extraordinary Pastoral
Activities, and Bishop José Costa Campos of Valenca,
national secretary for Catechetics. My talks with them
helped to formulate the problems which can arise either
from the objective situation or because of misunderstand-
ings. In some cases the criticism had been made, they
said, that the Crusade had distracted from a local pastoral

program and drawn away the priests and the lay workers needed to support that program. Such a result would
be unlikely in a diocese well provided with priests and a
developed Catholic Action. But where helpers were few and
resources already strained to the limit, it was necessary to
ensure a total integration of activities to prevent one good
work from harming another.

Another danger expressed by some bishops was that
the Crusade could be exploited by political, economic, and
other pressure groups, who would use it to advance their
own interests, to make it appear that the Church was urging the poor to be content in their misery and that it was
condoning the luxury in which a few lived while others
starved. Others were anxious to find a way to change the
attitudes of the many ignorant and superstitious people
who regarded the rosary beads as a kind of charm which
authorized them to continue to lead sinful lives. One bishop
spoke about bandits in the north of Brazil who carried a
gun in one hand and rosary beads in the other.

As far as such criticisms or reservations were concerned, none of them was particularly new to me, and I
had no problem in answering them. I assured the bishops
that nobody was more pleased than I was to know of the
determination of the bishops of Brazil to introduce pastoral programs which would assume part of the burden now
being carried by the Crusade, particularly the training of
catechists to do at least a part of the work of instruction
for which we had been forced to develop the popular mission. A co-ordination of efforts would be of mutual benefit.
The problem of exploitation of religion for partisan ends
is one with which the Church has always had to live and

presumably will always have to live. It is neither significantly greater nor less for the Crusade than for other religious
activities, and the close co-operation with the local clergy
guaranteed by the appointment of two priests to act as official liaison with the bishop ensures that the Crusade priests
will not allow themselves to be tricked into compromising
situations because of their lack of knowledge of specific
local conditions. As for the superstitious abuse of the rosary
beads, that is a part of a total atmosphere of ignorance and
superstition. The solution for this as for all superstitions is
not to abandon the religious practices of which they are a
perversion, but to lift the level of education and religious
instruction.

As I repeated these arguments and developed a continuing dialogue with these and other Latin American
bishops, I gradually came to realize that the mutual mis-
understandings were often deeper. The underlying criticism
was not that the Family Rosary Crusade was not accomplishing what it set out to accomplish, but that it ought to
be involved in a far bigger range of activities. These good
men were not criticizing me for seeking to strengthen family life through the practice of family prayer. They had no
objection to preaching devotion to the Mother of God. They
fully approved of the Rosary as the time-sanctioned method of expressing that devotion. What they were trying to
express was that there were many other pastoral needs in
their dioceses and that they believed the Family Rosary
Crusade could take care of more of them.

Once I saw the problem in that perspective, it was impossible simply to shake it off. Yet I was immediately torn by
conflicting emotions. I recalled the first basic decision I had

made as a young priest in Washington, when I was wondering whether I should not start a movement for greater attendance at daily Mass as a natural extension of the family Rosary. The decision I then made was to do one thing at a time, and it was a decision I had never regretted. The one thing on which I had since concentrated was more than a lifetime job, as events had proved. It had demanded superhuman efforts from my colleagues and myself, so that our physical and material resources were always strained to breaking point.

It was quite clear to me that the total transformation of their dioceses which some bishops in their zeal expected of the Crusade was quite unrealistic. To attempt it would involve an entirely different approach. It would mean allocating a team for several years to one place, and since I saw no way of maintaining more than two or at most three teams in action at any given time, that would be the end of the Family Rosary Crusade as a world movement.

I was, nevertheless, not so self-satisfied as to imagine that the instrument we had developed by trial and error was perfect in all its details. When a bishop said to me that the Council's updating of the Church called for an updating of the methods of the Crusade, I listened to him with respect and always asked for practical suggestions. The result of many such conversations and suggestions was a concrete plan of action. I asked one of the most brilliant Latin American sociologists, Father Renato Poblete, S.J., to make a study of the Crusade and suggest methods by which it could increase its contribution to the cause of religion in Latin America. A graduate of Fordham University's school of sociology, Father Poblete is attached to the Bellarmine Center for sociological research in Santiago, Chile.

As part of his work, Father Poblete interviewed a selected group of bishops in whose dioceses a Crusade had been
given. Two were from the Philippines, three from India, two
from South Africa, three from Australia, three from Canada, six from the United States, five from Panama, six from
Brazil, two from Venezuela, and three from Chile. Among
them were Cardinal Silva of Santiago, Cardinal Quintero
of Caracas, Cardinal Herrera of Málaga, Cardinal Gilroy
of Sydney, Archbishop Eugene d'Souza of Bhopal (Nag-
pur), India, Archbishop Hélder Câmara, Archbishop Philip
Pocock of Toronto, Bishop John R. Dearden of Detroit, and
Bishop John J. Wright of Pittsburgh. Father Poblete also
held individual and collective meetings with some of the
Church's most renowned theologians and sociologists, men
who played a big part in the shaping of the Council. They
included Father John Courtney Murray, Father Jean Dan-
ielou, Father Yves Congar, Father Bernard Häring, Father
Emile Pin, Father François Houtart, and Father Isaac Wust.

I cannot say that Father Poblete's report to me on the
views of the cardinals and bishops included many surprises.
I had heard time and again the same kind of praise of the
good produced by the Crusade, and I was pretty well aware
of its weaknesses. It was no shock, for example, to be told
that the whole operation depended excessively on myself,
that I should plan further ahead, that the work needed to
be institutionalized so that it would run smoothly under
its own momentum. On the contrary, nobody is more conscious than I am of these defects. The problem is a simple
one. Neither I nor anybody else has yet found the manpower and resources to make any other form of operation
possible. We have only Hobson's choice, either this way or

not at all. I must grasp each opportunity before the slender silk thread on which it hangs snaps. I must seize each petal as Our Lady tosses it toward me.

Nevertheless, the report has proved of inestimable benefit. First of all, it was a logical follow-up to the analysis made by Bishop de Smedt of Bruges in 1959, and it had the additional values of reflecting the views of many bishops and of presenting their thought as influenced by the Vatican Council. On the positive side, the cardinals and bishops interviewed were unanimous in approving the aims of the Crusade as touching a fundamental aspect of contemporary society: the need to unite the family and teach it to pray in common. They were equally unanimous in praising the good organization of all the steps of the Crusade.

For us in the United States, this may not seem so extraordinary, since we live in a society in which organization is universal in religious as well as civil life. But in most countries, the techniques used by the Crusade are a true revelation. It is an inspiration to a priest to see how easy it is to make a census of his parish, to take one small example, and to realize the many ways in which such a census, once made, can ease his burden and extend his pastoral help to his people. In the many places where laymen have traditionally no part in Church activity, the Crusade has also been a revelation by showing how easy it is to change that attitude, once you provide the proper motivation.

Approval of the value of the media of mass communication for instruction of the masses was also universal. This applied both to radio and television programs and to the use of the Rosary films in the popular mission. It was also agreed that the final rally had a definite place in the

program, on the sociological ground that a mass demonstration of one's faith is a positive act which expresses the
solidarity of a group and strengthens its morale.

While praising the over-all impact of the Crusade, not
a few bishops had criticisms to offer. Most were along the
same lines as those I had earlier heard from Brazilian and
other bishops and which had prompted the inquiry. In the
end, however, they boiled down into one of two categories.
They either asked whose job is it to continue to stoke the
fires that are lighted in a diocese by the Crusade, or they
asked to what extent are popular devotions legitimate in
the Church as purified and renewed by the Council, and
what form should such devotions take. Both questions are
legitimate. Both deserve an answer.

Fourteen

The Aggiornamento of the Family Rosary Crusade

I need hardly say that it is not possible to give the answer to the two big questions posed at the end of the last chapter off the top of one's head. Father Poblete's discussions and my own with theologians and sociologists during the final session of the Council in the fall of 1965 led to the decision to have a more formal symposium at the earliest possible moment. The occasion offered itself in March 1966 when the Center for Continuing Education of the University of Notre Dame was inaugurated with a week of meetings on the theological implications of the recently concluded Vatican Council. I took advantage of this opportunity to assemble all the priests engaged in the Crusade work in Latin America. Our evaluation session had the benefit of the thinking of some of the Church's most brilliant scholars, men who had come to Notre Dame for the theological conference.

Because of the Crusade's current concentration on Latin America, I was anxious that the thinking of that part of the world should be adequately represented. This was done by the presence of Bishop Mark McGrath, who presided over several meetings, of my Holy Cross colleague, Father Robert Pelton, head of St. George's College in Santiago, and of Father Poblete. Our other advisers included Father Walter J. Burghardt, S.J., Father Eamon R. Carroll, O. Carm., Father Bernard Häring, C.Ss.R., Father Arthur McCormack, M.H.M., and Father Thomas Barosse, C.S.C.

I think that the report by Father Poblete and the discussions at Notre Dame have already accomplished one very substantial benefit, and that is to clarify that such differences of opinion as may exist about the utility of the Rosary and the value of the Crusade are a reflection of a much wider divergence regarding the pastoral function of the Church. This is the same divergence which came to light at the Council, at times producing heated clashes. The Council urged liturgical and Biblical renewal, and some enthusiasts wanted this renewal to be applied immediately and in its totality at all levels in the Christian community. It soon became apparent, however, that two exaggerations are possible. A pastoral approach only for the masses, based exclusively on the traditional cultural aspects of the Christian message, can cease to be meaningful for members of highly educated and sophisticated groups, who feel the need for a more personal approach to religious expression. But a pastoral approach tailored to the needs of an elite, of the so-called "small community" of the well-instructed and actively engaged members of the Church, can be equally lacking in meaning for the masses.

Now the Church needs both these elements in order to be a Church and not merely a sect. The problem which the Council recognized was that these two necessary parts of the society of the Church were drifting dangerously apart from each other. Its efforts were directed to bringing them back closer to each other, so that each could learn from the other and give strength to the other. One of the ways it did this was by the chapter on Our Lady in the Constitution on the Nature of the Church, a chapter which emphasizes that Our Lady is not peripheral or accidental to the life of the Church, not the object of a devotion which challenges the centrality of God and of Christ, but an integral part of the Church's essential life.

The emphasis on the liturgy similarly forced our most progressive theologians to examine again the place of devotion to the Mother of God in our prayer life, and specifically the place of the Rosary as an expression of devotion to Mary. The result has not been to downgrade devotion to Mary but to insist on bringing it back more closely to the liturgical center and to purge it of extraneous growths which might leave it open to misunderstanding or deviation.

One of the points brought out at our Notre Dame meeting was that the Rosary as we recite it today is not the same as the Rosary preached by Saint Dominic with such success in the south of France in the early thirteenth century. It consisted at first only of a number of Hail Marys, and that prayer was considerably shorter than it is today. The other elements were added gradually, and there is no reason to assume that the particular form popular at the present time is necessarily definitive. Those who find it too conventional or repetitious for their liking have open to them an infinity of possible variations. Father Häring, the German

Redemptorist theologian, told us about an experimental formula which he had found very much to the liking of some of his friends. It stresses Scripture readings related to each of the truths of our faith commemorated in the fifteen Mysteries of the Rosary, combining these readings in flexible ways with the prayers we now recite. These prayers, the Our Father, Hail Mary, and Glory Be to the Father, I need hardly add, are themselves of course deeply scriptural.

Anxious to conduct our deliberations in an ecumenical atmosphere, I had invited a Lutheran pastor, Reverend Arthur C. Piepkorn, of Concordia Seminary, St. Louis, to give us the benefit of his advice. He not only approved of Father Häring's formula, but he told us that he had actually used a similar form of meditation on the Mysteries of the Rosary combined with scriptural readings in his own church, without labeling it as the Rosary. He believed that many Protestants would welcome such a prayer, and that the Rosary could thus take on a more ecumenical dress and serve as a bond of union instead of being divisive, as unfortunately it often has been.

Pastor Piepkorn insisted very strongly on a point that has sometimes been overlooked in the implementation of the decrees of the Vatican Council. Change has to be paced to the needs and conditions of each time and place. "We must never," he said, "take away from people anything that performs for them a spiritual function except in terms of replacing it by something better."

The application of this principle to the great masses of Latin America, living at a low level of education and religious instruction, usually with infrequent contacts with their priests, is obvious. For them devotion to Our Blessed Mother has been the bulwark of their faith, and I know of no better way to maintain and deepen that devotion than the Rosary. But I am absolutely persuaded that the message of the Rosary is not only for such people, but that it has profound significance as the ideal form of family prayer for countless others if properly explained to them and understood by them. Its message is not only for the simple. One of the most moving and edifying of my experiences in Rome during the Council was to spend an evening with Cardinal Suenens. This extraordinary man, one of the decisive influences on the entire direction and achievement of the Council, drew to his lodgings the cream of the great men gathered as Council Fathers and advisers. The conversation, always brilliant, changed according to the people and the circumstances. But the basic rhythm of the Suenens family did not change. The evening would start with a concelebrated Mass. Then would come a social interval to relax with the cardinal's hospitality and meet the other guests before sitting down to a modest dinner. And at the end of dinner, the recitation of five decades of the Rosary was followed by the sung "Salve Regina." Participating in this family gathering inspired me to new enthusiasm, to new conviction that not only has the Rosary survived the Council, but that it has been projected by it to a new pinnacle of importance in the Church.

Like Cardinal Suenens, I find absolutely no need to change the traditional structure of the Rosary for my own personal devotion. It remains full of endless inspiration for me in the form in which I learned to lisp it at my mother's knee. No matter how busy I am, no matter how many urgent business affairs call for my attention, I never let a day go by without reciting the fifteen decades. I do not even feel the need to dwell on the Mysteries to which the various decades are dedicated. The words of the prayer are in themselves enough to occupy my attention, enough to lift me from the distractions around to an awareness of the presence and the love of God the Father, God the Son, and God the Holy Spirit, to a sense of joining God Himself in paying honor to the woman whom He not only chose to be the Mother of His Son, but whose permission and co-operation He requested and invited in that supreme mystery of our salvation. Even though I repeat the same words, each time they are new, because they reveal to me another facet of a mystery that life is not long enough to explore to its depths or to exhaust.

While I myself feel no need for the kind of evolution suggested by Father Häring, I am certainly not opposed to development in principle. In fact, I see much to commend an evolution which would expand the Rosary from its present fifteen to a total of thirty-five Mysteries, so that we would have a more complete survey of the truths of our religion, beginning with Genesis and carrying right through the Bible. In that way we could have a weekly cycle, still reciting five decades each night in the family, as is the normal practice in families which say the Rosary.

One of the criticisms of the diocesan Crusades which emerged both from Father Poblete's survey of the bishops and from the discussions at Notre Dame was the danger of promoting a spirituality not sufficiently related to the existential situation of the listeners. In underdeveloped countries, some urged, more emphasis should be laid on the need for community life in order to permit normal structuring and activity of the family, instead of talking about the family as though it functioned without regard to the other social structures of which it is the most basic. Bishop Mark McGrath went so far as to say, speaking specifically of Latin America, that Catholics do great harm to religion by handing over to Marxists the leadership in improving material conditions.

I must confess that my reactions to this line of thought are mixed. On the one hand, I cannot deny that a certain minimum level of living is needed in order to maintain a normal family life. How can there be a home if there is not a dwelling of some sort, a hearth around which to kneel in prayer? The high incidence of promiscuity, of incestual relations, of abandonment of wives by husbands, and of many other evils against the home and family, is established beyond question for the mushrooming slums of Latin America's great cities. At the same time, I am not sure just how far the Family Rosary Crusade can become involved in the reformation of society, any more than it can spread its limited resources to a thousand other highly desirable activities. At most it can reformulate its message to give more stress to the social importance of the family not only in itself but in its relationship to the wider community of which it is a part. Yet at this point, I do not think we should be too apologetic. A major lesson of the Vatican Council was that spirituality had tended in modern times to become too individualistic, neglecting the social aspect of worship. This was the attitude with which I had constantly to contend in the early days. "Preach the Rosary by all means," people would say. "But why the Rosary in the family? Isn't it just as good if the individual members say their Rosary in private?" So here we were in those days insisting on the social value of prayer, the greater glory given to God and the greater benefit obtained by the worshipers when all the members of the family knelt down and prayed together, the very point stressed so emphatically by the Council in its Constitution on the Sacred Liturgy.

But quite apart from this, I have to insist that even people living in very primitive conditions can and do worship God. I think it is far too easy to project from the outside a picture that is quite different from the way it is seen by those involved. I can look back to my own youth, when poverty and hunger were on me and I didn't feel it, and I know it is the same for the poor people down there in Latin America. God knows how to take care of His creatures. When we went through it, we were happy to get a shadow of butter on a piece of bread, and a scrap of the white fat of bacon was as much appreciated as a steak today. I saw a man down there in the jungles of Africa, where all he had to do was to lie down on the ground with his family and wait for the bananas to drop right into his mouth all the year long. A man in Calcutta slept all night in the streets, and I saw him in the morning as I went for the bus. He was looking lovingly at the sun and praying, while back in New York was a man with aches and pains as he got out of his downy bed and no thought in his mind to thank God for anything. My father as a boy had to drive long hours through the night with his horse and cart, taking milk to Swinford to sell, but I'll bet he whistled and sang as he rode, his poor mother beside him to keep him company through the darkness. So I have a feeling that God fits each one of us at the right time and in the right way to carry what might be a greater blessing for us than the opposite would be.

At the Notre Dame meetings we also devoted consider-able time and thought to the complaint expressed by several bishops to Father Poblete that much of the tremendous impact of a Crusade on a diocese withered away in a rela-tively short time. One of the things that usually impresses the bishop and his priests, for example, is that we succeed in getting the men of the diocese and of every parish involved both in the popular mission as projectionists and instruc-tors, and in the campaign for pledges as door-to-door vis-itors. But when the Crusade team moves on to the next diocese, the men go back to their homes, and that is often the end of the organization and the end of their contribu-tion as a group to the life of the Church.

I have always given a simple answer to such complaints, which are nothing new, and that is that my associates and myself have always been very specific in our insistence that the post-Crusade is not our problem but that of the diocese itself. What we do is to activate the latent spiritual energies of the diocese by bringing together a series of techniques and a series of motivations. We can start a fire. We show them that there is an unused potential in the diocese, that the people are prepared, with the proper leadership and encouragement, to participate actively. But once the fire is started, it is up to the local leaders to keep it burning. If we were to stay in a given diocese for the length of time required to complete the in-depth training of a local organi-zation, I doubt if I could complete more than three or four Crusades in five years. That might be an excellent aposto-late, but it is not the one to which I have dedicated my life.

All of our discussions, nevertheless, have led me toward a refinement of our procedures which will, I believe, serve a double purpose. It will speed up rather than slow down the rate at which the message of the Crusade can be carried to the ends of the earth. And it will ensure that by the time a Crusade has been completed in a given diocese, local structures will have been formed in greater depth than previously, thereby giving a greater promise of their permanency.

The defect which I am now hoping to remedy is that the Crusade team has itself been doing too much of the work. In a typical situation, two priests and five lay helpers moved into a diocese. They obtained from the bishop two priests to act as liaison and to help them to execute their programs. But it was the Crusade team which assumed responsibility for all the work, which trained the technicians and the speakers, kept the card indexes and the files, and checked up on execution of each step of the program. The local clergy were undoubtedly involved, but we held their hands all the time. They admired the efficiency of the outside experts, but they thought of the operation as one executed by outsiders. They had a demonstration that this kind of thing can be done, but they did not do it themselves. They were intellectually convinced of its desirability but not emotionally committed to doing it.

That, I now believe, explains in large part why the demonstration provided by the Crusade was so often not followed by imitation. And the remedy I propose is to have a steadily increasing part of the program entrusted from the outset of the Crusade to local operatives, priests and laypeople. All that the Crusade will ultimately offer is one specialist and an elaborate do-it-yourself kit to replace the Crusade team with which we have been working in recent years in Latin America and elsewhere.

This reorganization has already begun. In January 1967 three Holy Cross priests, Fathers Joseph Quinn, William Persia, and Robert Rioux, joined forces in Madrid to work out the new program. Their first step was to enroll in a series of courses in Madrid's famous pastoral institute in order to acquire a deeper understanding of the mind of the conciliar Church. This knowledge will as quickly as possible be reflected in revised versions of the various manuals and handbooks used in the diocesan Crusades, the handbook for priests, the sermon outlines, the handbook for leaders, and the rest. New instruction material will also be prepared to permit the Crusade to function in its new form. In due course, any one of our Crusade priests will be able to go to a diocese to which the bishop invites him and supervise the training of a local team to conduct the Crusade in that diocese. What he will offer will basically be the blueprints for the operation and also the projectors and films to be used in the popular mission.

No doubt, each will have to stay longer in the diocese, but the net effect will be to speed up, because already the two formerly needed for one team will have become separate units working independently, and additional units will each require only one person instead of several, as before. And what is of at least equal importance is that the entire program will be carried out from start to finish by local people. This will involve a training in much greater depth than formerly of the local nucleus, and this nucleus will remain behind after the Crusade to continue the training of the additional local workers who were activated for the purposes of the Crusade.

Part of the do-it-yourself kit will be a continuing program to ensure long-term effects from the Crusade. I have long recognized the need for such a program, and several elements for it have already been developed. Many countries of Latin America, for example, have begun to celebrate the feast of the Immaculate Conception as Family Day. We provide a broad range of publicity materials and programs to dramatize this occasion and tie it into the Crusade in places where it has been held. The Rosary is recited on radio and television by typical local families, and the pledge to say it every day in the family is renewed.

Another method of ensuring the continuation of the impact of the Crusade has been devised by the Manila office of the Family Rosary Crusade, and I anticipate that it will be widely utilized elsewhere. The plan is now being executed by Bishop Bienvenido López, assisted by Father Borces, who had his training with us in Brazil, and Fabiola Ayala, who had spent several years on the Crusades in Latin America. It calls for the holding of a popular mission in Manila and subsequently in other cities in that part of the world. While middle-class and upper-class families can be reached by the other media of publicity harnessed by the Crusade and capable equally of being utilized in post-Crusade promotion, they are convinced that the only way to reach the masses of the very poor in underdeveloped areas is through outdoor movie programs.

For the first test, they are utilizing the techniques of the popular mission exactly as we have developed them in Latin America. The city is divided into sectors. The pastors of each sector are brought together, and projection sites are chosen. Men are selected to operate the projectors and to speak to the viewers at the end of each film, bringing out the connection between what they have seen and their own family life. Women are also recruited to visit the homes and motivate the people to come to the film showings. The fifteen Rosary films are being used for this test, two being shown each night. The final evening, after the fifteenth film has been shown, priests are available to hear confessions, and the proceedings close with a Mass or other religious ceremony. Reports from the Philippines state that in the first three sectors of the popular mission, attendances at the film showings total close to 990,930.

It is my hope that this kind of popular mission, which can be conducted completely by local personnel, will become a standard form of post-Crusade activity, to be repeated at yearly or two-year intervals. In many areas it can take the place of the traditional parish retreat or mission, reaching out to great numbers who never attended the church and consequently were untouched by that kind of mission. It is obvious, however, that its success will depend on the continuing availability of a supply of instructional films. Excellent as the existing Rosary films are, one cannot expect people to come back to see them time and again. In addition, it would be obviously desirable to have a wide range of films dealing with the sacraments, with the commandments, with the moral virtues, with the home and family life, with spiritual growth. Such films can carry the message of the Family Rosary Crusade all over the world both by means of the popular mission and on cinema and television screens.

It is for that purpose which, in the midst of all my other activities, I have clung to my toehold in the film capital of the world. Up till now, this book has contained only passing references to the Hollywood office of the Family Rosary Crusade. I have finally reached the point where I can briefly recount its story in the perspective in which I myself see it.

Fifteen

The Key to the Future

One's first impressions inevitably color one's subsequent attitudes toward a particular place, and I suppose that is part of the reason why I have always felt at home in the Hollywood–Los Angeles area. The people out there welcomed me from the word *go*. First there was Monsignor Cawley and his associates at the cathedral, then Tom Lewis, Loretta Young, Frank Mueller, Bob Longenecker, Senator George Murphy, Ann Blyth, Al Scalpone, Bing Crosby, Irene Dunne, Dolores Hope, Jack Haley, Rosalind Russell, and all those other wonderful people in the movie colony who had the courage and the love of God and His Blessed Mother to put their reputations and their careers on the line for an unpopular cause sponsored by an unknown priest.

My home in Hollywood had always been in the same place, at Immaculate Heart Convent, the mother house of the California Institute of the Sisters of the Immaculate Heart. Mother Humiliata, now superior general, has reaffirmed with equal warmheartedness the insistent assertion of her predecessors, Mother Regina and Mother Eucharia, that I am not a guest but one of the family. I can come and go, as my needs dictate, without a sense of imposing, with a confidence that I am loved and welcome.

Then there was Virginia Majors—a wonderful black lady who more than twenty years ago made a sacrifice for Our Lady far beyond any reasonable expectation. I had not been long in Los Angeles at the time, and I still had literally no resources. I was trying to get support for what would become "Family Theater," and I was simultaneously promoting family prayer by preaching triduums in city churches. This particular week, I had been invited for Sunday, Monday, and Tuesday by the Franciscan pastor of St. Joseph's Church in downtown Los Angeles, and he felt sorry for me when he saw me trying to dash around the city during the day, between sermons, in my efforts to get some action on the "Family Theater" movement.

This is no good, he thought to himself, because in Los Angeles more than anywhere else in the United States it is impossible to get around without an automobile. So he put a notice in his church bulletin the following Sunday. "Once Our Lady said, they have no wine, and she got an answer," he wrote. "Now she is saying they have no car. For Father Patrick Peyton, whom you heard proclaiming the love of Mary last week, is trying to arouse the whole of Los Angeles to the same love of Mary, and he has no car. So if some parishioner has an extra car, will he listen to the voice of Mary and give it to Father Peyton?"

A few days later the pastor called me. "When can you come to pick up your car?" I went over to the rectory, and he took me to a ramshackle place in a poor neighborhood, and there we met Virginia Majors and she handed me the keys to an old Buick. "You have another car?" I asked her. "No," she replied, "but that's all right. I can use the street-car." And in spite of my protests, she insisted. Not only that, but later she used to come over and help around the office in her free time, sweeping, scrubbing, cleaning windows, always happy to do whatever lay in her power to promote the cause of Our Lady. After about two years I was able to return the car, but by that time I fear there was little worth returning. I had put on an awfully lot of mileage, and I'm not the world's best driver.

The first office of "Family Theater" in Hollywood was a room at Immaculate Heart Convent, that and sundry telephone booths, and a corner in Doc Bishop's office or Tom Lewis's, or wherever among my friends there happened to be an empty desk at a given moment. Everyone agreed it was an impossible situation, but it was no more absurd than the rest of the operation, and it was simply out of the question to think of adding office rent to our other expenses. Then one day I met a lady who said her name was Mrs. Jacoba Buchenau. "You don't know me," she said, "but I know you. Some time ago you spoke to the girls who get together with Nellie Cantwell, the archbishop's sister, to make vestments to send to foreign missionaries. I am one of that group, and I heard you on that occasion. Then the other day I was having my hair done, and my hairdresser Mary Jordan was telling me about your need for an office. I think I may be able to help."

When Jacoba mentioned Mary Jordan's name, I knew where I stood. Mary and a friend of hers called Ruth Exley were deeply devoted to the family Rosary, and they used to attend every triduum I gave in the Los Angeles area. I had just given a triduum in the Blessed Sacrament parish at Sunset Boulevard, Hollywood, and I had asked the people to help by their prayers in the search for an office for "Family Theater." Jacoba came to see me and took me out on Sunset Boulevard in her car to a corner lot on which stood a frame building. "It's yours," she said. "There's a mortgage on it, but I'm going to wipe out the mortgage and let you have it free and clear." That was surely a gift from heaven. Jacoba had two daughters. If she had been worldly wise she would have figured that she should keep that property for them. But neither she nor her daughters thought in those terms. They were as happy as she was with their mother's decision. "It's for Our Lady," they said. And like so many others who made a generous gesture to Our Lady, they had no reason to regret it. One of the girls, Mary Jane, shortly afterward married Neil McQueen, a wealthy oilman. As I constantly preach, it is impossible to outdo Our Blessed Mother in generosity. When a person is motivated securely by faith, he can be sure of his reward.

We moved into the frame house at 7201 Sunset in 1948, the year after "Family Theater" went on the air, and it was there that all the subsequent programs of this great radio series were conceived and developed. Though the accommodations were far from lavish, we were very happy to have a roof over our heads. Finally, however, with the growth of this part of the city, the old frame building was condemned. This created a new financial crisis, but I was determined not to lose the toehold in Hollywood. Friends rallied round when they heard of the problem. Architects and engineers donated their services, and the contractor agreed to build at cost. The Raskob Foundation made the major contribution. The result is a beautiful building completed in 1960. It has a sound recording studio, a fine projection room and theater, film editing facilities, and a film storage vault, in addition to administrative offices. Many of the furnishings and much of the technical equipment also reached us as donations.

I had gone into "Family Theater" with some considerable reluctance in the first instance because the Mutual network had insisted on a formula which excluded the Rosary, and I feared I was getting away from my commitment to sell the Rosary as the ideal form of family prayer. Events soon showed me that I was not as far away from my goal as I had thought. The impact of the programs in favor of family prayer was tremendous from the start. In addition, I found that my public identification with the programs enabled me to project my continuing personal campaign for the family Rosary through the preaching of triduums to a far wider public than ever before. And it was "Family Theater's" participation in Ottawa's international Marian Congress of 1947 that opened the door to the first diocesan Crusade in London, Ontario, and the worldwide enlargement of the movement of which that was the predecessor.

My hand was really strengthened by the quick public acceptance and the long-term continuance of the public's approval of "Family Theater." The number of stations carrying the broadcasts doubled and tripled and quadrupled, finally reaching the phenomenal figure of seven hundred. The Armed Forces network beamed them to our fighting men overseas and sent them by shortwave behind the iron curtain. Networks and independent stations in other countries also used them. Awards poured in, the Thomas Edison

Award, the American Legion Award, the best program in polls conducted by such newspapers as the *Cleveland Plain Dealer* and the *Milwaukee Journal*. *Time* magazine called the series outstanding, and *Radio Daily* selected it as Mutual network's best of the year.

This was the atmosphere which enabled me to get time for special programs featuring the Rosary, like *The Joyful Hour* at Christmas and *The Triumphant Hour* at Easter. It also created a demand for *The Marian Hour*, a radio program with the avowed purpose of promoting devotion to the Mother of God. That series was inaugurated with thirty-seven original productions, and subsequently 190 of "Family Theater's" 482 scripts were edited in a different format and released as "Marian Theater" plays.

In the 1940s radio was still in its heyday, but in the last years of that decade it was becoming clear that it would soon be replaced by television as the primary medium of entertainment and information. I quaked at the thought, not that I objected to scientific progress, but that the financial implications were something my imagination refused to accept. I knew, nevertheless, what I had to do. I had committed myself to the harnessing of all the modern means of communication to sell the message of family prayer, and once television became an established fact, a way had to be found to include television also.

My first adventure in the field of television was a star-studded hour-long film called *The Triumphant Hour* and telling the same story of the Passion, Death, and Resurrection of Jesus as the earlier radio program of the same name. The Dionne quintuplets with their mother and the families of screen and radio personalities joined me in reciting the Rosary. The celebrities included Pat O'Brien, Maureen O'Sullivan, Jane Wyatt, Don Ameche, Roddy McDowall, the Bob Hope family, Morton Downey, Pedro de Cordoba, and Jack Haley. In a most unusual tribute to the quality of the offering, all the networks agreed to use it. During the 1950 Easter season, accordingly, it was carried at different times by NBC, CBS, ABC, and DuMont, as well as by many independent stations. The total audience was estimated at sixteen million for that first series of showings. "One of the most inspiring observances of Easter ever presented," was the verdict of the *Boston Post*.

The success of *The Triumphant Hour* encouraged me to plan a filmed version of *The Joyful Hour* for television showing for the following Christmas. The costs involved were staggering, twenty or more times as much as for a radio program of the same length, even though the stars contributed their talent free. The product did not produce revenue. The stations used it as a public service, simply providing the showing time without charge. Still, I felt forced to continue. The stakes were so great that I plunged ahead and left it to Our Lady to figure out how to meet the costs. And she always came through! So *The Joyful Hour* came along, with Ruth Hussey, Nelson Leigh, Lloyd Corrigan, and Pat O'Brien and his family. Again the approval was overwhelming. "It combines a rare spiritual beauty with the broad appeal of fine theater," was the summing up of the *New York Times*.

For the Easter of 1951 we were even more ambitious. We produced an hour-long dramatic film telling the story of the Resurrection and of Christ's victory on Golgotha, which is *Hill Number One*, the title of the show. The story was told by an army chaplain to a GI gun crew which had become discouraged in storming a hill. The stars were Ruth Hussey, Joan Leslie, Leif Erickson, and Gene Lockhart. Acceptance was even greater than that of the earlier films. *Variety* hailed its "strong appeal for young and old alike," and insisted that with this show, "Hollywood TV production need admit of no superior." It was shown on 102 television stations out of a possible 107, and the total audience was estimated at forty-two million. A *Billboard* magazine poll of television stations as to mail and phone response to religious films gave first place to *Hill Number One* with the tremendous score of 106 points, as compared with 63 points for the runner-up. And the runner-up was also a "Family Theater" film, *That I May See*, issued a few months after *Hill Number One*. No other film in the survey scored more than ten points.

I had at least succeeded in establishing one of the things I had set out to prove—namely, that there was a place for the message of family prayer on the new television medium, provided one went the right way about it. This was precisely what Jack Gould, television editor of the *New York Times*, said about that same time. "The leading producer in this field," he wrote, referring to religious presentations, "is the Reverend Patrick Peyton, a Catholic priest of Hollywood, who has made a number of superb religious films with top-flight motion picture stars. He, almost alone, has seemed to realize that with mass media the mode of presentation is every bit as important as the message."

During the following years I managed to raise funds to produce several additional films for television, and in every case the reception by the stations and by the public was excellent. One was *The World's Greatest Mother*, depicting important events in the life of Mary. Another, *Trial at Tara*, tells the story of St. Patrick. Yet another was an adaptation of Francis Thompson's beautiful poem "Hound of Heaven." It portrays a man who spent years in a desperate, fruitless flight in an effort to evade personal issues he feared to face.

With the concentration on the fifteen Rosary films during the middle and later 1950s, the television productions of "Family Theater" had to be curtailed. But they were never suspended. We made some thirty five-minute shorts and a number of inspirational spots. In addition the office was constantly busy with re-editing and redistributing year after year both the radio and the television programs. They continue in substantial demand, and the radio impact is beginning to climb once more, as radio carves itself out a steadily bigger audience in automobiles and even in the home.

The Hollywood office was also totally involved in all phases of the planning and production of the Rosary films and in the subsequent development of various other films made in part by combining segments of these films and in part from surplus footage. The two most important of these are *The Redeemer*, a full-length feature film portraying the Passion of Christ, and a shorter film called *The Promise*, presenting the events leading up to His birth. Unlike the typical Hollywood spectacular based on a Bible story, *The Redeemer* sticks to the facts as presented in the sacred text. For this reason it may have less entertainment value as judged by the commercial box office, but it serves the instructional function for which it was intended. It has been exhibited in many parts of the United States and in several foreign countries, and I am satisfied that it gives a further dimension to the monumental work represented by the fifteen Rosary films. As for those films, they were our providential introduction to Latin America. Without them we could never have achieved the basic instruction of the masses there in order to prepare them for the message of family prayer and the family Rosary. The attendance at showings of these films as part of the popular mission has passed the twenty-million mark, and their work has only begun.

The tremendous effort, both physical and financial, involved in the production and exploitation of the Rosary films, combined with the parallel effort to get the diocesan Crusade moving in Latin America and the need to spend a substantial time in Rome during the Council, caused other work in the Hollywood office to slow down, but it never stopped. On the contrary, the Council inspired me to new effort. "Let effective backing be given to decent radio and television productions," it urged in the Decree on the Instruments of Social Communication, "particularly those which are proper family fare. Catholic features should be intelligently encouraged, that through them audiences may be led to participate in the Church's life, and truths of religion may be instilled. . . . It should be a matter of concern that their offerings excel in professional quality and forcefulness."

As I studied these words, I saw each day more clearly the direct challenge to "Family Theater." In this operation we like to claim, without offence to any of the other organizations zealously committed to Catholic radio and television service in the United States, that we are unique in the volume of our work, the quality of our products, and the level of acceptance by American radio and television outlets. This last point seems to me overwhelmingly important. I know from bitter experience how hard it is to break in, how hard to assemble the expert teams, to deliver the kind of product that stations will use. I think I can claim that "Family Theater" never produced a show that did not win wide distribution, and its experience is that demand for most of its shows persists for a remarkable number of reruns. Its name has become a sort of hallmark, a standard of quality. It would be, humanly speaking, a shameful waste of assets and, religiously speaking, a deplorable refusal to follow a road obviously marked out for us by Providence, if we were now to withdraw from this vantage point.

"You will never be able to meet the cost," I am told time and again by people who look at the problems in purely economic terms. Superficially, they have a good point. Television swallows money, gulps it down with an insatiable appetite. To get $1,000 or $1,500 a week for "Family Theater" radio programs took superhuman efforts. How can one hope to get the $50,000 that a half-hour television show costs to produce even with donated talent? Yet I don't have to answer. The Council did that for me in the same Decree on Communications. "It would be dishonorable indeed," the Fathers solemnly warned,

> if sons of the Church sluggishly allowed the word of salvation to be silenced or impeded by the technical difficulties or the admittedly enormous expenses which are characteristic of these instruments. Hence the sacred Synod admonishes these sons that they are duty bound to uphold and assist . . . radio and television stations and programs whose main purpose is to spread and

> defend the truth and to strengthen the Christian
> texture of human society. This Council likewise
> urgently invites associations and individuals with
> great economic or technical prestige to give will-
> ingly and generously of their resources and tal-
> ents to the truly cultural and apostolic potential
> of these instruments.

I am totally convinced that if a thing is necessary, a way can be found to do it. The Council has said in the clearest words that this is necessary. The initial response to the most ambitious project of "Family Theater" since the Rosary films makes me believe that we are at least well started toward finding the way. The project is a series of thirty five-minute motion picture shorts based on the oldest and most eloquent of man's attempts to communicate his thoughts to his fellow men, the Psalms of the Old Testament. The idea originated with María Luisa Luca de Tena. She had long been attempting to translate it into written terms to make a book. When she came to work in the Hollywood office, she saw how much more appropriate was the screen for what she had in mind. Translated into modern images in the most modern of the communications, these renderings of the Psalms have been hailed with awe and enthusiasm by many entitled to judge. Some of them have already, before general release, won awards and honorable mentions, including the Bronze Medal of the Venice Film Festival, a tribute to artistic quality.

As I write, I have just completed arrangements for the showing of these films to a mass American audience under a unique arrangement with the WOR network, whose five stations in New York, Boston, Detroit, Memphis, and Los

Angeles reach a third of the United States television audience. This break-through was possible through the co-operation of the O'Neil family of Akron, Ohio. William F.
O'Neil, now deceased, was the creator of the General Tire
and Rubber Company, which he headed from 1915 until
his death, and he also became deeply involved in radio
when that industry expanded. I met him shortly after he
was named president of Yankee Network in 1942, and he
was a sincere friend and generous supporter of the Family Rosary Crusade for the rest of his life. His three sons,
Thomas, Gerald, and John, followed in his footsteps. All
are active in the rubber company, and they also control the
WOR network. General Tire is sponsoring the Psalms on
the network, thereby permitting me to recoup part of the
production costs. I have also got a sponsor in Brazil, the
Mercedes Benz automobile company. With these and other
sponsors throughout the world I see the possibility of creating a revolving fund that will permit the indefinite continuation of the production of religious and moral films for
television on a self-liquidating basis. Not all of these films
will necessarily be suitable for use in the programs of the
popular mission and its new extension as a post-Crusade
tool. Production will, however, be planned to ensure that
enough of them fit in the category of basic religious instruction, such as the Ten Commandments and the moral virtues, to provide the continuing flow of new material that the
post-Crusade programs will require. What is unique about
the arrangement with WOR is the kind of exposure which
Hathaway Watson, president of RKO General Broadcasting,
worked out for the Psalms. To dramatize the opening presentation, he combined five of the five-minute vignettes into

a half-hour theme, with a script spoken by Raymond Burr bridging the transition from each Psalm to the following one. The program is called *The Search*, and it portrays an old man's quest for the innocence and faith of his childhood. The man is strolling in a forest, free for a time from the pressures of his daily life, and he is challenged by the cry of the Psalmist to cast his mind's eye backward over that life to a childhood which reveals itself in the form of the innocent boy that this man once was. As the man moves through the forest and through his life, his search, guided by the theme of one Psalm after another, the boy pursues him, gradually getting closer to him. And as the man's soul fills with the desire to become again what he once was, the boy finally catches up with him, and they fade out hand in hand in a restored faith and confidence. The total effect is of a beautiful, peaceful meditation on the innocence of child-hood lost by the pressures and distractions of the world, yet with the possibility always present that man can again turn to God and regain what he has foolishly thrown away. It is thus not only a search but a finding. So successful was *The Search* that two added films, *The Find* and *The Fulfillment*, were planned to compose a trilogy. *The Search* is the only American film selected by the International Catholic Radio and TV Association at the 1967 film festival at Monte Carlo.

After this spectacular start, Mr. Watson showed the entire series of thirty Psalms during a thirty-day peri-od. One Psalm was shown twice every day at appropriate intervals, so that at some time each viewer would have the opportunity for five minutes of uplift and meditation in a context appropriate for people of all faiths and even people of no specifiable faith.

During the summer and fall of 1967, "Family Theater" was involved in widespread television and radio activities. The *Prince of Peace* television series, a composite of the fifteen Rosary films plus the newer films, *The Promise* and *Recife Smiles*, features myself in dialogue with a famous Hollywood star at the conclusion of each story and is provided as a public service to television stations. Nationwide television release was scheduled beginning the week of December 10, 1967. A ninety-minute television special for St. Patrick's Day was also to be produced for us.

On radio we released the *Stories of the Saviour*, a series of fifteen short shows narrated by Raymond Burr and produced by "Family Theater" with music by the famed concert pianist Amparo Iturbi. A series of twenty-six one-minute selected prayers, recited by various well-known personalities, was also syndicated across the nation.

These undertakings were made possible thanks to Patrick Frawley and Paul Fassnacht of Technicolor, Bob Stabler, producer of *Death Valley Days*, Ed Lynett and Cecil Woodland of the *Scranton Times* and radio station WEJL, Lionel Baxter of the Storer Broadcasting Company, and Jack Haley Jr. of Wolper Productions, to name just a few of the many who helped us.

It is incidents like this which bolster my conviction that the "Family Theater" office in Hollywood is not only there to stay but will play a progressively bigger part in the Family Rosary Crusade. Twenty-five years have passed since that fateful Sunday in January 1942 when I committed myself to devote my life to a single purpose: to repay Mary's delicacy to me by working without respite to strengthen family life through daily family prayer and especially the recitation of the prayer so dear to Mary, her Rosary. At that time I did not have a single penny of backing, nor did I have the skills, the experience, the contacts which one might prudently and reasonably demand, speaking in human terms, as an essential prerequisite for success in this enterprise.

The resources, human and material, have nevertheless never been lacking. If there is always less than my ardor aspires to, there is always enough to keep progressing. For my story has one basic lesson, if it has no other. Millions, literally millions of people are always ready to help Our Blessed Mother. They belong to every race, every nation, every class, every walk in life, every level of prosperity and poverty, outside the Catholic Church as well as inside. They are the Brothers and Sisters of the Vincentian Institute in Albany and their students who were my first helpers, the Sisters and students at the College of St. Rose in Albany, and the Holy Cross seminarians who worked for Mary during their summer vacations in Deer Park, Maryland.

They are the bishops of the United States who responded to the early halting letters in which I timidly expressed my ambition to be a salesman for Our Lady. They are the pastors who invited me to preach triduums to their flocks. They are the scores of priests who gave years of their lives, some of them their entire lives, to participate as full-time cooperators in the Family Rosary Crusade. Most of these were my colleagues of the Congregation of Holy Cross, and to them goes out my heartfelt thanks, and to the superiors who released them and who recognized from the beginning until now that the Crusade is a sacred trust of Holy Cross. Other priests were not from Holy Cross, and to them my debt is also immeasurable, men like my soul brother and first partner, Father Francis Woods, like Bishop Bienvenido López and Father José Borces in the Philippine Islands, Father Xavier Echenique in Madrid, Father Francis Bennett from New Zealand, who worked on the Rosary films both in Hollywood and in Spain, and Father James B. Reuter, S.J., who had been a prisoner-of-war with Father Lawyer in the Philippines and who later worked in the Hollywood office.

To these priests I must add Father James D. Roche, S.J. Before becoming a Jesuit, Jim was one of Hollywood's talented script writers and directors, endowed with a rare knowledge of a dozen of the exotic specialties required to make a film. He served in the navy during the Second World War, transferring of his own choice to submarines. He had already had experience in Hollywood, and he was in charge of censorship clearance of film production at the first Bikini atomic tests. He came to work as a volunteer at "Family Theater" in 1949, at the same time as Joe Russell, who is still there. Jim is normally gentle, but his artistic temperament can come through. He wrote the script of *The Triumphant Hour*, doing a complete first draft over a weekend because I had to have it Monday to get a quotation of the cost of production. He took that with good grace, but when it came to casting, the two of us nearly had a stand-up fight. I had set my heart on having Patricia Kennedy, sister of the genial young man who would later become president, play the part of Our Blessed Lady. Patricia was then and for a considerable time working in the "Family Theater" office, and she seemed to me to have just the right combination of qualities for the part. Jim liked her, too, and respected her talents, but for his own mysterious reasons he turned thumbs down. "You can't," he said to her, when I attempted to argue. "You're too tall." Patricia was very calm, and she asked a very reasonable question. "How do you know how tall Our Lady was?" "I don't know," he stormed back, "but you're still too tall. And besides, you have a Boston accent." I guess that was the clincher. Jim won out. After several years he left us to join the Jesuits, has recently returned to Hollywood after serving in the Far East, and is once again giving us the benefit of his talents on a part-time basis.

The briefest listing of those who helped me realize my dream must stress the Spanish Misioneras whose contribution was invaluable in opening up the Spanish world and in many other ways. Close to my heart, too, are the Irish and American girls who happily flew like the swallows to whatever part of the world needed them: Terry Fellowes, Gertie Lally, Pearl Buckley, Pat Spanbauer, Dorothy Kahl, Genevieve Campion, and Frances Delaney. And speaking of Ireland's help, I must mention the name of Bridie Doherty, not only because her husband, Joe, and she have always a home for me, but because what she has accomplished for the Crusade would fill a book, a book that I sincerely hope can one day be written. And what words of praise and tribute could do justice to all that I owe and all that I feel in gratitude and appreciation to all my co-workers and their immediate circle of friends and benefactors in the Family Rosary Crusade offices of Albany, Hollywood, Madrid, Manila, Rio de Janeiro, São Paulo, Caracas, Bogotá, Panama, and Sydney, Australia!

As for the motion picture, radio, and television stars who made possible by their generosity so much of the good which "Family Theater" has done, their names alone would cover pages. I remember with particular affection those who appeared on the first radio shows. It required a great courage and integrity at that time for an idol of the entertainment world to stand up before a microphone and proclaim himself a believer in prayer and an advocate of family prayer. The change of climate in this regard in the interval is one measure of the excellence of the job these men and women did in selling the idea of family prayer to the public of our country.

Nor was the contribution of the entertainment industry confined to the donated services of the stars. I have mentioned such behind-the-scenes giants as Tom Lewis, Al Scalpone, Bob Longenecker, Doc Bishop, Jim Roche, and others in our early years. Tom Lewis and his team went back to their own work when they got "Family Theater" launched, but they did not forget us. Years later, Tom has become a full-time unpaid worker in "Family Theater," dedicating his knowledge and skills to a great new launching that will establish us on television as securely as he then did on radio. He believes totally in the series on the Psalms, and he is convinced that we can get airborne by pursuing the program of which they are the start. And Al Scalpone is always on call, quick to respond when I appeal for the benefit of his vast talent.

Particularly vivid in my memory is the dinner we held at the Beverly-Hilton Hotel in Hollywood in 1962 to celebrate the twentieth anniversary of the Family Rosary Crusade. I was overwhelmed once again at the generosity of these wonderful people of the entertainment and business worlds who fifteen hundred strong packed the main ballroom in a touching tribute to our cause and, of course, to Our Lady. The highlight of the evening came when Patricia Kennedy

Lawford read a telegram from her brother, President John F. Kennedy. It said:

> OUR WARMEST CONGRATULATIONS ON THE 20TH ANNIVERSARY OF YOUR WONDERFUL WORK. YOUR SUCCESS IN STRENGTHENING FAMILY TIES THROUGH PRAYER HAS UNDOUBTEDLY BROUGHT THE WORLD CLOSER TO THE PEACE WHICH WE ALL DESIRE. MAY THE FUTURE CROWN YOUR EFFORTS WITH EVEN GREATER SUCCESS.

It is a precious souvenir which I will treasure all my days.

Such are some of the people who proved that help is not far away when you ask in the name and for the honor of the Mother of God. Others are the bishops, priests, nuns, and laypeople who found the money to stoke the furnace. I have mentioned a few, but they are only a tiny fraction of all whose good works are recorded in the Book of Life. And when I say this, I think not only or not primarily of the wealthy donors, much as I appreciate their generosity, but of the tens of thousands who have stinted themselves year after year to send their dollar bills or their two dollars each time I launch an appeal from Albany. I think of the secretary who manages to save five dollars a month for Mary out of a small salary, of the file clerk who walks to and from work when the weather allows and drops the bus fare in a little box to send on when it builds up to ten dollars. It is this sense of love and sacrifice, which I find at all levels all across the nation, in thousands of wonderful housewives, office staffs, working men; it is their story I have told you rather than my own when I have tried to describe twenty-five years of the Family Rosary Crusade. They, not I, have made the

Crusade what it is. They, not I, guarantee its growth and perpetuation for the family, for family prayer, for the family Rosary, for the honor of the Mother of God, for the glory of the God whom she joins us in eternal praise and adoration.

Epilogue

The story does not end here. During the following nineteen years, until his death on June 3, 1992, Father Peyton continued to develop and oversee the work of Family Rosary in Albany and Family Theater Productions in Hollywood. He produced fourteen additional TV programs, including two three-part series on the Rosary, one featuring Princess Grace and another featuring Loretta Young. He also conducted seven more Rosary Crusades—his 1985 crusade in the Philippines attracted two million people.

In October 1991, as the Soviet Union dissolved, Father Peyton launched a "Rosary for Russia" campaign. During this time Family Rosary collected more than two million rosaries and distributed them to people in countries that were part of the former Soviet Union. Before it was over, another million rosaries were distributed to people in these and other countries throughout the world. This global Rosary program continues today as "Rosaries for the World."

Just a few months before his death, Father Peyton commissioned his last TV series. Aimed at young people and their parents, these five half-hour programs interweave a contemporary story with a biblical story taken from a

Mystery of the Rosary. Father Peyton was able to review and approve all five scripts, and Family Theater produced the first film of that series before his death. The five films, titled *The Choice, The Visit, The Journey, The Search,* and *The Hero,* have since won several awards and have had more than 2,500 broadcasts on over 250 TV stations, three cable networks, and 1,500 cable systems throughout the United States. *The Search* and *The Hero* were screened for and discussed by more than 1,200 youth as an official event at World Youth Day 1993 in Denver.

In 1993, Family Theater produced *A Most Unusual Man.* Biographical as well as memorial, the film relates Father Peyton's incredible ministry through media, and details his work to enlist hundreds of Hollywood stars to perform in his more than six hundred radio and TV programs. This hour-long program is hosted by Bob Newhart, Ann Blyth, Jane Wyatt, Ralph Edwards of *This Is Your Life,* and the late Macdonald Carey.

In 2019, Family Theater Productions will release the official documentary on the life of Father Patrick Peyton, C.S.C. This comprehensive look at the life of this humble and holy priest will complement the story found here in *All for Her.*

The ministries founded by Father Peyton continue his mission to encourage families to pray together every day, and especially to pray the Rosary. In 2000, Family Rosary and Family Theater Productions joined administrative offices, under the new title Holy Cross Family Ministries, to simplify the corporate entities and enhance efforts to serve the spiritual well-being of all families. Holy Cross Family Ministries has a presence on five continents, in seventeen countries and through twenty-four active ministry centers. Bringing the good news of the family to the digital continent has been a significant, challenging, and promising area of growth for Holy Cross Family Ministries. The themes of Father Peyton's ministry now reach millions of twenty-first-century families through websites, social media, multiple apps, short-format videos, and full-feature documentary and live-action films.

In 2017, Holy Cross Family Ministries acquired CatholicMom.com. Founded by Lisa Hendey, the website has created an online community of Catholic parents to share insights on living their faith with their family.

***

Father Peyton's life still inspires families around the world not only through his ministries, but also through his cause for sainthood. On December 18, 2017, Pope Francis declared Father Patrick Peyton, C.S.C., to be "Venerable." People around the world have shared their testimonies of Father Peyton's holy life and heroic virtues. Many continue to share the favors received through his intercession and pray that he will be canonized and recognized as the "Saint for Family Prayer."

Father Peyton's conviction that families everywhere would be more unified through daily prayer, and especially the Rosary, was imbued in every part of his priestly life. For more than half a century, he shared his vision that "The family that prays together stays together." That message contains as much power and grace for families today as it did for his family in Ireland more than one hundred years ago. May you and your family be inspired by his story and pray together daily. Father Peyton's great hope was that families around the world, praying the Rosary, would lead to real peace. He conveyed this hope in his second signature phrase, "A world at prayer is a world at peace." Please join families around the world in praying for the realization of this dream through the intercession of Mary, the Queen of Peace, and Venerable Patrick Peyton, her beloved and faithful son and champion of the family Rosary.

Index

Note: *page numbers in italics indicate photographs.*